Identity and Capitalism.

For Mam and Dad

Identity and Capitalism.

Marie Moran.

Los Angeles | London | New Delhi
Singapore | Washington DC

Los Angeles | London | New Delhi
Singapore | Washington DC

SAGE Publications Ltd
1 Oliver's Yard
55 City Road
London EC1Y 1SP

SAGE Publications Inc.
2455 Teller Road
Thousand Oaks, California 91320

SAGE Publications India Pvt Ltd
B 1/I 1 Mohan Cooperative Industrial Area
Mathura Road
New Delhi 110 044

SAGE Publications Asia-Pacific Pte Ltd
3 Church Street
#10-04 Samsung Hub
Singapore 049483

Editor: Chris Rojek
Assistant editor: Gemma Shields
Production editor: Katherine Haw
Copyeditor: Jane Fricker
Proofreader: Lynda Watson
Indexer: Elizabeth Ball
Marketing manager: Michael Ainsley
Cover design: Shaun Mercier
Typeset by: C&M Digitals (P) Ltd, Chennai, India
Printed in India at Replika Press Pvt Ltd

Library of Congress Control Number: 2014937806

British Library Cataloguing in Publication data

A catalogue record for this book is available from
the British Library

MIX
Paper from
responsible sources
FSC
www.fsc.org   FSC® C016779

ISBN 978-1-4462-4974-1
ISBN 978-1-4462-4975-8 (pbk)

At SAGE we take sustainability seriously. Most of our products are printed in the UK using FSC papers and boards.
When we print overseas we ensure sustainable papers are used as measured by the Egmont grading system.
We undertake an annual audit to monitor our sustainability.

Contents

About the Author

Dr Marie Moran is a lecturer in Equality Studies at the UCD School of Social Justice, Dublin. She has an interdisciplinary background, with a degree in English Literature and Psychology from Trinity College Dublin, and an MSc and PhD in Equality Studies, combining sociology, political theory, cultural studies and political economy. Her main areas of interest are the development of cultural materialism as a sociological paradigm, ideology and power in capitalist societies, and the social and political theory of equality, on all of which she has also published. She is also engaged in a number of broadly anti-capitalist activist campaigns in her home town of Dublin, and is a founding member of Debt Justice Action Ireland, and the Irish chapter of ATTAC, both of which attempt to 'disarm the power of the financial markets' through public action and popular education programmes.

Acknowledgements

There are very many people I want to thank for their help and encouragement in writing this book. First, to those who helped me with the academic nuts and bolts. This book began life as a doctoral thesis, under the patient and careful supervision of John Baker at the UCD School of Social Justice. John's intellectual insights, rigorous feedback and generosity of time and spirit have been an enormous source of help and encouragement to me, and indeed, made this book possible. Thank you John, for your unwavering and continued faith in me, and for setting me on the course I continue today. I want also to thank Jim McGuigan, who has long been an intellectual inspiration of mine, and more recently, a good friend. I have benefited enormously from his active encouragement and stern advice, and take heart from the fact that we are like-minded creatures with a similar admiration for the work of Raymond Williams (though I, apparently, am more 'prolix' than Jim, and have a terrible tendency to meddle needlessly with words). Very many thanks to Harry Browne, who supported me enormously through the summer of 2013 in particular, and in the final stages of editing. Reading drafts while on holidays, even, Harry unravelled historical knots, made incisive interventions and spurred me forward. And to Andy Storey – I could not have finished this book without you. In the final weeks, Andy read and commented on every single chapter, with a sharp eye and a sharper pen – confirming, in many cases, Jim's worst suspicions, but rooting them out, so no one else would be subjected to such boring verbosity (that's the dictionary definition, Jim). Thank you Andy, for your huge generosity, support and attention to detail. John, Jim, Harry and Andy, I am truly indebted to all of you.

Many other people have offered great support and assistance to me over the course of writing this book. I want to thank Kathleen Lynch and all the staff and students of Equality Studies, and latterly, the UCD School of Social Justice. In particular, I want to thank Maureen Lyons and Judy Walsh, for their enduring support and much valued friendship. I am also very grateful to Andrew Sayer, for his deeply generous and insightful guidance during my four-month visit to Lancaster University, and for prompting me – mixed metaphors aside – to leave behind postmodernism. In addition, I would like to thank my editors at SAGE, Chris Rojek and Gemma Shields, for the support and encouragement they gave me while writing this book, with special thanks to Gemma for her patient assistance, helpful feedback and unwavering enthusiasm. Special gratitude goes to the crew of Debt Justice Action Ireland and ATTAC Ireland, with whom I worked over the course of writing this book: thank you all for being great friends and inspirational proof of collective, anti-capitalist activism.

For other practical and scholarly help when I needed it most, thanks to Conor McCabe, Edel McAteer, Vincent Browne, Gavan Titley, Pilar Villar Argáiz, Theresa O'Keefe, Niamh McCrea and Eoghan McDermott. A special thanks to Eileen Drumm for lending me her house in Cork for two crucial weeks of writing, even though she had never met me.

To my much loved friends, Laura Craig, Lorna Powell, Sinead O'Dwyer and Su O'Mara, thank you for always cheering me up, filling me in, bringing me out and keeping me sane. I would like to give special mention to Keith Darragh, for his 'motivational' text messages, emails and phonecalls. I will quite literally never forget them. And to Pete Drumm, thank you for your huge kindness, practical support and for always making me laugh when I most needed to. You are one in a million.

Finally, to my family. Jean, your continual positive reinforcement, encouragement and steadfast faith in me has been a constant source of strength. Brian, thank you for your practical and humorous outlook, your steady support, and the sense of perspective you have given me over the course of this book. Kate, even though as a 15-year-old you probably doubt this, you are a constant source of happiness in my life, and you make me remember the importance of having fun. If you ever come to me in the future for advice on whether or not to write a book, I will most likely, therefore, advise the latter. Dad, thank you for giving me my love of reading, writing and arguing, and a strong belief in social justice. Chapter 2 in particular is for you, as you instilled in me, from a very young age, the power of words – I hope I do you justice. And Mam, thank you for your unconditional love, generosity, sense of fun, but most of all, for your optimism. You helped me to keep going during some tough times, and I will always be grateful.

I would like to acknowledge receipt of the National University of Ireland (NUI) grant towards publication, for which I am very grateful. I would like to thank the editorial board of *The Sociological Review*, as well as their publishers, Wiley, for permission to reuse extracts from the article 'Raymond Williams and Sociology', which appeared first in *The Sociological Review*, February 2014, 62(1): 167–188. I am also grateful to Jim McGuigan, with whom I co-wrote the article, for allowing me to use these extracts in this volume. Finally, I want to thank Andrew Sayer for allowing me to use some of his wording from an email exchange we had on the merits of Boltanski and Chiapello's concept of a spirit of capitalism, reproduced here in Chapter 3.

Be careful when speaking. You create the world
around you with your words.
~ *Quote attributed to the Navajo storytelling tradition* ~

Introduction

IDENTITY: THE SPIRIT OF THE TIMES?

Since the 1950s, western societies seem to have become preoccupied with questions of identity. Evident first in the field of psychology, by the 1990s identity had become a central concern across a range of political, cultural, commercial and academic spaces, animating discourse and informing practice in disparate ways. Authoritative voices proclaimed identity to be the dominant political logic of the age (Brown, 1995; Fraser, 1997b) as questions of cultural, ethnic, religious and sexual identity took political centre stage, seemingly supplanting older class-based or ideological allegiances. Meanwhile the equality and anti-discrimination legislation of most western politico-legal systems came to be organised around these identity categories, and, from the 1960s in particular, a range of 'new' social movements mobilised around experiences and expressions of identity. In this period, identity also came to be viewed as the defining personal issue of the time (Giddens, 1991). Television shows demonstrated the centrality of individual identity to lifestyle and fashion, and self-help books elevated the search for one's 'true' identity to key psychological status. Identity also became the source of an array of popular anxieties, bound up with the perceived threat to self and sanity represented by the notion of an 'identity crisis', and, in another context, the growing hazard of 'identity theft'. Many prominent social theorists who have viewed identity in historical perspective have argued that identity has been somehow emblematic or definitive of the late modern world: a zeitgeist, a 'cultural logic' of the times. As Bendle (2002: 1) has put it, 'there is a pervasive sense that the acquisition and maintenance of identity has become both vital and *problematic under high modernity*'.

There have been many attempts to explain the contemporary salience of identity, and investigations into why it has become both 'vital and problematic' in late modernity. Theorists of the so-called 'postmodern', 'post-industrial' or 'network' society have looked to the evolution of information and communications technology, transformations of social class, the continued rise of individualisation, or the disruptive forces of globalisation to account for the centrality and turbulence of identity concerns across so many domains of contemporary life (Inglehart, 1990; Pakulski and Waters, 1996; Žižek, 1997; Beck and Beck-Gernsheim, 2002; Castells, 2004). Meanwhile, other theorists working broadly within a poststructural paradigm, and influenced especially by the work of Foucault (1977) and Judith Butler (1990), have argued that identity, by its nature, is intrinsically both vital and problematic. As Bauman has put it,

To say that modernity led to the 'disembedding' of identity, or that it rendered the identity 'unencumbered', is to assert a pleonasm, since at no time did identity 'become' a problem; it was a 'problem' from its birth – was *born as a problem* (that is, as something one needs do something about – as a task), could exist only as a problem ... (1996: 18–19)

These theorists have invested much critical energy into examination of the 'construction' of identity and the manner in which identity is 'performed' rather than simply available as a pre-given source of meaning and self-knowledge. The identity of an individual or group is not, they claim, 'essential' to it, but is a 'social construction' or even a 'fiction'. This type of understanding has become routine in social, political and literary theory, to the extent that while 'identity-talk' continues unabated, and university modules and academic articles on 'identities' proliferate, the emphasis rests on the constructed, discursive, fluid, contingent and fragile nature of identity. In these accounts, identity is *by definition* a project and a problem.

Recent years have seen a backlash against this attention to and agonising over questions of identity, both politically and conceptually. The financial crash and economic crisis of 2008 have purportedly revealed the weaknesses of an identity-based politics, and shown up its irrelevance in the face of the dominant economic structures that govern contemporary life. But even before this, it was claimed that we now live in a 'post-identity' – or even 'post-post-identity' – world (Lloyd, 2005; Millner, 2005). In this post-identity world, we have apparently tired of identity struggles, even as they remain with us. Nicholson (2008: 4) writes that 'identity politics seems now to be largely dead, or, at minimum, no longer able to command the kind of public attention that it did from the late 1960s through the late 1980s'. The term itself has been argued to have become over-inflated, over-used, and ultimately meaningless (Brubaker and Cooper, 2000).

Yet despite this, it seems we cannot do without the notion of identity. Although the more overt forms of identity politics have receded, identity nonetheless remains a central political concern into the second decade of the twenty-first century, animating discourses of multiculturalism, nationalist politics, the women's movement and LGBTQ organisations. Questions of identity continue to pervade social and political thought, with a plethora of academic books and journal articles published on the subject each year. Google Books throws up 29 million entries for 'identity' in the twenty-first century alone (with less than a million entries returned for 'social class' in the same period). Even a 2012 *Wall Street Journal* and *New York Times* best-seller recently declared it 'your passport to success' (Graham, 2012). Despite, then, a growing scepticism towards the concept of identity and value of identity politics, identity nonetheless remains a forceful concern in politics, culture and society, continuing to animate social movements, legislation, political declarations, television programmes, popular fiction, film, self-help books, the therapeutic industries and academic and literary studies. What Gilroy (1997: 301) proclaimed at the end of the last century continues to hold true today: '[w]e live in a world where identity matters. It matters both as a concept, theoretically, and as a contested fact of contemporary political life'.

IDENTITY IS A NEW IDEA

An interesting feature of most of the literature on identity, whether celebratory or critical, is the underlying assumption that in modern societies people's identities have always mattered at least to some very minimal extent, but that for better or for worse, the experience and expression of identity have become more prominent in recent years, trumping alternative political, social and cultural concerns. Thus while Brubaker and Cooper complain that a recent academic obsession with identity has distorted the unremarkable fact that '[p]eople everywhere and always have particular ties, self-understandings, stories, trajectories, histories, predicaments' (2000: 34), others have celebrated the recent attention to questions of identity, with Alcoff applauding the fact that '[t]he constitutive power of gender, race, class, ethnicity, sexuality, and other forms of social identity has, finally, suddenly, been recognized as a relevant aspect of almost all projects of inquiry' (2006: 5). The shared assumption of both the celebratory and critical accounts seems to be that where questions of identity were once peripheral, they are now central, and that where the experience of identity was once neglected, it is now prioritised. This rests on the more basic assumption that the *very capacity* to 'have an identity' – or multiple identities – is a universal aspect of what it means to be human, albeit one that can vary according to the historical and cultural context. Thus Jenkins comments, although 'public concern about identity may wax and wane', that concern is always, inevitably present, for 'without identity there could simply be no human world, as we know it' (2008: 27). Even theorists who assert the socially constructed, inessential nature of personal and social identity nonetheless assume that the *search* for identity, or the collective or individual attempt to build, consolidate, mark or construct an identity – however 'fluid', 'negotiated' or even 'fictive' that identity might be – is a human or social capacity, that pre-existed our extensive current reflection on what exactly an 'identity' is. This assumption is not just academic. While writing this book, I was regularly met with the confident assertion that, while individual identities may change, 'get lost', or enter crisis, this fundamental sense of self – this capacity to 'have an identity' – is a constitutive and defining feature of personhood.

Against such assumptions, this book makes the perhaps surprising and controversial claim that identity never 'mattered' prior to the 1960s because it did not in fact *exist* or operate as a shared political and cultural idea *until* the 1960s. The very word identity, as we know and use it today, only emerged into the popular, scientific and political imagination and associated discourses in the second half of the last century. In historical perspective, the idea of identity, particularly as it is elaborated in the associated categories of 'personal' and 'social' identity, is a surprisingly novel one. This is the first key claim of this book.

The second key claim is that this emergence of identity as a significant social, political and everyday concept cannot be understood separately from the context in which it emerged. When we look closely at the contexts of usage of the 'new' term identity, we find that it emerged in two key spaces – firstly, in new patterns of consumption, particularly those associated with individualism, 'lifestyle' and distinction (where these in turn were underwritten by new popular psychological discourses of personal transformation and personal stability); and secondly, in a series of political shifts that responded to and shaped the politico-economic landscape of western capitalist societies, as demands for universal redistribution were gradually displaced by demands for group-based recognition. In this respect, identity is best understood as a 'keyword' in the sense intended by Raymond Williams – that is, to paraphrase, a word whose problems of meaning are inextricably bound up with the problems it is used to discuss (1983: 15). This formulation derives from the broader 'cultural materialist' framework within which Williams worked: a keyword, in this cultural materialist sense, is not merely an important or fashionable word, but a key element of a wider social transformation, capturing, embodying and expressing new, historically and socially specific ways of thinking and acting. Developing this cultural materialist analysis, this book shows that what we now think of routinely as 'personal identity' actually only emerged with the explosion of consumption in the late twentieth century. It also makes the case that what we now think of as different social and political 'identities' only came to be framed as such with the emergence of exclusive group-based politics, new social movements and 'multiculturalism' in the 1960s and 1970s. The idea of identity, as we now know it, cannot be separated from the cultural political economy of the capitalist societies in which it came to prominence.

In effect, then, this book is concerned with what kind of identifications people make, and how people experience – and are encouraged to experience – their sense of self in a capitalist context. The claim is not that people's 'identities' came to matter more in late capitalism, but that identity itself came to operate as a new and key mechanism for construing and experiencing a sense of self, and its relation to others. Important work has been carried out by Michel Foucault, Nikolas Rose, Judith Butler and others on the processes of 'subjectivisation' – that is, the various practices and discourses which work to constitute individuals as particular subjects. The emphasis is typically on various disciplinary processes, which derive from the (apparently 'voluntary') self-subjection of the individual to certain discursively legitimated norms about how one should behave, perform, desire, self-present and relate to others. The claim is that these various processes of subjectivisation work to create particular *identities*, whether gendered, 'racialised', heteronormative or classed. This presupposes the very idea of identity as a core sense of self and groups that I argue to be historically very recent. For the fact is that the idea of identity as we now know it emerged long *after* many of the disciplinary processes of modernity discussed by Foucault and others came into being. Therefore it is not simply that a given 'identity' is the effect of a particular form of subjectivisation, but that the very idea of identity is itself bound up with the *possibilities* for subjectivisation in contemporary western societies. Where the 'subjectivisation' arguments are used to demonstrate the construction of a particular subject in terms of a particular identity via certain disciplinary mechanisms or 'technologies' of modernity, this book makes the case that the idea of identity *is* one such mechanism or technology, rather than the product of such disciplinary practices: it is only comparatively recently that one can be subjectivised as a (type of) person who is capable of possessing and expected to possess an identity at all. How precisely this mechanism operates in a capitalist context is the subject of this book.

SETTLING THE 'VEXED QUESTION OF IDENTITY'

The argument that identity is a contemporary keyword begins from recognition of the novel and often conflicting ways in which the word began to be used at a certain point in its history, despite the concealment of this shift by the nominal continuity of the term. As Chapter 1 will demonstrate, the word identity was not used in the ways it is now used before the 1950s and 1960s. However, the great majority of work on the subject of identity does not acknowledge the novelty of the very idea of identity as we now understand it. Instead, for the most part, 'personal identity' and 'social identities' − two key ways in which the term is now used − are treated as historically persistent concepts, and attention is directed instead to how we should explain the formation, constitution and treatment of these 'identities' in the current historical juncture. It is routine within the literature to distinguish between different theoretical perspectives on or accounts of identity, whether essentialist, intersectional, deconstructionist, symbolic interactionist or some other. These various theoretical perspectives offer valuable if competing ways of thinking about the social and political sources and implications of identity claims and identity formations today. However, the approach developed in this book is at odds with the implicit assumption of these debates, which is that identity's very existence pre-dates these theoretical interpretations and explanations of its nature. Against this more commonplace understanding, this book suggests we need to investigate *the emergence of the very idea of identity*: its naturalisation, the uses to which it is put and the work it currently does.

The two fundamental arguments made in this book − that identity is a historically recent idea, and that it has been born and evolved in a particular way in relation to the cultural political economy of capitalist societies − can help us to make sense of the contemporary salience of identity, and to adjudicate on many of the debates around identity that have exercised politics and academia over the last decades. That is, they go some way towards settling what many have referred to as 'the vexed question of identity'. One of the most prominent of these debates concerns whether identity should be considered 'essential' to individuals and groups, or whether it is in some sense 'socially constructed'. Although much of value has been written by the 'essentialists' and the 'social constructionists', what neither position does adequately – if at all – is locate the idea of identity in its historical context. As Zaretsky (1995: 256) complains, these debates, 'though important are nonetheless *internal* to the politics that characterize our time. They presuppose identity as the central content of politics and do not historicize it. Therefore, these debates do not provide the means to situate and evaluate the politics of the present, as only an historical perspective can.' The assumption that identity always 'existed' or always mattered serves to obscure some of the work that the very concept of identity *itself* does in contemporary politics – and it does this work *whether* a particular 'identity' is construed as essential to the individual or group, or viewed as a social construction.

The historical novelty of the idea of identity as we now know it has been obscured by the fact that identity came to reframe and reshape a range of already existing and historically persistent concerns about the self and its similarity to or difference from others. Addressing these concerns through the use of the category of identity was a decisive shift that continues to be active and performative. It does not simply reflect a new or superficial linguistic fashion, but actively operates upon these concerns – it 'does something' to them. Specifically, this book will argue that what it does is to enable essentialist classification of individuals and groups: it offers a way of saying 'I really am this kind of person', or 'you really do belong to that group'. This recognition of the idea of identity as a classificatory device in contemporary history rather than as an intrinsic property of persons and groups provides a means of going beyond the 'essentialism vs social constructionism' debates that have been dominant within the social theory of identity. It shows that the debate itself is misguided, as both sides presuppose the very (recent) idea of identity as we now know it, and fail to recognise that it is *the idea itself*, rather than the groups or individuals to which it refers, that is inescapably essentialist in its operation as a classificatory device.

A second key debate constituting the 'vexed question of identity' concerns the political utility of mobilisation around experiences or expressions of identity in an era of advanced capitalism that continues to be characterised by great inequalities of wealth and power both within and between societies. This has been described by Nancy Fraser in terms of a 'bitter split' between a 'social left' who regard the emphasis on identity as a distraction from the proper politics of class and analyses of capitalism, and who believe that identity politics conceal the material bases of oppression and fracture any coherent, class-based movement; and a 'cultural left' who defend the political and theoretical insights of cultural analyses, and the often realised potential of identity politics to bring about increased social, political and material equality for excluded and disenfranchised groups, as they mobilise primarily around gender, sexuality, 'race' or ethnicity (1997b: 3). This 'split' has allegedly contributed to a weakening of the left in the latter years of the twentieth century. This book will also throw new light on this debate, by offering a fundamental reframing of the issues, and a new starting point from which to pursue the relevant questions. It offers a means of exploring the *articulation* of the idea of identity to the cultural political economy of capitalist societies, thereby enabling us to examine how exactly this device – this way of thinking, organising and acting – has been operationalised, culturally, politically and commercially, in a capitalist context. Instead of asserting the priority of economic over cultural concerns, or of class over identity concerns, or vice versa, this approach allows us to explore and evaluate their inter-relation – by examining how the *idea of identity* is used and acted upon to great political and commercial effect within capitalist societies, in ways which do not always or automatically reinforce a capitalist logic, but which may also challenge it.

INTRODUCING CULTURAL MATERIALISM

The 'social versus cultural left' debate is also played out in academic or disciplinary terms, in the contrived but growing opposition of 'cultural studies' to 'political economy', as well as in a number of debates which oppose 'identity politics' to 'social class'. One of the main reasons identity theory has achieved such academic prominence, we may conjecture, is precisely because it has been perceived to offer an alternative means of understanding and explaining forms of group oppression and social inequality that does not rely upon what are often viewed as economically reductive or determinist categories of class associated with traditional sociological and Marxist theory. Accordingly, for many theorists of identity, it would be anathema to ask precisely the question of this book – what has identity got to do with capitalism? In this way, the social theory of identity has been associated with an anti- (or 'post') Marxist perspective, and has formed part of that larger academic split to which I have referred, which, at its broadest, can be characterised as 'culture' vs 'economy'. However, this split rests on a number of false associations, including – of particular relevance to the argument of this book – the association of economism with materialism and the association of culturalism with idealism. As Chapter 3 will explain, both the culturalist and the economistic positions fail to adequately conceptualise the causal power of ideas in a material context, either overemphasising the determining power of the material context, or engaging in a form of unhelpful idealism which views ideas as autonomous forces, quite independent of (or even constructive of) the material context. This culture/economy, idealism/materialism split is itself implicated in the more general reluctance to view identity in the relation to material social conditions of the capitalist societies with which it has evolved since roughly the 1960s.

A central task of this book is, therefore, to articulate a framework for analysis which enables us to take seriously the power of ideas in their material context, and thus explore the articulation of the idea of identity to the cultural political economy of capitalism. In order to do so, this book develops Raymond Williams's cultural materialist paradigm, as a means of exploring directly the connections between ideational and structural change, and the way in which they are necessarily bound up together. Rather than simply account for 'culture' within a materialist paradigm, this approach shows how ideas, language and signification are not simply produced by (and thus the 'effect of') material conditions, but exist as forms of practical consciousness themselves, and in virtue of this, have causal powers. In addition, this book offers the notion of a 'social logic of capitalism', which emphasises the meaningful social practices that people engage in, that serve not only to reproduce and legitimise the 'abstract' logic of capital accumulation, but also various social institutions and relations in capitalist societies. This framework allows us to address how the cultural and the ideational operate in a capitalist system; how people are socialised into a capitalist way of life; and how ideas can support the reproduction of capitalism or, alternatively, offer forms of resistance to it.

While the book focuses on a particular form of ideational change in its exploration of the emergence of the idea of identity, what I hope will become clear is the potential of this approach to be fruitfully applied to other prominent ideas and discourses in contemporary capitalist societies. Prioritising neither culture nor economy, and indeed, challenging notions of their mutual exclusivity, this cultural materialist approach seeks to demonstrate that political economy 'is through and through cultural without ceasing to be material', and that 'culture' is both material and economic 'in its production, distribution and effects, including effects on reproducing class relations' (Young, 1997: 154). 'As I understand it', continues Young, 'this has been the project of the best of what is called "cultural studies".' In engaging with these issues this book hopes not only to advance an understanding of how identity relates to contemporary capitalism, but also to contribute to the ongoing development of cultural materialism as 'the best of cultural studies'.

STRUCTURE OF THE BOOK

Chapter 1 makes the case in greater detail that identity, as we now know it, is to all intents and purposes a *new* concept, that emerged in popular, political and scientific discourse in roughly the mid-twentieth century. It argues that although the issues that we now associate with identity have always mattered politically and socially, the characterisation of these issues *in terms of identity* is novel, and furthermore, involves a use of the word that is itself substantively novel.

Chapter 2 carries out a 'keyword' analysis of identity, tracing its changing meanings from the earlier sense of the continuity of a particular entity over time, to the notions of personal and social identity with which we are familiar today. It also begins the work of exploring what the category of identity itself 'does' – that is, how it operates as a device that classifies according to what is considered essential to an individual or group. In addition, it suggests a way out of the 'essentialism–social constructivism' impasse that has dominated the social theory of identity. This analysis of identity as a contemporary keyword furthermore provides a particular and substantive rationale for the investigation of the evolution of the term in its historical and material context, and therefore a rationale for the exploration of the evolution of 'identity' in relation to the cultural political economy of capitalist societies that forms the subject of this book.

Chapter 3 draws on and develops the relatively neglected 'cultural materialist' paradigm articulated by Raymond Williams, and sets out a framework that allows us to explain how capitalistic ways of being and knowing can operate across multiple spaces in capitalist societies, forming, shaping, animating or otherwise guiding social norms, ideas and practices, behaviours and institutions. This is what I call the 'social logic of capitalism'. In addition, it offers a means of exploring how different ideas and practices can either promote or challenge this 'social logic of capitalism', by emphasising the practical power of ideas themselves. This, then, is the framework that will be deployed to explore the practical operation and use of the idea of identity in capitalist societies. This approach advances the 'keyword' analysis already carried out, by moving it from a lexical dimension to a more fully social one.

Chapter 4 explores the 'pre-history' of the idea of identity in capitalist societies, examining the shifting social, political and cultural formations and struggles that would eventually give rise to the need for, and culminate in the use of, the word identity as we now know it. It shows that the category of identity emerged at the endpoint of a longer historical development in western thought, which conceptualised *the subject* in different ways over centuries, each of which depended on notions of biological, psychological or cultural essentialism. Specifically it was the movement from the idea of an autonomous self, created by nature, to the idea of a social self, created by the environment or 'culture', that eventually gave rise to the notion of identity as we now know it.

Chapter 5 explores the evolution of identity politics, tracing the emergence of the idea of social identity, and the notion that there are such things as 'social identities', to the new social movements of 'gender' and 'race' of the 1960s. It demonstrates that the notion of social identity provided a new way of thinking politically about the experience of grouphood, functioning both as a clarion call to those who had both experienced oppression on account of their collective heritage, and as a source of pride and political mobilisation in challenging this. It also shows how the idea of social identity, and the notion of 'cultural identities' more particularly, emerged as a useful political resource for groups who sought to defend their customary and valued ways of life against the onslaught of capitalist globalisation. Ultimately, it shows how the idea of social identity did not precede, but emerged as a key part of what we now know as 'identity politics'.

Chapter 6 examines the emergence of the idea of personal identity, tracing its meanings and uses to the intensified contexts of consumption associated with twentieth-century capitalist societies. It shows how the idea of identity offered a useful way of asserting both similarity with and difference from others via practices of emulation and distinction in the 'mass society', effectively displacing class differences onto cultural domain. It makes the case that once people are persuaded that they 'have' an identity – in part by its very invention – they are motivated to try to find it. In the 'consumer society' of late twentieth and early twenty-first century capitalism, the 'psychological' problem of finding an identity finds a ready solution in engagement in practices of consumption, which allow for the visible marking of that identity, thereby 'finding' and 'marking' it at the same time. Ultimately, then, this chapter argues that the idea of 'identity', and specifically 'personal identity', did not pre-exist but emerged alongside and as part of these practices of consumption which have come to characterise twentieth-century capitalism.

Finally, Chapter 7 evaluates the contemporary salience of identity in contemporary capitalist societies from an egalitarian perspective. It examines the extent to which the category of identity can be deployed as a mode of resistance to the social logic of capitalism, in the fields of both politics and popular culture, and offers an historicisation of the political uses and values of the idea of identity in the evolution of capitalism from organised to neoliberal capitalism. It makes the case that though there is some scope for resistance, the social logic of capitalism is itself often articulated through the concept of identity in a way which makes it likely to dovetail with capitalist concerns and social relations. The chapter concludes with some suggestions for how 'identity' might be incorporated into a broad struggle for equality today.

1

Historicising 'Identity'

INTRODUCTION

Identity, particularly as it is elaborated in the associated categories of 'personal' and 'social' identity, is a relatively new concept in western thought, politics and culture. The word itself emerged in popular, political and scientific discourse only in the second half of the twentieth century, and was not discussed at all in these contexts prior to this. Until the 1950s, or even the 1960s and 1970s, there was no discussion of sexual identity, ethnic identity, political identity, national identity, corporate identity, brand identity, identity crisis, or 'losing' or 'finding' one's identity – indeed, no discussion at all of 'identity' in any of the ways that are so familiar to us today, and which, in our ordinary and political discussions, we would now find it hard to do without.

This claim that 'identity' is to all intents and purposes a new concept is controversial, and for many, will be counter-intuitive. Nonetheless, this surprising realisation is also very epistemically fruitful. Recognition of the historical novelty of our contemporary notion of identity sheds light on a number of debates and uncertainties about the experience and expression of identity today. Firstly, it helps resolve some of the key disputes animating social and political theory, including whether 'identities' should be conceptualised as 'essential' to individuals and groups, or socially constructed; and whether it is a divisive or solidaristic force in contemporary group politics. Secondly, it provides insight into the changing cultural and political formations of late capitalist societies, and how people are encouraged to experience their sense of self, and their relations to others in that context. In sum, it goes at least some way towards explaining why identity is both 'vital and problematic in high modernity' (Bendle, 2002: 1).

Quite how recognition of the novelty of the word, and indeed, concept of identity could illuminate so many complexities around the contemporary experience and expression of identity is not something that can be immediately elaborated upon here, but will be revealed over the full course of this study. This first chapter begins this work, and in so doing, introduces the theoretical frame-work that allows us to trace the evolution of words and meanings in a social context in a way which sheds light upon both. Specifically, then, this chapter explores the emergence of the *word* identity into the contemporary political, popular and scientific lexicon, making the case that what we have witnessed is not the mere popularisation of an already existing word across new domains of practice, but the importation of an older word into these domains in a way which has involved a significant change of meaning, albeit one that was masked by the nominal continuity of the term. Ultimately, this chapter will argue that what occurred was not merely the popularisation of an older term, as is widely assumed, but the invention of an idea: the idea of identity.

IDENTITY: FROM ABSENCE TO PRESENCE

The assertion that 'identity' is a historically recent concept, and that the very notion of 'identity', as we now know it, was unavailable prior to the 1960s, seems far-fetched. It runs directly up against a commonplace treatment of iden-tity today, which is precisely to view the very capacity to 'have an identity' as a basic and universal feature of the human condition. Identity just is who we are and who we know ourselves to be, whether that is in terms of our indi-vidual personalities and sense of self – roughly, 'personal identity' – or in terms of the social groups to which we are assigned or identify – roughly, 'social identity'. How could that not be a historically persistent feature of humanity? Furthermore, it is hard to imagine a society, however primitive, in which ques-tions of personal and social identity didn't matter. As Calhoun comments, '[c]oncerns with individual and collective identity are ubiquitous ... [we] know of no people without names, no languages or cultures in which some manner of distinctions between self and other, we and they are not made' (1994: 9).

It is from such a position that a number of commentators have criticised contemporary theoretical accounts that have assumed or proclaimed identity to be a historically recent concern that only came to prominence in late or postmodernity. (Giddens [1991], Woodward [1997] and Castells [2004] provide some well-known accounts of this kind of claim.) Jenkins, for example, urges us to be 'very sceptical' of the claim that 'identity [has] become more marked and more significant over the last few decades' and argues forcefully that con-cerns about identity are an endemic aspect of the human condition (2008: 20). 'It is nothing new', he writes, 'to be self-conscious about identity: about what it means to be human, what it means to be a particular kind of human, what it means to be an individual and a person, whether people are who and what they appear to be and so on' (2008: 36). He accuses postmodern theorists of forget-ting 'the fundamental importance of systematic inquiry into the observable realities of the human world' (2008: 36), arguing that their position is simply unconvincing. After all, he comments, 'didn't people know who they were, or think about it, before the twentieth century?' (2008: 35). This belief is supported in scientific and quasi-scientific ways in the vast amount of popular and clinical psychological accounts of 'human nature', 'human development' and human well-being which regard the need for and expressions of identity as universal and cross-cultural human concerns (Max-Neef, 1991; Sen, 1999; Akerlof and Kranton, 2000; Sen, 2000; Kail and Cavanaugh, 2010).

Similar critiques have been made of recent social theory which views 'identity politics' as a novel historical phenomenon. Calhoun (1993, 1994), for example, accuses those who claim that issues of identity are new to social movements of historical myopia. He challenges what he sees as the consensus view that issues of identity did not feature in 'old' social movements, providing evidence of the pertinence of issues of identity to nineteenth-century labour movements, and asserting that 'we need to recognize how profoundly early workers' movements were engaged in a politics of identity' (1993: 395). This view is supported by O'Neill (1998) and Aronowitz (1992), who suggest that questions of identity and recognition have always been central to labour and working class politics. Calhoun also argues that movements organised princi- pally around identitarian social categories are not new: 'the notion that identity politics is a new phenomenon ... is equally false' (1994: 23), he writes, pointing to women's movements, the establishment of communes, anti-colonial resist- ance and nationalistic politics as evidence of identity-based social movements in existence up to 200 years ago. Others too have made similarly revisionist arguments, including Hetherington (1998: 30), who questions the assumption that 'identity politics' are emblematic of 'new' social movements, asserting that 'feminism, environmentalism, peace movements, anti-racist campaigns, animal rights movements and so on are not new; they have existed for at least two centuries within Western societies'. These theorists all effectively challenge the claim that identity politics are a recent phenomenon, by tracing the issues and movements we today label as identity politics back to the 1800s. '"Identity poli- tics" and similar concerns', writes Calhoun, 'were never quite so much absent from the field of social movement activity – even in the heydays of liberal party politics or organized trade union struggle – as they were obscured from con- ventional academic observation' (1993: 388). Thus for Calhoun, while identity concerns are 'ubiquitous', '[s]ocial science has paid [them] only intermittent attention' (1994: 23).

There are also countless studies documenting the identity challenges of older civilisations, including the Greeks, the Celts and the ancient Mediterraneans (Gruen, 2011; Demetriou, 2012; Andrade, 2013; Gibson et al., 2013). Many more studies examine the politicisation of identity concerns historically, includ- ing, prominently, the identity struggles of colonised nations from the 1700s (Canny and Pagden, 1987; Katten, 2005), and the identity struggles of the wom- en's movement and of women more generally in and prior to the twentieth century (the journals *Women's History Review* and *The Journal of Women's History* return over 1300 articles between them on the subject of women's identities in historical context). Questions of identity seem absolutely central to early studies in psychology and sociology, as they grappled with the problems of individual deviance and normality, and the development of the individual in relation to her/his social environment (Ernst and Harris, 1999; Wagner, 2001; Thomson, 2006; Bourne Taylor, 2007). Jenkins (2008: 31) points out that 'an established sociological and psychological literature about identity goes back to the turn of the century and before: James, Cooley, Mead, Simmel come to mind immediately'. He also goes on to refer to the work of Locke, Shakespeare and Indian philosophers of the 1500s, admonishing that 'we sacrifice historical perspective if we neglect the variety of intellectual traditions that have reflected on identity: there is nothing intrinsically new about these issues'. Williams (2000) has made similar observations, and indeed, we might add to Jenkins's list of social and political theorists the work of Mary Wollstonecraft, W.E.B. du Bois, John Stuart Mill, Sigmund Freud, Frederic Nietzsche, amongst others, all of whom are widely agreed to have contributed significantly to our understanding of identity. Literary fiction too seems to be replete with historical examples of a concern with identity. In *The Nineteenth Century Novel: Identities*, Walder (2001) and his co-contributors discuss the significance and centrality of questions of identity in the well-known novels of Gustave Flaubert, Henry James, Bram Stoker, Kate Chopin and Joseph Conrad. Virginia Woolf, Ernest Hemingway, Robert Louis Stevenson and numerous others are also regularly announced to have written intensively on the subject of identity (cf. Benjamin, 1993; Cornes, 2008; Strong, 2008), with Cornes (2008: 5) positing that this literature reflected 'an obsession with individual identity [that] pervaded Western world thinking in the nineteenth and early twentieth centuries'. Meanwhile, undergraduate and postgraduate courses routinely offer modules on identity in nineteenth-, eighteenth- and even seventeenth-century fiction.

However, closer reading of these original texts reveals the startling fact that none of these theorists, scientists, activists or writers credited with discussing or explaining identity ever actually used the word identity themselves. Though the term appears in more recent discussions, summaries and reviews of their work, this is typically without any acknowledgement or awareness of the fact that the original authors did not themselves deploy the term in the manner in which it is used today. This is not to suggest that the word identity was *never* used in any of these texts – it was. Crucially, however, *it was used in a very particular sense*, and indeed, what we would now see as a very narrow sense, to mean the sameness of an entity to itself, or the sameness of an entity over time. Consequently, almost without exception, where the term 'identity' does appear in these texts now assumed to be 'about' identity, it is incidental, and never the subject of any substantive discussion in itself. The only place a discussion of identity appears as a substantive topic in itself prior to the 1950s is in studies in analytical philosophy, where philosophers puzzled over the persistence and sameness of an entity – whether human or inanimate – over time. The connection between this narrow sense and the later uses with which we are now familiar will be elaborated in Chapter 2. But for now, the important point is that those writers, theorists and scientists who we now believe to have discussed questions of personal and social identity as we now know and use the concepts never, in fact, discussed identity at all.

Contemporary scepticism of such a claim runs deep, so let us consider some specific examples, beginning with the fields of psychology and sociology with which discussions of identity are often associated. Freud has been identified by the Oxford University Press (2008) as a key theorist of identity – 'there is little doubt', they tell us, but 'that he has radically altered how modern people think about themselves and their identity' – yet a comprehensive search of his entire volume of work reveals only a few uses of the term identity. In each case, it is not the contemporary sense of the term that we find, but the older sense of 'the sameness of an entity to itself'.[1] So for example, we see Freud (1920: 61) use the phrase 'identity of perception', which he explains as 'a repetition of that perception which is connected with the fulfilment of the want', thereby using 'identity' to indicate an *equivalence* between perception and want, and not 'identity' as we now know it. Indeed, Erik Erikson, who could conceivably claim credit for being among the first to use the term identity as we now understand it, writes, 'First a word about the term identity. As far as I know Freud used it only once in a more than incidental way, and then with a psychosocial connotation' (1959: 109). Introductory textbooks in the fields of psychology and sociology regularly make a similar mistake where they cite Charles Cooley, George Herbert Mead and William James for their important contributions to our modern understandings of identity (Hall, 1992; Kellner, 1995; McIntyre, 2006; Matthewman et al., 2007; Jenkins, 2008). Yet investigation of their key texts reveals that none of these authors actually use the word identity in the sense suggested by these contemporary reviewers. For example, in Chapter 10 of *The Principles of Psychology*, entitled 'The Consciousness of Self', James discusses the problem of 'personal identity', remarking that 'ever since Hume's time, it has been justly regarded as the most puzzling puzzle with which psychology has to deal' (1890: 334). However, it continues to be the problem of the sameness or the persistence of the self that James discusses in this context – and though arguably James develops and provides a more social understanding of this abstract philosophical problem, he clearly does not discuss identity in its fuller contemporary sense, instead defining the feeling of identity as 'the experience that "I am the same self that I was yesterday"' (1890: 332). He continues,

> the sense of our own personal identity, then, *is exactly like any one of our other perceptions of sameness among phenomena*. It is a conclusion grounded either on the resemblance in a fundamental respect, or on the continuity before the mind, of the phenomena compared ... And accordingly we find that, where the resemblance and the continuity are no longer felt, the sense of personal identity goes too. (James, 1890: 334, my italics)

This clearly reveals that what is at stake here is an understanding of identity as the persistence of self over time. Similarly, a search of Cooley's *Human Nature and the Social Order* (1902) and Mead's *Mind, Self and Society* (1934) – both assumed to be centrally concerned with the sociology of identity – reveals no instances of use of the term at all.[2]

There are similar findings in relation to the subjects of 'race' and gender, with which the notion of identity tends today also to be closely associated. W.E.B. du Bois, who is so regularly credited with being a key theorist of identity that several books have been written on the topic, does not once use the term in his important work *The Souls of Black Folk*, which is widely understood to form the core of his contribution to understandings of identity (Nicholson, 2008). In his Introduction to 'W.E.B. du Bois: Of Cultural and Racial Identity', editor Robert Gooding-Williams (1994: 168) claims that 'Du Bois's writing continues to shape our own thinking about issues of racial and cultural identity. To engage Du Bois, then, is to engage many of the concerns, questions, and perspectives which animate contemporary debates about these issues.' In fact, it is incredible that so many reviews of du Bois's work cannot do without the term identity, even though the term did not appear once in his key texts they review. The same issue is evident in contemporary feminism which looks to its earlier or foundational tracts for evidence of formative feminist thinking on the subject of identity. For example, Gunther-Canada (2001: 4) argues that one of Wollstonecraft's great achievements was to 'envision an autonomous political identity for women', and to base her argument on an understanding of how the 'female identity' is formed through childhood. But the word identity is not used once in *A Vindication of the Rights of Woman* (Wollstonecraft, 2002 [1796]), nor indeed elsewhere in her writings (cf. Butler and Todd, 1989). Virginia Woolf is also widely imagined to have confronted the problem of female identity, as indicated by Marina Benjamin (1993: 1) when she chooses to open the first chapter of her work, *A Question of Identity: Women, Science, and Literature*, with the following excerpt from Woolf's *A Room of One's Own*:

> Imaginatively she is of the highest importance; practically she is completely insignificant. She pervades poetry from cover to cover; she is all but absent from history. She dominates the lives of kings and conquerors in fiction; in fact she was the slave of any boy whose parents forced a ring upon her finger. Some of the most inspired words, some of the most profound thoughts in literature fall from her lips; in real life she could hardly read, could hardly spell, and was the property of her husband.

Yet even though this passage is the opening piece in a chapter also entitled 'A Question of Identity', it does not seem to strike the author as strange that Woolf herself does not use the word identity in order to address the 'woman question', either in the cited passage or elsewhere in *A Room of One's Own*.

More broadly, there is a striking absence of the term identity from that nineteenth-century literary fiction which is now also widely assumed to be about identity. Despite explicit claims to the contrary, there is no evidence of the word identity in any of those 'great' nineteenth-century 'identity' novels like Flaubert's *Madame Bovary*, James's *The Portrait of a Lady*, Chopin's *The Awakening* and Conrad's *Heart of Darkness*. Similarly, when Jenkins refers us to a key passage of Shakespeare's *As You Like It* in order to demonstrate the 'long history' of reflections on identity, it is significant that the piece he cites does not contain the word identity at all, though Jenkins proceeds glibly – and blindly – as though it does:

> All the world's a stage, And all the men and women merely players: They have their exits and their entrances; And one man in his time plays many parts. (Cited in Jenkins, 2008: 31)

And this pattern can be found yet more widely still: a search of the archival record of *all* published output for the UK and Ireland,[3] which includes books, journals, periodicals and newspapers, reveals that the word identity appeared in the title or as a subject keyword in very few published items prior to the 1950s (featuring in an average of one item published every four years). Where it did appear, closer inspection reveals that it was not in the sense we now know and use the term, but again, in that older sense associated with analytical philosophy as, for example, in *Identity and Reality* (Meyerson, 1930), or (relatedly, as we will see), in the sense of a 'mistaken' identity, as in *Concealed Identity* (Richmond, 1938). Interestingly, once the term identity is excluded from the 'keyword' search, items which have subsequently been tagged by the cataloguer as being 'about' identity, but which did not use the term identity itself, are excluded. While this unsurprisingly throws up a smaller number of items, it also removes some telling items from the list, including *I Passed for White* (Lee (Pseudonym) and Hastings Bradley, 1955) and *The Ghetto* (Wirth, 1928). Questions of ethnicity, which are now routinely understood as questions of identity, were not, so it seems, understood as such a mere 50 years ago.

This dearth of discussion or even use of the word identity was evident in other domains too, as investigation reveals that politicians, marketers, activists and ordinary people engaging in day-to-day activities seem to have rarely used the word identity prior to the 1960s, and when they did, again, it was not in the way we use it today.[4] Of course, this type of search is potentially boundless, but searches of political speeches, magazines and newspaper articles from the first half of the century give a good indication insofar as they do not yield any evidence of such use of the term identity. These findings are corroborated by a small number of other observers who have identified a distinct and noticeable absence of the term identity in public and political as well as academic contexts prior to about 1960 (Mackenzie, 1978; Gleason, 1983; Fearon, 1999).

Suddenly, however, all this changed. In the 1950s, books with identity in a sense we now easily recognise started to appear, as for example, *Identity and Interpersonal Competence: A New Direction in Family Research* by Nelson N. Foote and Leonard S. Cottrell Jr in 1955 (on the subject of interpersonal relationships), and *On Shame and the Search for Identity* by Helen Merrell Lynd in 1958. Lynd immediately cites Erikson and his use of identity in her introduction, writing that 'so great has been the impact of the changes of recent years that it is possible for an innovating Freudian psychoanalyst, Erik H. Erikson, to say that the search for identity has become as strategic in our time as the study of sexuality was in Freud's time' (Lynd, 1958: 14). The rest of the introduction reads like any introduction to the problems of identity today, making similar claims about its social and personal formations, and its great significance as a contemporary social concern. Interestingly, her comments here suggest that identity had become a common and familiar term beyond its academic use, something which was not reflected in the number of books published at the time of her writing. Yet this, too, would soon change. Erikson had not yet written his famous *Identity and the Life Cycle* (1959) but he had written *Childhood and Society* (1950), to which Lynd specifically refers. In the following years, an increasing number of books were published which deliberately deployed the term identity in the psychological sense set out by Erikson, followed in the early 1960s by a scattering of books that dealt explicitly with the subject of cultural or ethnic identity/ies, including *Politics, Personality and Nation-Building: Burma's Search for Identity* (Pye, 1962) and *Modern Islam: The Search for Cultural Identity* (Von Grunebaum, 1962). Much as a few isolated kernels of corn 'pop' as the oil heats in the pot, the examples from this 'warming-up' period were only an indication of what was to come. Indeed, the full evolution of the new senses of the word identity would be clustered together in a loud and chaotic eruption in the following decades. From this point on we see an exponential increase in the number of items published with identity in the title or subject matter, from the publication of an average of one item on identity every four years prior to the 1950s, to a peak of 533 items in *one year* in 2007.

As Figure 1.1 shows, after a steady increase from the 1950s to 1980s, the number of publications with identity in the title itself rose dramatically during the 1990s; 46 were published in 1990, 207 in 2000 and 237 in 2010.[5] Others too have documented this huge explosion in the use of the word identity. Brubaker and Cooper (2000) have traced a vast increase in the number of people writing about identity since the 1970s, evident in the number of articles published on the subject and even the emergence of new journals explicitly devoted to identity. In his review of the growth of the usage of the term identity in the social sciences, Gilligan (2007) notes that while in 1970, 0.1% of all articles, books and book reviews indexed by the International Bibliography of Social Sciences (IBSS) had 'identity' in the title, by 1990, the figure had risen to 0.4%, and by 1999, had jumped to over 0.9%. Fearon (1999) also notes that the number of dissertations published with the term identity in the abstract

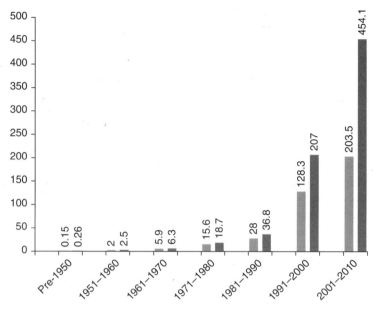

■ Average no. of Publications PER YEAR with 'Identity' in title only
■ Average no. of Publications PER YEAR with 'Identity' in title/subject matter

Figure 1.1   Average number of publications on 'identity' in the UK and Ireland per year

increased at an average rate of 12% per year between 1986 and 1995, while Gleason (1983: 918) claims that even 'by the 1960s, the word identity was used so widely and loosely [in the social sciences] that to determine its provenance in every context would be impossible'. As Brubaker and Cooper have pointed out, what is surprising about much of this work is that it has been carried out by people whose training and background lies emphatically 'outside the "homelands" of identity theorizing' (2000: 4), to the extent that the language of identity and identity crises can be found in the medical and natural sciences as well as the social (2000: 38, fn 15). There has been little or no abatement of academic work on the subject of identity since any of these measurements were taken, though there may be a decrease in the rate of expansion. As Alcoff recently put it, 'identity is today a growth industry in the academy' (2006: 5).

Crucially, however, it is not just academics or literary figures talking about identity. As Brubaker and Cooper note, the language of identity has rapidly proved highly resonant across a number of domains, 'diffusing quickly across disciplinary and national boundaries, establishing itself in the journalistic as well as the academic lexicon, and permeating the language of social and political practice as well as that of social and political analysis' (2000: 3). Gleason (1983: 931) carefully documents what he sees as an 'enormous popularization' of the term in public, political and everyday as well as academic discourse from the middle of the twentieth century, while Fearon (1999) notes especially the recent 'ordinary language' usage of the term, and calls for an analysis which is attentive to these uses. Mackenzie (1978: 15) even goes so far as to discuss the 'murder' of the word identity in 'semi-popular discourse from about 1971'. Within a very short space of time, suddenly everybody seemed to be talking about identity. African American, feminist and gay and lesbian movements declared their newly articulated pride in their 'identities', politicians discussed 'national identity', multicultural festivals celebrated 'ethnic identities', teens agonised over their 'individual identities' and middle-aged white men went through 'identity crises'. David Riesman, in the 1961 preface to his widely read book on changes to the American 'social character', *The Lonely Crowd*, referred directly to 'the current preoccupation with identity in this country' (1961 [1950]: lx). A few years later, Malcolm X spoke directly to his followers about the identity concerns of African Americans (while, significantly, as will be discussed further in Chapter 5, Martin Luther King never mentioned identity once). And in 1977, the black feminist lesbian organisation, the Combahee River Collective, produced the famous 'Combahee River Collective Statement', often credited with being one of the archetypal texts of 'identity politics', asserting:

> We realize that the only people who care enough about us to work consistently for our liberation is us ... This focusing on our own oppression is embodied in the concept of identity politics. We believe that the most profound and potentially the most radical politics come directly out of our own identity, as opposed to working to end somebody else's oppression. (1979 [1977]: 365)

Identity-talk continues unremittingly today. There is explicit discussion of identity in media talk shows, in self-help and popular psychological literature, in online profiles and in television and film. The word identity appears in multiple book and music titles,[6] and films dealing with identity theft, swapping or loss have proliferated in recent years (*The Bourne Identity*, *Identity Thief* and the eponymous *Identity* are some recent high-profile examples). Online searches using the words 'losing', 'searching for' or 'finding' identity throw up a huge array of websites, blogs, adverts, online discussions and help-groups which claim to have an answer. This includes but is not limited to quasi-religious sites which proclaim themselves to be 'dedicated to providing information and resources to help people find their purpose and identity'; blogs about 'losing identity', in marriage, in mental health disorders, and in a range of common but traumatic experiences associated with family life, immigration, career and expected life trajectory; and a variety of sites providing advice and encouragement on issues of self-esteem and self-worth on the subject of 'searching for an identity'.[7] Fashion and consumption is directly and explicitly linked to identity, with, for example, Gok Wan, the presenter of the highly popular British Channel 4 make-over show *How to Look Good Naked*, writing in The *Guardian*, 'Fashion is about costume and identity, it's about being who you are ... fashion and image is so subjective, it's not down to my opinion. It's about confidence. It's about understanding your identity, and why you do certain things' (Carter, 2008). The language of advertising, marketing and the corporate world has also become heavily inflected with explicit references to identity, evident in the vast number of practical manuals and guides published on the development and management of brand and corporate identities, and indeed, the emergence of a veritable industry on the subject. The home page of 'identity builders' *Keen Branding* tells us it is 'dedicated to helping our clients in all aspects of creating, building, growing and fully realizing the potential of each corporate and brand identity through our specialized services for brand identity development, corporate identity development, [and] corporate identity design'. Other similar companies include *BIG – Brand Identity Guru, Identity Works, Brains on Fire* (which interestingly uses the language of social movements as well as identity) and *Kontrapunkt*, who claim on their home page that 'Identity is the core of business strategy'.[8]

IDENTITY: A SIGN OF THE TIMES?

How should we explain this huge explosion in use of the term identity across academic, political, popular cultural, commercial and literary spaces from roughly the 1960s? And what does it tell us about the longevity or otherwise of identity concerns? Those accounts which posit a new salience of identity in western societies, evident in the shift to identity politics, multiculturalism and identity-based forms of consumption in particular, tend to pay little attention to the explosion of use of the term itself. We might reasonably conclude that their assumption is that as the issue of identity has become more important, so too, obviously, has the language. People talk about it more, and theorists analyse it more precisely because it matters more today than it ever did.

Jenkins, however, turns this assumption on its head. He argues that in fact what has happened is that the 'identity theorists' have run away with themselves, projecting their own identity concerns onto the world they view. He attributes the ostensible new importance of identity to 'the conceits of western modernity, and its intellectual elite' who externalise their new-found fascination with identity concerns onto modern society more generally (2008: 34). Given the documented explosion of academic uses of the term, it is not hard to see why Jenkins might assume this to be the case. This does not, however, explain the popular explosion of the term, which Jenkins also acknowledges. Here he finds himself arguing that the growth in a popular discourse of identity is a function only of the development of information and communication technology. He claims that 'it's probably ... true that the *volume* of discourse about identity has reached new magnitudes, if only because global noise and chatter about everything has increased with the population and the widening availability of communication technologies' (2008: 31). This provides him with a means of acknowledging a growth in a popular discourse of identity while maintaining that the true importance or value of identity has not changed. This argument is largely unconvincing, not least because it does not explain why other historically persistent concerns or experiences are not talked about to the same degree. It is also difficult to reconcile the claim that the contemporary salience of identity reflects nothing more than an increased popularity of the term with the growth in social movements organised around identity, and the clear increase in identity-based marketing and consumption from this time. Jenkins, however, is emblematic of a wider perception, and one with which I was regularly confronted in academic and lay circles while writing this book. And indeed, this interpretation is not surprising given the widely held contention that identity 'always mattered'. If this were the case, how could the huge 'noise' and 'chatter' around identity represent anything more than its popularisation as a word?

These two readings of the contemporary salience of identity are dominant today – either identity matters now more than it ever did, and its prominence in contemporary discourse reflects this; or identity has always mattered, but we are simply – for better or worse – paying it increased attention. What both perspectives miss is the key point established here: it is not just that identity is now discussed *more* than it was previously, but that prior to the 1950s, identity was simply not discussed *at all* in the ways it is now. And what is important to recognise in all these academic, political and popular contexts is not just that the word identity was being used extensively where it had not been used before, but that these uses themselves carried a significant change of meaning. No longer referring simply to the persistence of an entity over time, or even to a quasi-legal form of identity as in a 'mistaken' or 'concealed' identity, what is at stake here are the two uses of the term with which we are so familiar today: 'personal identity', to refer to personality and individuality, and 'social identity', to refer to assignment to or identification with a particular social group. Thus, although from our current vantage point it is widely perceived that this contemporary emphasis on identity involves an *increase* in the use of the term identity, in fact what is at stake is a *new* and original use of the term.

This reveals that the non-use of the word identity prior to the 1960s in the contexts in which it is now used was not simply accidental but quite sensible. It was not simply that the word was not fashionable, or that we just simply had not thought to use it, but that crucially, identity did not mean then what it means now. Instead, those participating in social movements, writing about self and society, thinking about their relationships with others and their association with different groups, expressed their concerns in alternative terms – concerns which are *now* but which were not then axiomatically considered or explicitly expressed in terms of identity. So although Jenkins and others are right in saying that issues that we now associate with the idea of identity have always mattered politically and socially, the characterisation of these issues in terms of identity is novel, and furthermore, involves a use of the word that is itself substantively novel. Thus in response to Jenkins's question, 'didn't people know who they were, or think about it, before the twentieth century?' the answer is: of course they did – but they did not frame or consider these issues in terms of identity. The same applies to the question of the persistence of identity issues in social movements – Calhoun and Hetherington are quite right to say that groups mobilised around questions of gender, ethnicity and nation for centuries prior to the emergence of a series of 'new' social movements around identity, but the fact remains that the protagonists did not explicitly consider these issues as issues of identity, nor did they, it seems, expressly identify membership of these social categories as particular *identities*. And although feminists, political theorists, philosophers, psychologists and social scientists have always, to a greater or lesser extent, been concerned with questions of self and society, groups and social categories, and our individual and collective self-understandings arising from each, it seems clear that they did not expressly regard these as issues pertaining to 'identity' until the second half of the twentieth century. The key point remains both that identity did not mean then what it means now, and that the issues *now* discussed in terms of identity are not in themselves either entirely new or newly important; rather it is their framing and discussion in terms of identity which is novel and widespread.

IDENTITY IN CONTEXT: A CULTURAL MATERIALIST FRAMEWORK FOR ANALYSIS

This important point has achieved very little recognition. Indeed, it is surprising that so many have puzzled over the 'problems' of identity, yet do not pick up on the novelty of the term or its uses, leaving it instead to three or four writers working at the fringes of the identity 'tradition' in the academy, namely, Mackenzie (1978), Gleason (1983), Fearon (1999) and Brubaker and Cooper (2000). (Gleason is a historian, famous for his work on the history of American Catholicism, while Fearon is a political scientist who has specialised in political violence and democracy – his article on identity remains unpublished. Mackenzie had a background in classics and political sciences, and never published again on the subject of identity. Only Brubaker and Cooper work within the 'subject area' of identity in the social sciences.) Furthermore, the fact that each of these authors has written on the subject in different decades, without any widespread acknowledgement of this novelty of the term in the interim, points, I believe, to the deeply entrenched notion that the term identity has always more or less meant what it means now, and that 'identity', as such, has always mattered.

Working against the grain of this common appraisal of identity concerns, these commentators represent a special case insofar as each of them recognises, as Gleason puts it, that '*identity* is a new term as well as being an elusive and

ubiquitous one' (1983: 910). However, despite this, it is the case that none completely grasps the significance of the word's proliferation and meaning change
in its historical context – mainly, I will now suggest, because each continues to
see the *word itself* as the problem. As Mackenzie puts it, identity is a word that
'express[es] everything and nothing about personal and social anguish in the
last third of the twentieth century' (1978: 101). Recognising both its changing
meanings and vast proliferation of uses across multiple contexts, Mackenzie and
Fearon both encourage us to pin down or capture the meanings of the word.
'It would be a victory', says Mackenzie, 'if one could ensnare the concept, settle an appropriate use of the word' (1978: 102), which he attempts to do by
mapping the structure of 'links and sequences' within which the word identity
is used (1978: 104). Meanwhile Fearon aims to 'distill a statement of meaning
of "identity" from an analysis of current usage in ordinary language and social
science discourse' (1999: 2).

  For Gleason and Brubaker and Cooper, however, this project is misguided.
Given the level of 'generality and diffuseness' of the term, contends Gleason,
'there is little point in asking what *identity* "really means" when matters have
reached this pass' (1983: 914). But it is Brubaker and Cooper (2000) who have
put forward the most sustained attack on the word identity itself. In their
paper 'Beyond "Identity"', they diagnose identity as an inflated and ambiguous
concept that has lost any useful meaning. Tracing its diffusion across lay and
academic contexts, they complain that we have arrived at a point where 'all
affinities and affiliations, all forms of belonging, all experiences of commonality, connectedness and cohesion, all self-understandings and self-identifications'
(2000: 2) are conceptualised in terms of the idiom of identity. Distinguishing
between identity as a 'category of practice' – that is a category of 'everyday
social experience, developed and deployed by ordinary social actors' – and as
a category of analysis – that is, an 'experience-distant categor[y] used by social
analysts' – they argue that its contemporary popularity as a category of practice
does not require its use as a category of analysis (2000: 4). But this important
point has not been recognised or heeded, they contend, as the everyday 'hard'
or 'essentialist' uses of identity have been unthinkingly imported into the social
scientific lexicon. To make matters worse, these 'hard' understandings are in
conflict with the 'soft', 'constructivist' understandings currently in vogue in academic analysis, where the term identity has already followed its own complex
internal development. For Brubaker and Cooper, then, identity refers to everything and means nothing.

  Although they acknowledge the ordinary practical uses of the term identity
as it is deployed by a range of lay actors 'in some (not all!) everyday settings
to make sense of themselves, of their activities, of what they share with, and
how they differ from, others' (2000: 4), these uses do not concern Brubaker and
Cooper. Instead their concern rests with the analytical categories required to make
sense of all those affinities, affiliations, self-understandings and self-identifications
that are currently bundled together in the 'blunt, flat, undifferentiated', not to

mention contradictory, vocabulary of identity (2000: 2). They stress on a number of occasions that what is at issue is 'not the legitimacy or importance of particularistic claims, but how best to conceptualise them' (2000: 34). On these grounds, they argue that we should dispense with the problematic language of identity and replace it with a range of concepts better suited to the difficult analytical task of understanding how 'identity' operates as a category of political and social practice. They do not believe there is anything important going on with the reference to so many issues in terms of identity, nor indeed with the proliferation of practical uses of the term – for them, 'identity' is simply an analytical mistake.

In each of these cases, it is clear that the focus rests on the problematic relationship of the word to the concept. For Brubaker and Cooper, the word identity unhelpfully conflates too many disparate and contradictory concepts – our purposes are better served as analysts by eschewing identity and selecting some more precise and accurate words to capture the relevant concepts. Mackenzie makes this formulation of the problem explicit when he asks whether we should consider identity as 'a new label for an old concept? A new label for a new concept? Or merely a with-it word … used not to convey meaning but to give tone?' (1978: 18). While each of these alternatives has a ring of truth, none completely captures what has happened with the emergence of identity as a term, since crucially, none acknowledges the changing behaviours and politics accompanying the changing use and meaning of the term. The meaning change in question coincided not just with a massive explosion of the use of the term but also with the proliferation of an array of actions, behaviours and interests to do with what we now understand as 'identity'. As will be explained in greater depth as the book proceeds, the word identity came to be used in contexts in which questions of group and selfhood were themselves becoming problematic – that is, in 'new' social movements around 'race' and gender; in the intensified contexts of consumption that have come to characterise the 'consumer societies' of contemporary capitalism; and in the widespread popularisation of psychology and the emergence of a 'self-help' industry. Thus, current uses and meanings of the term emerged at the same time as these political, social and cultural issues to do with questions and expressions of self- and grouphood became much more significant. This tells us that the word identity *as we now know it* came into being at the same time as the issues concerning the experience and expression of identity (or rather, the issues we *now* consider in terms of identity) became notably prominent in political and social life.

These contexts of use are at best overlooked in these explanations, as, on the whole, they do not take adequate account of the particular and changing circumstances in which the word identity came to be used. Brubaker and Cooper offer a token contextualisation, but their emphasis remains firmly on identity as a category of analysis rather than a category of practice. Only Gleason addresses this issue and these connections with any seriousness, as he turns, in the final part of his paper, to 'the matter of causes', and asks 'why did *identity* so quickly become an indispensible term in American social commentary?' (1983: 922). He identifies the new prestige of the social sciences and the popularisation of Erikson's work on identity as key factors, but argues that the 'decisive cause' was the way in which the 'word identity was ideally adapted to talking about the relationship of the individual to society as that perennial problem presented itself to Americans mid-century' (1983: 926). His analysis, however, is mainly suggestive, and is stymied by his lingering belief that the word itself is a problem.

This inattention to the contexts of use is reflected in the curious dismissal of or disregard for the everyday uses of the term – or what Brubaker and Cooper refer to as the uses of identity as a category of practice. It is either seen as a relatively inconsequential offshoot of the academic development, as is the case with Gleason and Mackenzie, or is deliberately bracketed out of the analysis altogether, as is the case with Brubaker and Cooper. Only Fearon suggests that we should pay more attention to these everyday uses, arguing that 'Brubaker and Cooper and Gleason are giving up too soon on both popular and "popular academic" usage' (1999: 7). In this Fearon is right, but because he tries only to pin down what identity 'means' in everyday language, he remains trapped in the word-concept binary and pays insufficient attention to the context, tracing these meanings in abstraction from the changing circumstances of their use.

These issues are all connected. That is, this inclination to view the word identity as problematic is a product of a failure to properly contextualise its new and changing uses – a failure to look at the word 'identity' in action. For it is not alone a question of new or old words and concepts, but also a question of new and changing events, conditions and issues: the new use of identity is not simply indicative of changing meanings of a word, but this new use and these changing meanings are themselves bound up with a changing reality. Identity, I suggest, is not simply a new word to describe old issues, nor an old word invested with new meanings, but a word that carries and encapsulates a new way of thinking about and engaging with a range of social, political and human concerns, which in turn, changes and affects the concerns and the conditions which give rise to them.

A shared but hidden assumption of these theorists who recognise the novelty of use and meaning of the word seems to be that that to which identity refers precedes its naming (albeit in a messy and complicated way). Hence Brubaker and Cooper's admonition that 'people everywhere and always have particular ties, self-understandings, stories, trajectories, histories, predicaments', but it is a mistake to reduce all this diversity and complexity to the 'flat, undifferentiated rubric of "identity"' (2000: 34). Fixing the term by pinning down its meanings, or throwing it out and replacing it with other equivalent but sharper words, is seen to provide better access to the concept it is supposed to capture. Thus as Mackenzie grasped the issue, 'I realized that I was moving from word to concept; and that there were difficult conceptual questions, for which the word "identity" (whether personal, political or social) might prove as good a label as any other' (1978: 50). This book takes issue with this belief – identity is not just any old word, or as good (or bad) as any other, but is purposive and active: it calls into being and shapes that which it seems only to describe. Or to put it another way, that to which identity now refers did not precede its naming in these terms. Consequently, and against Mackenzie's claim, no other word would do – and *the word itself*, properly investigated, reveals why this is so, as this book demonstrates.

For all these reasons I suggest it is most helpful to consider identity a 'keyword' in the sense intended by Raymond Williams; that is, as a word related in complicated ways to the changing social reality it at once attempts to describe and forms an intrinsic part of. In the important introduction to *Keywords*, Williams clarifies the special character of a keyword, which is that 'the problems of its meanings [are] inextricably bound up with the problems it [is] used to discuss' (1983: 15). These problems of meaning and the problems it is used to discuss are historically specific, and thus we would expect the list of keywords to change over time, alongside the changing cultural, political and social beliefs, values and problems of the moment. As indeed it does – the word identity does not appear in Williams's original *Keywords* (1976), nor the revised second edition (1983), though it appears in later emulations of his work (Wolfreys, 2004; Bennett et al., 2005).[9] The foundational claim of *Keywords* is that language change, and specifically meaning change, is a part of, and provides insight into the nature of, social and cultural transformation. As Bennett et al. (2005: xvii) explain,

> For Williams the point was not merely that the meanings of words change over time but that they change in relationship to changing political, social and economic situations and needs. While rejecting the idea that you could describe that relationship in any simple or universal way, he was convinced it did exist – and that people do struggle in their use of language to give expression to new experiences of reality.

In this way, and as I will explain, Williams turns ordinary understandings on their head so that what might otherwise appear to be problematic difficulties of meaning are revealed to be better understood as a solution, or the key to analysis and wider understanding. Thus where Brubaker and Cooper urge us to 'throw out' the word identity, on the grounds that it is confused and confusing, Williams's inclination is to find in precisely this semantic complexity a unique insight into the social changes with which the new and sometimes conflicting uses of the word are bound up. This 'cultural materialist' approach, then, is the approach I propose to take in investigating and explaining the contemporary salience of identity in western, capitalist societies.

CONCLUSION

The widespread and deeply entrenched failure, with the few notable exceptions mentioned here, to recognise that identity is to all intents and purposes a new word – or more exactly, an old word used in new ways – rather than one that has simply and unproblematically increased in usage, reveals another, important set of assumptions that are key to the historical argument of this book. That is, the widespread assumption that the word identity always meant what it means now reflects and is the product of a deeper, underlying belief that that to which it refers – 'identity' as we now know it – always existed. This is the consensus view on identity: it tells us that identity concerns have *always* featured in human societies, but that in contemporary, western societies, these concerns have come to matter more, trumping alternative political, social and cultural concerns; that where identity was once peripheral, it is now central, and where it was once neglected, it is now prioritised – 'in fashion' so to speak. Where these dominant readings differ is on the extent to which they view the movement of identity from periphery to centre, from neglect to priority, as a product of 'real' social changes, or a new social scientific and popular fascination with all things identitarian. This understanding that identity, somehow, always featured, itself rests on the more basic assumption that the experience and expression of identity is a universal experience and expression; that 'having an identity' – whether stable and unchanging or complex and fractured – is a basic and constitutive element of the human condition.

Against this interpretation what this book shows is that identity never 'mattered' prior to the 1960s – at least not as we know and understand identity today – primarily because it didn't in fact *exist* or operate as a shared political and cultural idea until the 1960s. That is, the very idea of identity, as we know and use it today, only emerged into the popular, scientific and political imagination in the second half of the last century. So far I have traced this emergence mainly in terms of the appearance of the very word itself across a range of political, popular, literary and academic sites. However, as I have argued, the word emerged into popular and scientific use precisely as the bearer of new meanings. It is these new and changing senses in which the word came to be used that I trace in the next chapter. But more than this, developing a cultural materialist perspective means viewing changing meanings as intrinsically part of the social context in which they are expressed, utilised and which they shape. More formally, a key principle of the paradigm of cultural materialism is that the emergence of significant social concepts – keywords – cannot be understood separately from the cultural, political and economic contexts in which they emerge. It is only in exploring these contexts of emergence and use that we can fully understand the power of identity today. And as we will see, many of these contexts are deeply connected to the cultural political economy of capitalist societies. In particular, as I will show, changes around consumption patterns and opportunities for marking distinction or sameness, and changes in the forms of politics that characterise these societies, both provided the context and created the need for the idea of identity as we now know it. But that is to jump ahead. Before exploring the idea of identity in context, we must identify and understand its changing meanings, as it is these meanings which provide the cipher to the social changes captured, carried and propagated by the idea of identity in capitalist societies. This is the subject of Chapter 2.

Notes

1. Searches of the original German texts as well as their English translations similarly reveal little or no evidence of the word 'identität' – which translates directly as 'identity' – see http://www.gutenberg.org and http://users.rcn.com/brill/freudarc.html.
2. The single use of the word identity in Cooley clearly indicates that it is identity as sameness that is at stake: 'We cannot feel strongly toward the totally unlike because it is unimaginable, unrealizable; nor yet toward the wholly like because it is stale – identity must always be dull company' (Cooley, 1902: 153).
3. Trinity College library is a 'copyright library' and thus holds legal deposit for all 'books' (including journals, periodicals and newspapers) published in the UK and Ireland. The 'Stella' search engine made available by the library sorts publications within this database by number of items (with the key search term) by year.
4. There were some occasional and incidental uses, as, for example, with the phrase 'an identity of interests' – a use which persists though which hardly springs immediately to mind in discussions of 'identity' today.
5. Although this method of searching is clearly not comprehensive, nor entirely satisfactory in other ways, it does nonetheless indicate the general movement and change in the use of the term identity over the years in question. Similar searches carried out using Google Books or Amazon reveal similar shifts, but are harder to quantify reliably as Amazon in particular is sales-based, and often thus lists duplicates of the same book where it is retailed by different sellers.
6. On 24 June 2009, for example, a search for 'identity' on Amazon.com threw up 500,564 books, 1602 DVDs and 2102 MP3 downloads tagged with the label identity.
7. See, for example, http://www.seekingpurpose.com/, http://aishaiqbal.blogspot.com, http://www.livingmanicdepressive.com/, http://www.experienceproject.com/groups/Feel-As-If-I-Am-Losing-My-Identity/3961 and http://www.tolerance.org/handbook/beyond-golden-rule/searching-identity.
8. The website for these companies are available at http://www.keenbranding.com/, http://www.brandidentityguru.com/, http://www.identityworks.com/, http://www.brainsonfire.com/ and http://www.kontrapunkt.dk/.
9. Williams himself acknowledged the intrinsically open-ended character of his project, and approved of the addition of new keywords with changing times, as specifically indicated by the inclusion of blank pages at the end of each published copy.

2

'Identity': A Keyword Analysis

INTRODUCTION

Keywords: A Vocabulary of Culture and Society was, as the subtitle suggests, originally written as an appendix to *Culture and Society* in 1958, though it was not published in full-length book form until 1976, with a second edition appearing in 1983. It was in *Culture and Society* (1958), and *The Long Revolution* (1961), that Williams's understandings of culture and its relation to social transformation first emerged, and these understandings colour, often implicitly, the understandings and impetus of *Keywords*. Williams's intention in developing a list of keywords was to provide a socio-historical lexicon that gives insight into and is made relevant by the key social issues of the time, and as such, much of the work involves substantive tracings of changing meanings and uses, rather than in-depth engagement with the philosophical and methodological claims and suppositions which make the very idea of a keyword sensible. Nonetheless, the rightly famous introduction indicates the sense and substance of his theoretical framework, and when read alongside *Culture and Society* and *The Long Revolution*, a clearer picture of the theoretical grounds and social ontology underpinning the notion of a keyword emerges.

Although Williams did not explicitly set out an official set of characteristics of a keyword, close reading of his work makes it possible to identify a set of partially overlapping features or attributes which we may consider necessary for a term to qualify as a keyword. The first part of this chapter sets out these characteristics. The second part begins the keyword analysis of 'identity', tracing the developing and sometimes conflicting meanings and uses of the term over time. The third part sets out the three dominant senses of identity today: legal, personal and social identity. The final part uses the keyword analysis to clarify some key contemporary debates around identity, and specifically whether it should be understood to be 'essential' to individuals and groups, or 'socially constructed'.

CHARACTERISTICS OF A KEYWORD

The first characteristic of a keyword, as indicated by its name, is that it is a significant or important word. Durant employs Williams's own practice of taking the definition and etymology of the word provided by the *Oxford English Dictionary*, and offers the following definition of a keyword as:

> (a) a word serving as a key to a cipher or the like ('The key-word of these inscriptions'); and (b) a word or thing that is of great importance or significance; spec. in information-retrieval systems, any informative word in the title or text of a document, etc., chosen as indicating the main content of the document. (2006: 3)

This provides two overlapping senses in which a keyword should be understood as significant. Firstly, it is a vital, pivotal or even indispensable word in a particular text, indicating an overall sense or purpose of that text; and secondly, it operates as 'a key to a cipher', unlocking some of the mystery or valuable information hidden within a particular code or cryptic text. *How* it 'unlocks' the pivotal meanings and purposes of a text is related to its other features.

A second characteristic of a keyword is its complexity, or what sometimes manifests as an indeterminacy or multiplicity of meaning. We can pick out two senses in which Williams understands a keyword to display 'problems of vocabulary' such that its meanings may be indeterminate or contested. The first is in terms of the 'particular' meanings of words; that is, 'the available and developing meanings of known words' (1983: 15), which are discernible from the use of the word in practical discussion and written text, and include both historical and contemporary uses. The second is in terms of the 'relational' meaning of the word; that is, 'the explicit but as often implicit connections which people were making, in what seemed to me, again and again, particular formations of meaning – ways not only of discussing but at another level of seeing many of our central experiences' (1983: 15). A keyword, then, displays a range of meanings and senses, not all of which are compatible. As Durant comments further: 'Williams's keywords present a cluster of interlocking, contemporary senses whose interaction remains unresolved across a range of fields of thought and discussion. Interaction between the senses can lead to cross purposes and confusion in public debate' (2006: 4).

According to Williams, interaction between the senses occurs in two ways, as also noted by Durant (2006). On the one hand, there are what we might call the synchronic relations between meanings, such that different meanings coexist in a single historical moment, and in a particular instance of use. This might occur when different senses arise and are meaningful at the same time within a single use of a word, with both senses required in order to communicate the meaning, as, for example, with the word 'class' (denoting both 'rank' and 'group'). It is the synchronic meanings that most analysts tend to be concerned with when they attempt to 'pin down' or 'capture' the meanings of identity. On the other hand, however, there are also what we might call diachronic differences of meaning; that is, contrasting meanings within different historical instances of use, rather than within a single use of the word. For Williams, however, this distinction between diachronic and synchronic difficulties, between changing meanings over time, and polysemy in contemporary use, is largely an analytic one, as he sees the diachronic and synchronic differences in meaning as inextricably related. Williams is especially attentive to the persistence and continuity of these older meanings, and to the 'process through which new ways of exploiting the meaning potential conventionally available in a word cumulatively alter the meaning of that word' (1983: 8). The complexity of the words comes from the fact that historical senses coexist with contemporary senses which are themselves derived in various ways from the older yet still persistent meanings. Durant, looking at Williams's entry for alienation, writes: 'Difficulties arise, in effect, because a range of senses that have followed different historical paths now coexist, sometimes with one or more parallel technical senses as well as a range of other, lay senses that cut across each other in unpredictable ways' (2006: 10). What matters here is not so much how these different meanings combine in a single word, but rather how speakers draw from the tapestry of meaning in a way that might not always be apparent to others, or which resonates in different and perhaps unintended ways with the audience.

This complexity is often not recognised as such. In fact, keywords are *familiar* words: there is typically no rush to define them where they are used; no insistence upon clarification of their meaning. This familiarity may be taken as a third characteristic of a keyword. Indeed, what is considered to invest each keyword with its peculiar force is its widespread deployment and usage across a whole array of specialised and lay contexts, such that it forms part of 'a general vocabulary ranging from strong, difficult and persuasive words in everyday usage to words which, beginning in particular specialized contexts, have become quite common in descriptions of wider areas of thought and experience' (Williams, 1983: 14). This familiarity both masks and contributes to its very complexity. As Williams writes, behind such familiarity,

> We find a history and complexity of meanings; conscious changes, or consciously different uses; innovation, obsolescence, specialization, extension, overlap, transfer; or changes which are masked by a nominal continuity so that the words which seem to have been there for centuries, with continuous general meanings, have come in fact to express radically different or radically variable, yet sometimes hardly noticed, meanings and implications of meaning. (1983: 17)

The simple 'popularisation of identity' argument considered in the previous chapter is problematic precisely because it misses the history of meaning change of the word identity, and reads semantic continuity where it is only nominal. Our familiarity with the word today obscures this deep diachronic complexity that renders it so important and problematic in contemporary discourse.

A fourth characteristic of a keyword is that its problems of meaning are historically and contextually specific. For starters, the complexity of meaning is directly related to the particular uses of the term in that moment in time. The fact that quite often the dictionary definition fails to capture the specifics of a contemporary usage, or that the changing meanings are only apparent with reference to a historical dictionary, is testament to the historical character of a keyword. Coupled with this, the meanings are also *contextually* specific to the society in which they are deployed: the problems a keyword is used to discuss are of a specific nature in that they concern 'the practices and institutions which we group as culture and society' (Williams, 1983: 15). The difficulties of the words cannot be resolved by reference to some clarifying glossary of terms; rather, their complexity derives directly from their use in the discussion of problems of culture and society, and thus any attempts to resolve their complexity are also attempts to resolve the problems with which they are bound up. They are therefore also 'controversial' words in that their complexity and resolution are bound up with the real-life problems they are used to discuss. In addition, keywords often have a normative tenor, as they are typically deployed in discussions of central beliefs and values of the contemporary moment; of the 'things that matter' in a given society. This is why the list of keywords is referred to by Williams as a 'vocabulary of culture and society'. 'This', writes Williams, 'significantly, is the vocabulary we share with others, often imperfectly, when we wish to discuss many of the central processes of our common life' (1983: 14).

It is the combination of these characteristics − significance, complexity, familiarity, active use in discussions of the problems of culture and society, and normative import − that captures both Williams's distinctive approach and insight, and the reasons why a particular word should be understood to be 'key' in the sense intended by him. Language strains and changes at the limits in order to enable new ways of seeing and acting, and is stretched in order to accommodate new practices and experiences. A keyword thus demonstrates how 'some important social and historical processes occur *within* language' (Williams, 1983: 22) as meanings change and the use of language both enables and restricts, encourages and forecloses upon different ways of thinking about what is feasible, possible, worthwhile, or desirable. In Durant's interesting phrase, keywords provide 'the material of thinking', by which he means that a keyword provides not only a material archive of past and contemporary meanings for analysis, but also 'the tools for further new thinking: that is … the material resources out of which concepts for cultural debate are formed' (2006: 4).

It should now be apparent that identity constitutes a contemporary keyword. As with other keywords, our familiarity with the term masks what are in fact a range of different, oppositional or even incompatible meanings. It is on the grounds that complexity is often hidden behind a facade of familiarity that Williams suggests it is a useful exercise to 'pick out certain words, of an especially problematical kind, and to consider, for the moment, their own internal development and structures' (1983: 23). This exercise helps unravel some of the complexities of both the word and the idea of identity, as it has come to form part of the key vocabulary people use to make sense of and shape their personal and social lives.

I am not the first to attempt this project of updating Williams's keywords, either generally or in relation to the particular term 'identity', with the most prominent recent example coming from Bennett et al. (2005). However, most of these efforts do not capture the spirit of Williams's approach.[1] In the original, Williams's genealogy of each term showed clearly how the meanings of the word changed and developed in ways which were only intelligible in terms of the more general practices and beliefs legitimated and in circulation. As the word changed, so too did the 'reality' – the change in meanings and uses of the word did not simply represent a new way of looking upon that reality but a change in the very facets of that reality, of what makes up and makes meaningful everyday life. However, many have missed the bigger insights associated with this small and unassuming term, and deploy it today in a fairly descriptive way, reciting its various meanings and uses without – as Williams crucially did – linking these to the changing values, beliefs and practices of that historical moment. In what follows, as over the remainder of this book, I treat identity as a keyword in a manner which emulates not just the style but also, more importantly, the spirit of Williams's approach.

THE HISTORY OF THE WORD 'IDENTITY'

Identity is a familiar term in the contemporary social and political lexicon, and though it is used to refer to what is widely imagined to be a complex *subject*, the *word* identity is not usually itself understood to be difficult. Indeed, the term is used casually and easily – 'its very obviousness seems to defy elucidation: identity is what a thing is! How is one supposed to go beyond that in explaining it?' (Gleason, 1983: 910). So although questions of personal, group, national and corporate identity are recognised as complicated and problematic today, the very use of the term identity in reference to 'who I am' or 'who we are' is not. Attention typically centres on addressing these former questions, and the related philosophical, metaphysical and political issues they are understood to give rise to, rather than on the very use of identity to *refer* to these matters to begin with.

Yet, despite the widespread assumption that it is the substance of identity rather than the word identity that is problematic, identity is demonstrably a complicated word. As we have already seen, the term identity was originally used to indicate 'the sameness of an entity to itself'. This was not understood to be a property specific to persons, but rather a formal quality of any type of entity. This original meaning of identity persists today, but it is relatively rare, as expressions like 'an identity of interests', though still in use, are more typically expressed in terms of two parties having *the same* interests. The adjective 'identical' tends to be used to express an exact equivalence between two separate and distinct entities – as for example, identical twins, identical handwriting – but rarely to indicate the sameness of an entity to itself (we are far more likely to say 'that's the same man I saw yesterday' than 'that man is identical to the one I saw yesterday').

Beyond this limited use, we can today discern a number of contemporary uses of the term identity, which diverge in varying degrees from this original sense. The first of these is what we might call the 'legal' sense of identity, used to refer to the official invocation of a person as a particular person, identifiable through identity papers, finger-printing and other forms of 'ID'. The second of these is the 'personal' sense of identity, used to refer to a core aspect of an individual, or those combined essential features of a self that make it unique and differentiate it from all others. The third is the 'social' sense of identity, used to refer to membership of a social category, such that different social categories, and most typically categories of 'race', ethnicity, gender, 'culture', sexual orientation and religion, are themselves construed as different 'identities'.

Each of these contemporary senses departs in particular ways from the original senses, and indeed, the latter two, 'personal' and 'social' identity, are far enough from the earlier senses that we cannot easily recognise them in the earlier definitions and accounts of identity. These recent uses have not yet been fully captured by the most comprehensive historical dictionary of its kind, the *Oxford English Dictionary* (OED), upon which Williams himself so faithfully relied.[2] Fearon noted this at the end of the twentieth century, when he pointed out that the OED is 'reporting an older meaning of the word that is ... narrower than our present concept of identity' and that 'even the most relevant entry' in the OED does not adequately capture our contemporary senses of personal and social identity (1999: 7–8). Even in its most recently updated online edition from November 2010, the OED has not yet fully captured these three common contemporary senses of identity in a satisfactory way, which is evidence not only of the historical novelty of these senses, but also, I believe, of a general confusion around the longevity of what we now take axiomatically to be 'identity' issues. For it is the case that the OED exhibits in its historical tracing a compression of what are different and newer meanings into more persistent older meanings, both anachronistically reading evidence of contemporary meanings in older instances of use of the word, and failing to identify properly new pathways of meaning that have developed and solidified into these three reasonably distinct uses so familiar to us today. This may in part be explained by the fact that the original sense of the term identity still persists in our contemporary uses, and is close enough to *some* of these not to raise suspicion or uncertainty. However, it is far enough from these original uses to raise some questions: specifically, it is not clear why the word identity should have developed from its narrow sense to its modern senses, that is, from signification of an abstract or formal quality (roughly, 'sameness') to a substantive quality which may be personally or collectively possessed. This development of the term from its original use to its contemporary uses, particularly as manifest in 'personal' and 'social' identity, provides insight into the contemporary substantive problems of identity which are imagined to be quite distinct from the term itself (or, at least, whose connections are not properly recognised). It also helps explain why it is specifically the term *identity* that is used to refer to a core element of self and social categories, and opens the way for exploring what such framing actually does to our understandings of self- and grouphood. As I will show, it is not the case, as Mackenzie suggested, that the word identity is potentially 'as good a label as any other' (1978: 50) for capturing our experiences of self- and grouphood today, but that, in fact, 'identity' does some very particular work in framing these experiences.

The first recorded use of the word identity was 'This likenes, idemptitie, or equallitie of proportion is called proportionallitie', and dates to 1570. It is this use of identity to reference the quality of sameness that is set out in the first definition provided by the OED (second edition), which defines identity as 'The quality or condition of being the same in substance, composition, nature, properties, or in particular qualities under consideration; absolute or essential sameness; oneness.' The dictionary gives a range of examples from the next three centuries to illustrate this sense of the term, including the question from Harris (1751), 'Is it not marvellous, there should be so exact an identity of our ideas?'; and a century later the claim in Herbert Spencer's *The Principles of Psychology* (1872), that 'Resemblance when it exists in the highest degree of all … is often called identity.'

The specific linking of this quality of sameness to the human person is first recorded in 1638, in Rawley's translation of *Bacon's Life and Death*, where he writes, 'The Duration of Bodies is Twofold: One in Identity, or the self-same Substance; the other by a Renovation or Reparation.' The OED traces this particular use of the term through the seventeenth, eighteenth and nineteenth centuries, citing Locke in his claim that '[t]he Identity of the same Man consists … in nothing but a participation of the same continued Life' (1690), and Hume, who wrote in 1739 that 'Of all relations the most universal is that of identity, being common to every being whose existence has any duration.' According to the OED, then, these uses indicate a second sense of the term identity, for which they offer the definition: 'The sameness of a person or thing at all times or in all circumstances; the condition or fact that a person or thing is itself and not something else.' However, it appends the terms 'individuality' and 'personality' to that second definition without any evidence that the term identity was intended in this sense at the time. With the exception of one quote (see below), all the uses relayed depend upon a change of *application* rather than meaning from the first sense, indicating that the quality of sameness and the notion of the persistence of an entity had become an issue in considerations of the self or the person, thereby making sensible the use of the already existing notion of identity to meet this need. Indeed, this is evident from Hume's 'Of Personal Identity', where he points out, in reference to both 'plants and animals' and 'a self or person', that 'we have a distinct idea of an object, that remains invariable and uninterrupted through a supposed variation of time; and this idea we call that of identity or sameness' (2000 [1739]: 144). This is what analytical philosophers sometimes call 'numerical identity' to refer to the persistence of the human person despite changes to its qualitative state (including, for Hume, an individual's perceptions and impressions). As Shoemaker explains, the phrase 'numerical identity' means 'the relation each thing has to itself and no other thing'; he continues, 'the phrase "one and the same" ... always expresses numerical identity ... Non-philosophers, when offered a discussion of identity, are often puzzled and disappointed to find that it is identity in this "logical" sense that is under consideration' (Shoemaker, 2006: 40). All but one of the illustrative quotes provided involve this notion of personal identity as 'numerical identity', and not personality or individuality – at least, not as we now know and use these terms. This is easily demonstrated by inserting either 'personality' or 'individuality' in the place of 'identity' in each of the quotations from Rawley, Hume, Locke and others: we see that this completely changes the sense of each quotation, and in some cases, renders them nonsensical.

Williams's entry in *Keywords* for 'individual' is here illuminating, as he points out that 'individual originally meant indivisible' (1983: 161). 'That now sounds like paradox', he continues: '"Individual" stresses a distinction from others; "indivisible" a necessary connection' (1983: 161). 'Identity' as 'the quality of sameness in the human person' is clearly closer to the notion of 'indivisibility' than it is to 'individuality', though it does not seem to be the case that the OED in fact intends this earlier usage. It seems more likely that it *does* mean 'individuality' in its current sense of the sum of attributes, traits and disposition of a particular person, or the distinct character of a person, given their pairing of it with 'personality'. What is significant about the transition from 'indivisible' to 'individual' for our purposes here is that this, as Williams points out, represents a shift of emphasis from some continuity or sameness of self, to an emphasis on the difference or distinction of that self from others. Williams argues that 'the development of the modern meaning from the original meaning is a record in language of an extraordinary social and political history' (1983: 61). Something similar may be said of 'identity', as it evolves from this earlier sense of the quality

of sameness in a person to its contemporary sense of a distinctive set of characteristics, motivations and personality.

Although the OED errs by appending 'individuality' and 'personality' to this
second sense of 'personal identity', anachronistically reading the new sense of
the word in these older uses, it is nonetheless the case that we can *begin* to see
changes of this type in the final citation given in the OED for this entry. This
is the citation from E. Garrett's *At Any Cost* (1885): 'Tom ... had such a curious feeling of having lost his identity, that he wanted to reassure himself by the
sight of his little belongings.' Here we can identify some transitions in meaning
which foreshadow the sense of identity as we know it today. Firstly, we see that
the notion of identity seems to have moved from referencing an abstract formal
property of a person to a substantive human attribute – something a person can
possess, and indeed lose. Secondly, we see here the association of identity with
personal belongings, and in this a transition from what we might call an endog-
enous understanding of identity, where identity is understood in terms of the
relation of an entity to itself, to an exogenous one, where one's identity derives
at least in part from one's relation to the external material world. And finally,
we see something of that shift from an emphasis on continuity or sameness of
self, to an emphasis on the difference or distinction of that self from others,
that Williams also noted in the etymology of 'individual'. But this transition is
liminal rather than complete in Garrett's formulation. The full emergence of
the sense of personal identity as something that can be sensibly associated with
'personality' and 'individuality' would not occur for another 70 years.

There is, however, evidence of what we might register as a transitional
sense of identity in use around this time, which provides a bridge between
that earlier notion of personal identity as the continuity of a self, and the later
uses of personal identity to signify personality and individuality with which
we are familiar today. I shall refer to this (with some reservations) as the 'legal'
sense of identity. This legal sense refers to the idea that a person is factually
and evidentially the person s/he claims or is taken to be, and exhibits some of
the same shifts we see in Garrett's formulation. The OED does not provide a
record or definition of this sense on its own terms, but collapses it into that
first definition of identity as the quality of sameness in a person. Nonetheless,
it is arguably this distinctive 'legal' sense of identity that animates several of the
citations provided by the OED, as well as a range of other uses not recorded
by the OED from around this time. The work of Charles Dickens provides
some particularly telling examples. Thus, in *David Copperfield* (1850), we find
the passage:

> My mother had a sure foreboding at the second glance, that it was Miss
> Betsey. The setting sun was glowing on the strange lady, over the garden-
> fence, and she came walking up to the door with a fell rigidity of figure and
> composure of countenance that could have belonged to nobody else. When
> she reached the house, she gave another proof of her identity ...

And in *Great Expectations* (1867), we find:

> After overhearing this dialogue, I should assuredly have got down and been
> left in the solitude and darkness of the highway, but for feeling certain that the
> man had no suspicion of my identity. Indeed, I was not only so changed in the
> course of nature, but so differently dressed and so differently circumstanced,
> that it was not at all likely he could have known me without accidental help.

And also:

> He was taken to the Police Court next day, and would have been immedi-
> ately committed for trial, but that it was necessary to send down for an old
> officer of the prison-ship from which he had once escaped, to speak to his
> identity.[3]

While none of the instances cited above as yet indicate identity in the sense
of personality, they clearly all point to that 'legal' sense of identity – that is,
the ascertainment or proof that one is the person one appears or claims to be.
That this differs – albeit subtly – from that original sense of personal identity
is evident from the fact that *these* uses of identity refer us to a substantive
attribute of the person, rather than a noun of condition, and call up the unique
(and recognisable) differentiation of that self from others, rather than simply its
continuity or sameness with itself. Thus in general in this period of usage in
the latter decades of the nineteenth century, we see the beginning of a number
of shifts which, while not yet fully formed, become integral to the notions of
'personal' and 'social' identity that were to emerge in academic, political and
popular usage from the 1950s and 1960s. These shifts are anticipated, but not
properly traced and distinguished by the OED.

The most recently updated online edition of the OED from 2010 evinces
a greater awareness of these distinctions of meaning, though it has not yet
completely resolved the issue, nor fully caught up with our three dominant
contemporary senses. It now differentiates two senses of 'personal identity',
adding a new entry, 'Who or what a person or thing is; a distinct impression
of a single person or thing presented to or perceived by others; a set of characteristics or a description that distinguishes a person or a thing from others',
to their original definition. However, of the full set of citations provided for
this new definition, only two could be said to manifest that later psychological sense of 'personal identity'. These come from the years 1965 and 2005, and
thus correspond exactly with the period identified here for the emergence
of this new use. All the others call up that transitional 'legal' sense of identity,
as for example in the citation, 'But, as to the proof of identity, whatever is
sufficient to satisfy a jury, is good evidence' from 1789. The OED continues
to offer no corresponding definition for such a sense of identity as a legal
persona in itself – instead it exists by implication only in a series of 'identity

compounds' such as identity '-papers', '-card', '-fraud' and '-theft' that speak of its verification. And despite offering this new definition, the OED continues to append the words 'individuality' and 'personality' to that original sense of 'personal identity' as 'the sameness of a person or a thing at all times', while at the same time moving the only quotation (from Garrett) that provided any rationale for this at all to the second definition. Thus we see that even in the most recently updated version, the OED does not adequately distinguish between what we might usefully call 'numerical identity', 'legal identity' and the newer psychological sense of 'personal identity', and through anachronistic uses of illustrative historical quotations, forces a lexical shift that has not in fact taken place.

Another curious feature of the OED's entry for identity is that even in the most recently updated 2010 version, it offers no definition of what we might refer to as 'social identity' at all. As is the case with the notion of 'legal identity', the concept of social identity exists by inference only in a small number of identity compounds that imply its existence; that is, in references to 'identity politics', and the 'identity struggles' associated with rap music and racially inflected art from 1979 onwards.[4] There is no reference to different social 'identities', which is how the notion of social identity has typically manifested itself, particularly in the proliferation of sociological and political literature which takes racial, gendered, religious and ethnic 'identities' as its subject. This almost wholesale omission of the sense of 'social identity' from the OED is surprising, and relevant because it reflects some of our current assumptions and confusions about identity – including that identity always 'meant' more or less what it means now, and that both personal and social identity as we now know it always 'existed'. Interestingly, something the OED does not indicate is the *volume* of use of a particular word, and thus the flurry of use of the term identity from the 1960s is not apparent from the etymology it provides of the term. There clearly remains a case to delineate the three dominant, and widely used, current senses of identity to which I now turn.

CONTEMPORARY SENSES OF 'IDENTITY'

The transition of identity from 'the sameness of an entity to itself' to refer to personal or social attributes of humans is complex. But it is my contention that this early sense is nonetheless distinct – to varying degrees – from the three senses with which we are familiar today, though the original meanings persist in and help shape these contemporary senses in important ways. Let us now look directly at these three contemporary senses of legal, personal and social identity. As I have already discussed the legal sense of identity in some detail in getting to this point, and because it has a longer history than the other two contemporary senses, I will focus my attention primarily on the 'new' senses of personal and social identity, which have emerged since the middle of the last century.

The 'legal' sense of identity

The first dominant contemporary sense of identity, as we have seen, is what I call 'legal identity'. This is the sense that animates the notions of 'identity cards' and 'identity papers', as well as the more recent notions of 'identity theft' and 'identity fraud'. It is therefore the sense that is invoked in the notion of identifying oneself as a particular person and in the notion of 'concealed' or 'mistaken' identity. These uses, as we saw, stretch back to at least the mid-nineteenth century, as evident from Dickens's writings, and the small range of books published on the subject in the first decades of the twentieth century (see Chapter 1). While all of these uses presuppose a system of certifying that a person is so-and-so, or more simply the cognitive capacity to do so, they do not seem to presuppose any concrete account of what it is to be that person. The sense of identity invoked here then is simply 'who you are', and carries within it connotations of verification – it is not enough to simply be the same person as you were the day before (the 'numerical' sense); this simple fact must now be proven. The emphasis in this sense thus lies with the notion of verification, which is why I refer to it as legal identity. However, while it could be argued that 'who you are' here is not strictly a *legal* construction, but is instead a pre-legal status that the legal apparatus is supposed to capture, I nonetheless retain this term for its connotation of the official and formal naming, recognition and even interpellation of a person as a particular person. So while some of the terms associated with this sense of identity are new (for example, 'identity theft') the idea of identity which it invokes is not fully new, existing at least since the 1850s – if not earlier, given its relatively close connection to the original sense of the term. However, it develops the original sense of the term as it invokes a substantive legal persona that differs in some important way from that original sense.

Interestingly, the more recent notions of identity theft and fraud, rather than the earlier notions of mistaken or concealed identity, reveal most about the substantive character of this sense of identity. While the terms on the face of it refer directly to theft of the actual papers and documents which legally verify an identity, the contemporary experience of identity theft seems to signify some more intrusive, personal loss that has the capacity to impact upon that person's whole life.[5] While the magnitude of the impact of identity theft today is certainly linked to the development of new forms of information technology and personal information security, as well as to increased levels of electronic surveillance and documentation of the population – what Foucault (1998) refers to as 'biopower' – it also nonetheless seems to point to a new sense of personhood – 'identity' – that can be lost or stolen, rather than merely insufficiently marked or identifiable (as the simple absence of verifying papers suggests). As already suggested, and as will become further apparent, this legal or quasi-legal sense of identity, evident not only in allusions to identity papers and identity theft but also in less official invocations of recognition of a particular person as that person, could be registered as a transitional meaning, as it exhibits clear connections to and overlaps with both the earlier sense of personal identity as 'numerical identity', and the contemporary sense of 'personal identity' to which I now turn.

The 'personal' sense of identity

The second dominant contemporary sense of identity is the use of identity to refer to a set of psychological and sometimes physical characteristics that are understood to define a particular person. I refer to this as 'personal identity', and distinguish this from the other sense of personal identity that the philosophers puzzle over by reserving the notion of 'numerical identity' to account for that. Personal identity still retains a link to that original sense of identity as it presupposes that the entity in question is the same as it was the day before. Or, as philosopher W.V. Quine (1980) posited, 'No entity without identity'. This demonstrates, as Shoemaker puts it, 'that our grasp of the nature of things is at least partly a grasp of what counts as being the same thing of that kind' (Shoemaker, 2006: 42). However, this understanding is implied and recessive rather than dominant in this new use of the term identity. What is significant about this sense are the unique characteristics, traits, dispositions possessed or exhibited by that entity, or rather, person. What differentiates this sense from that more legalistic one is that it is the *content* of the identity rather than the fact of the identity that is at stake. In this personal sense of identity, then, we find an even more pronounced movement from an abstract quality to a substantive attribute than is apparent in the legal sense, further evident in the widespread tendency to speak possessively of one's identity ('*my* identity as such-and-such …'). Thus it is here that we see an obvious break with the older senses of identity: though this sense of personal identity implies that the entity in question is the same entity as itself, it does not settle nor pivot on this point, but instead directs our attention to the content or character of that entity. It is not the fact of sameness to a self, or the persistence of that self which is at stake, but *that which makes* the self unique, special, different from all others.

Fearon (1999: 25) offers the following, somewhat unwieldy, definition of this contemporary sense of identity:

> Personal identity is a set of attributes, beliefs, desires, or principles of action that a person thinks distinguish her in socially relevant ways and that (a) the person takes a special pride in; (b) the person takes no special pride in, but which so orient her behavior that she would be at a loss about how to act and what to do without them; or (c) the person feels she could not change even if she wanted to.

A simpler way of expressing this would be to say that identity is currently used to refer to a core quality or essence of an individual, or those combined, essential features of a self that make it unique and differentiate it from all others. It is the fact that these features are somehow core and definitive that makes them potentially both a source of pride (or, indeed, stigma, as Goffman [1963] insightfully explored), *and* key to who one is, while remaining in some way unchosen and unchangeable. This notion that identity refers to the core, definitive features of an individual is evident in the contemporary popular discourse of 'asserting', 'finding' or 'being true' to one's identity. In everyday language, identity is often used to mean 'who you *really* are', which, if challenged, is understood to have deeply destabilising and traumatising effects. In many ways, this is a *psychological* sense of self, and as such, is the sense of self imagined to be under threat in the notion of an 'identity crisis'. This, of course, is what Erikson captured with such incredible popular resonance and force in his 1950s publications on the topic. These features indicate that 'personal identity' is implicitly positioned as a valuable possession, which carries with it largely positive connotations. It is no longer a neutral or purely descriptive noun of condition. This is especially important because the controversial or complex nature of many keywords is 'especially prominent [when] change is motivated by valorisation of a word away from any neutral descriptive sense' (Durant, 2006: 12). This sense of identity as positively definitive of self is apparent in many contemporary practices and discourses: in the court cases where achieving legal protection depends upon proving a fit between a supposed underlying identity and the outward appearance (Tirosh, 2007); in the self-help books which recommend establishing and celebrating the personal behaviours, beliefs, values and preferences that will enable one to 'find' one's identity and grow in self-esteem and self-worth (Graham, 2012); and in the proliferation of fashion magazines and 'make-over' television shows that link style and appearance to identity, confidence and self-invention (Weber, 2009; Hearn, 2008). In each case we see that it is the unusual or striking personal features or attributes, the personal preferences, the characteristics and personality traits, the individual desires of (and their particular expression by) an individual which are imagined to constitute and *substantiate* (i.e. fill the content of) the identity. So where the OED presents 'individuality' and 'personality' as part of the original sense of the term, I suggest instead that this represents a new sense of the term.

But how precisely does the notion of identity correspond to notions of individuality and personality? The connection between this notion of personal identity and individuality is clear enough, for both are used to refer to the unique set of characteristics that make somebody a particular person. The connection is less straightforward with personality, however, and indicates a set of tensions within this new sense of identity. As Goldie (2004) suggests in his genealogy of the term, 'personality' typically connotes the *superficial* characteristics of an individual – something which goes against the association of identity with some core or essential features or attributes. In this respect, identity seems to have a greater affiliation with 'character' from which personality is often differentiated, as the former is taken to refer to something deeper, more noble and more worthy than personality (Covey, 1989). Indeed, this 'Victorian' idea of character, as it carries both a sense of deeply rooted attributes of an individual, and moral connotations of duty and responsibility (Collini, 1985), has also been largely displaced by the notion of identity. However, it seems that where the notion of character is reworked in the idea of identity, it comes without the sense of duty or responsibility that typically accompanies the 'Victorian' notion of character, and the idea that one's core character must be worked upon, and a 'good character' earned. While there is a clear shift in norms here, from improving one's character to simply celebrating one's identity, there is another more significant point here too: in contrast to character, identity is increasingly used to refer us to a more malleable sense of self, which may be chosen, shaped and altered in line with one's preferences rather than one's morals. Identity, in some contemporary uses, connotes something more flexible and fluid than character – and this shift is occurring not alone in contemporary discourse, but also in contemporary theory. This is what Brubaker and Cooper rail against when they argue that the prevailing constructivist stance is precisely to see identities as 'constructed, fluid and multiple' (2000: 1). Thus there is something of a liminal tension between the supposed permanence or fixity of the 'character', traits and disposition which constitute an identity, on the one hand, and both the superficiality of 'personality' and the burgeoning recent possibilities for 'choosing' an identity, on the other. I discuss these issues further at the end of this chapter, and in the social context of capitalist 'consumer societies' in Chapter 6.

There is a final feature which is important to this contemporary personal sense of identity, and it is this: it is not simply the *existence* of these features (the content) which constitute the identity, but their active recognition, marking or *identification*. This related term, identification, is central to our contemporary and historical senses of identity. The first definition of 'identify' provided by the OED is 'to make identical (with, to something) in thought or in reality; to consider, regard or treat the same'. Here then is the link with the original sense of identity, and we see continued evidence of this today in the uses of 'identify' to signify 'empathise' (e.g. 'I identified with the victim') or 'associate' ('we identify garlic with France'). However, the subsequent definitions seem to have a greater affinity with how we use the word identity today. Here OED offers: 'To determine (something) to be the same with something conceived, known, asserted, etc.; to determine or establish the identity of; to ascertain or establish what a given thing or who a given person is; in *Nat. Hist.* to refer a specimen to its proper species.' It is these latter senses of the term identify which play an important role in our contemporary sense of identity. While there is a clear and direct connection between 'identify' and the legal sense of identity, in the practice of verifying that one is the person one appears to be, there is also a connection between 'identify' and the personal sense, which gives rise to a different set of practices. This has to do with the visible marking of 'an identity', and the setting of it apart as special, distinctive and different to others. Thus whereas in relation to the 'legal' sense, identification still concerns verification of the fact that you are the person or entity you claim or appear to be, and thus the marking of the *sameness* or continuity of an entity, in this new sense of personal identity it is primarily about the marking of *difference*, and specifically, those practices of distinction associated with lifestyle, 'taste' and fashion. Again we see this in those make-over television shows which emphasise drawing attention to one's personal identity, in 'MTV' popular culture which encourages idiosyncratic fashion choices, in lifestyle media which promote setting yourself apart from rather than 'keeping up with' the Joneses, and more generally in the deliberate choices by individuals to wear those clothes, drive that car and attend those cultural events that they are encouraged to believe best represents their identity.[6]

In sum then, we may say that 'personal identity' today connotes a substantive property rather than a formal property or noun of condition, and is concerned with what is unique, special or distinctive about the self. Psychologically, this is bound up with the notions of self-esteem, self-knowledge and identity crises, while in everyday life and popular culture, it is connected with the active identification or marking of this 'identity' as distinction.

The 'social' sense of identity

The third dominant contemporary sense of identity is 'social identity'; that is, the use of identity to refer to membership of a given social category, and in particular those broad sociological categories including race, gender, ethnicity, sexuality, religion, disability, age and class. Fearon (1999: 2) also picks out this sense of identity animating contemporary discourse, which he argues refers us to 'a social category, a set of persons marked by a label and distinguished by rules deciding membership and (alleged) characteristic features or attributes'. It is this sense which renders sensible current talk of the existence and significance of different 'identities' in complex societies. In many of these cases, the term identity is used to stand in directly for the very social category or group itself, rather than the associated experience of being a member of either. Thus when someone speaks of 'intersecting' or 'multiple' identities, what they are typically referring to is the intersection or multiplicity of different social categories *qua* groups – for example, black women, or British Muslims – or an individual's experience of being part of two different social categories or 'identity groups' simultaneously. In recognition of this, Fearon (1999: 13) suggests 'a simple definition' which he sees as widely operational, 'that says an identity is just a social category, and to have a particular identity means to assign oneself to a particular social category or perhaps just to be assigned to it by others'. While this sense and use of identity is clearly evident in mainstream discourse, it is also naturalised in contemporary sociological and political writing. This point is illustrated in the vast amount of books or articles written with identity in the title or keyword (as documented in Chapter 1): many of these do not in fact discuss the concept of identity at all, but are instead focused on the issues associated with a *particular* 'identity'; that is the issues deriving from membership of a particular group, and how that group is constructed or treated within dominant discourse and understandings.[7] There is little reflexive awareness within these accounts of the historical specificity of the use of the term identity to refer to different groups or social categories. Thus these accounts are typically not alert to any potential implications or effects of treating these social categories or groups *as* identities, since this is not understood to be anything new or out of the ordinary to begin with.

A significant feature of this social sense of identity is that, as with the personal sense of identity, its use to refer to a particular social category involves a shift from a conception of identity as a formal property or noun of condition to its conception as a substantive property. Thus we have 'German identity', 'masculine identity', 'Asian identity', 'Catholic identity', 'lesbian identity' and so on, where in each case the identity is a substantive property manifest in the group, signifying 'what it means' to be a member of that group. Furthermore, as with personal identity, it is the content or characteristics of that social identity that are particularly emphasised over the mere fact of having an identity. Thus, a second significant feature of this social sense of identity is that these characteristics are understood to be somehow essential to, or definitive of, that category or group. As a consequence of this, these characteristics are notable for the manner in which they are *common* to all the members of the group (or other people considered to have the 'same' identity), rather than – as was the case with personal identity – for the way in which they set an individual apart from a group, thereby rendering them in some way distinctive. Thus when someone speaks of 'my identity as a woman', for example, they are classifying themselves as a member of a social group, rather than (as in the personal sense) providing an account of their unique set of personal characteristics. However, at the same time there is also an obvious parallel with the personal sense of identity, as the characteristics that constitute a particular group 'identity' are also those that serve to differentiate that group from others. Thus although it is this basic, constitutive core similarity with others from the same social category, and the awareness of and action on this behalf, that is understood to make up the collective (but also, therefore, the derivative individual) identity, at the same time, questions of difference from other groups and from an undifferentiated (often hegemonic) mainstream are also at stake. The social sense of identity therefore emphasises both difference and commonality: what is brought into play by the use of the term identity is the idea that all the members of the group are the same in some important way, and can be distinguished from others on that basis.

A final significant feature of this social sense of identity, as was the case with personal identity, is the importance of marking this identity, and specifically its 'recognition' politically. In fact, this is so much the case that the terms 'identity politics' and 'recognition politics' are often used interchangeably. At issue is the marking and then valorisation of this sameness or important similarity between the group members. Thus, the practice of identity politics is widely associated with the recognition and positive re-evaluation of different 'identities'. In this respect, identity now operates increasingly as a symbolic resource – to name a social category as an identity invests it with symbolic capital – which is exchangeable for political rights, academic authority and positive visibility. Again, although the sameness of the group members is what is most obviously or visibly at stake in this marking of group identity in recognition politics, questions of difference also arise here in important ways. For in effect, although the primary 'move' in identity politics is the creation of political identification through the marking of similarity with others, the actual practice of identity politics also typically involves the politicisation or celebration of how that collective identity is 'different', both from other groups, and from dominant or normatively proscribed ways of being and acting.

IDENTITY AND ESSENCE

One of the main shifts of meaning of the term identity, from its original to its contemporary senses, is its movement from signification of an abstract to a substantive property of people. From signifying the quality of sameness, identity now signifies some substantive essence or features that serve to identify an individual or group for who they 'really' are. But there is some difficulty in pinning down what *kind* of a word identity now is. While in its earlier uses it operated as a noun of condition, it is now used in ways which suggest it could be a concrete noun (an observable, material entity, as suggested in the reference to different 'identities'), or an abstract noun like 'happiness' or 'personality', possessed by individuals or groups, but nonetheless intangible for that. Answering the question of what kind of a word identity is will enable us to grasp more fully how and why identity operates as a powerful and highly active keyword today.

In their influential paper on the subject, Brubaker and Cooper are also concerned with this general issue. They argue that what is significant – and problematic – about the everyday treatment of the term identity is the tendency to 'reify' it – that is, to treat identities as if they really exist. One of their concerns with the use of identity as a category of analysis is that it repeats this 'everyday' error, with detrimental effects for social scientific analysis. Brubaker and Cooper draw parallels with the work of Bourdieu and Wacquant on the category of race in order to explain their concern. 'The problem', they write,

> is that 'nation', 'race', and 'identity' are used analytically a good deal of the time, more or less as they are used in practice, in an implicitly or explicitly reifying manner, in a manner that implies or asserts that 'nations', 'races' and 'identities' 'exist' and that people 'have' a 'nationality', a 'race', an 'identity'. (Brubaker and Cooper, 2000: 6)

However, what is key for them is that 'just as one can analyze "nation-talk" and nationalist policies without positing the existence of "nations", or "race-talk" and "race"-oriented politics without positing the existence of "races", so one can analyze "identity-talk" and identity politics without, as analysts, positing the existence of "identities"' (2000: 5). Thus the problem for Brubaker and Cooper is that analysts now also act as though identities really exist, when in fact they do not.

In making this case and subsequently calling for the eschewal of the analytical category of identity on these grounds, Brubaker and Cooper argue that the category of identity is in many ways like the category of race. I will suggest that though there are important parallels and connections, the category of identity is in important ways *not* like the category of race; and that achieving clarity on this point helps us understand more fully what kind of word identity is, and how and with what effects the idea of identity is used today. Let us look at this argument now in some greater detail.

Robert Park (2009 [1950]) famously argued that though there are no empirically verifiable, objectively observable things called 'races', the fact that people refer to races as though they were empirically real means that we should treat them as such, and analyse them on the terms in which they are produced and understood. This is precisely the kind of argument that Brubaker and Cooper want to challenge in relation to identity. Their argument is instead similar to that put forward by Robert Miles (2009), who rejects race as an analytical category on the grounds that it enables and naturalises the same putative biological distinctions which make racism meaningful, and upon which practices of racism depend. The equivalent argument, for Brubaker and Cooper, is that just as we can reject the idea of race as giving rise to the fictitious belief that the social world is divided by distinct 'races', so we should reject the idea of identity as giving rise to the fictitious belief that the social world is divided by distinct 'identities'.

This theoretical move has not so far been widely made in relation to 'identity'. A substantive body of work has indeed been carried out 'deconstructing' (if not entirely rejecting) identity, but this tends to centre on deconstructing *particular* 'identities' – 'female identity', 'black identity', 'gay identity' and so on – *rather than the very idea of identity itself.* This is not the case for race, which has received serious critical attention as an actual idea. This difference between the treatment of 'identity' and 'race' is evident in the growing tendency for sociologists to put race in inverted commas, to talk only about 'race' as a construction, and to distance themselves from any sense that they somehow believe its fictions. In distinction to this, only rarely do we find 'identity' in inverted commas, even where the author takes a markedly constructivist stance towards particular 'identities'. This demonstrates the fact that what is generally perceived to be a social creation or construction is *not* the very category of identity, but instead the packaging of a particular historically and socially specific set of attributes, beliefs and characteristics *as* a putative 'identity'. The equivalent theoretical move in relation to race would be that theorists have no real problem with the *idea* of race, but only with the construction of particular groups as distinctive races – which is not the case. This difference in the treatment of race and identity is because identity is in fact a different *type* of category to race.

Let us consider this. Both race and identity are classificatory categories. But whereas race specifies the substantive grounds on which one is categorised, 'identity' does not – in fact, having an identity in this social sense just specifies that you belong to a particular group, or can be assigned to or associate oneself with a particular social category. Designation of an 'identity', then, also depends on *other* systems of classification, and in itself does not supply these grounds or criteria. In relation to the 'social' sense of identity, different social characteristics provide the basis upon which one classifies and categorises by 'identity' – categories such as gender, ethnicity, sexuality, class and 'race'. The fact that 'race' is one of the bases on which an 'identity' is categorised gives lie to the argument that the category of identity operates in the same way as the category of race: instead, identity functions as an 'empty' classifier that needs to be 'filled' by some other, substantial social characteristics attached to a particular social category. Identity functions only to categorise someone *as of a particular kind*, but does not specify what that kind is. To define someone or some group in terms of a particular identity is simply to classify them, and it is to classify (as arguably *all* classification proceeds) by grouping together as of a kind those who exhibit some claimed necessary or 'essential' characteristics. Attribution of an 'identity' entails defining, marking or 'constructing' a particular kind of person, but does not entail specifying what that kind must be. While to classify according to race entails indicating that a person or group 'has' or belongs to a particular 'race' – for example, 'Caucasian', 'Black', 'Asian' – to classify by identity only entails that those classified each display the characteristic that is *subsequently* considered to constitute that 'identity'. For any attribute or combination of attributes can provide the basis for an identity, so long as they are considered essential to or definitive of those who are then considered to have a particular identity on that basis. It is subsequently these 'identities' – i.e. these features that are imagined to constitute a particular kind – that are subject to deconstruction within socially constructionist accounts of identity. The classification of individuals into coherent groups on the basis of some shared (and essential or fixed) social or biological characteristics is deconstructed, but the very idea of identity itself, *precisely as* a classificatory mechanism, is not.

Identity, therefore, cannot be considered to be equivalent to 'race', nation or ethnicity but is one of the ways of thinking (and perhaps the currently dominant way) in which these and other 'fictions' materialise and crystallise. As an idea, it enables people to make sense of, structure and take ownership of the experience of being classified by race, ethnicity, sexuality, gender or any combination or intersection of these, by providing a means of thinking about race, gender and so on in terms of real social groups, of which the individual – on account of displaying such characteristics herself – can subsequently recognise herself to be a part.

The new senses of identity indicate a shift from a formal property to a substantive property of individuals and groups, evident in the widespread tendency to speak of one's own identity in possessive terms, and equally, of a range of social identities – female identity, black identity, gay identity, black female identity and so on. In each case, the 'identity' in question refers us to the definitive, core or essential character of that individual or group. However, what this usage masks is *the very operation of the category of identity itself* in enabling this kind of essentialist thinking. Thus, though identity is treated most commonly as a substantive property of individuals and groups, in fact, identity is a classificatory device, that classifies according to what is considered essential to a particular person, type of person, or group.

This argument that we should recognise identity as a device that classifies according to the perceived essential attributes of an individual or group, that in the process then come to be understood as 'an identity', thus demonstrates the implicit essentialism of *all* uses of identity. What should now be clear is that the concept of identity is itself an essentialist concept: from its earliest senses right through to its current active uses, it is premised fundamentally on the notions of sameness, oneness and how these constitute – or are essential to – a given entity. Of course as also documented, as the twentieth century progressed, the very obvious links between 'identity' and oneness or indivisibility were gradually eroded, as identity began to be used in a number of other ways, and specifically, as a different type of noun. And as identity moved from signifying a formal to a substantive property, its application was extended, giving rise to the legal, personal and social senses of identity I have delineated here. Experiences of selfhood, of being a particular person, of self-perception and self-esteem, and of group membership all existed prior to their description in terms of identity. However, consideration of all these issues and experiences in terms of identity changes or adds to our perception of these issues and experiences – by construing them specifically in an essentialist way. It emphasises, in the legal case, the fact that your personhood remains constant throughout your life; in the personal case, that you possess a unique set of characteristics that remains the same through time; and in the social case, that there is a set of characteristics that is the same for all of the members of a particular group. Thus although identity is now also used in ways which connote the marking of difference or distinction, it came into being as an essentialist concept – indeed, as the very embodiment of an essentialist impulse. The marking of difference thus depends in the first instance on establishing the fundamental sameness of the entity (whether an individual or group) in question, and it is the concept of identity that allows us to do this. Hence we see that the very construal of gender, 'race', ethnicity, sexuality and so on as 'identities' is already an essentialising move, even when the focus rests on questions of 'difference'.

This recognition then throws light on the 'essentialism vs social constructionism' debates that dominate contemporary academic discussions of identity. In fact, the category of identity is not appropriately approached within this opposition, for it implies that 'identity' pre-exists both ways of understanding its constitution. However, to speak of an individual or group identity is precisely to make the claim that certain features or characteristics – which may be social or cultural and not only biological[8] – are essential to that person or group. Identity is an essentialising mechanism that offers a particular way of construing or experiencing self- or grouphood, and does not pre-exist this categorical practice. Thus where it is commonplace, for example, to construe 'selfhood', 'gender' and 'ethnicity' as 'primary identities' (cf. Jenkins, 2008: 41), I suggest rather that the mechanism of identity offers one particular way of thinking about and inhabiting each of these subject positions, by looking for and asserting the defining or core features that one must exhibit in order to count as such a person or a member of such a group. Significantly, by taking the existence of an 'identity' as a given and then asserting its inessential, fragmented or fluid nature, social constructivists often miss this important point that to speak of an individual or group 'identity' in the first place is precisely to make the claim that certain features or characteristics are essential to that person or group. In his introduction to *Social Theory and the Politics of Identity*, Calhoun (1994: 13) draws the key lines of battle. Social constructionism, he writes,

> challenges at once the ideas that identity is given naturally and the idea that it is produced purely by acts of individual will … social constructionist arguments also challenge 'essentialist' notions that individual persons can have singular, integral, altogether harmonious and unproblematic identities … [They also] challenge accounts of collective identities as based on some 'essence' or set of core features shared by all members of the collectivity and no others.

As we can see from this, such constructionist stances are remarkably *un*constructionist about the very idea of identity. By accepting that people can have, or feel themselves to have, 'identities' at all, social constructionists begin from an essentialist position, though the conflation of 'identities' with groups on the one hand, and individual selves on the other, obscures this. This means that the social constructionists find themselves in a position where they must constantly argue for the constructed, fluid, unfixed nature of 'identities' since the opposite of this is assumed by the very use of the term. However, *the very idea* of identity is already essentialist in the manner of which these contemporary critical accounts complain. It is therefore something of a pointless exercise to expend so much critical energy debating whether an identity should be considered essential or not when the very emergence of identity as a contemporary way of thinking about the self and society is already intrinsically, and by definition, essentialist. This remains the case even where the identity in question is posited to be 'intersectional'. (For more on this, see 'the crisis of identity in academia' in Chapter 5.) If 'identity' means the persistence and continuity of an entity, and the recognition of the specific features which persist and constitute that entity, then the argument should be around whether it is *useful* to think of a person or a group in terms of an identity, as opposed to in terms of some other idea – and *not* around whether an 'identity' is essential or socially constructed.[9]

Given that, in fact, it is the self and the group that pre-exists these opposing understandings, what is really at issue here is whether groups or individual selves can be usefully or legitimately understood in an essentialising way – that is, as having any universal, definitive, 'core' features or components. This is an important political issue and carries important consequences for groups whose supposedly constitutive features – that is, whose 'identities' – are characterised as natural to them. For example, this is the case for women who resist the ascription of a biologically caring or nurturing 'identity' on the grounds that this restricts their autonomy and real opportunity to participate in the 'masculine' public sphere. But this debate should be engaged in on its own terms, and does not need the confusing use of 'identity' to designate the features of that group which must then be argued to be fluid, unfixed and socially constructed – i.e. not an 'identity' at all. Thus what this discussion of identity has shown is that it is in fact inappropriate to consider whether an 'identity' is essential to a group or socially constructed, for identity is by definition an essentialist concept. It *is* however appropriate to consider whether selfhood or a particular group can be essentially defined and reducible to some basic core, or whether that 'core' – and the conception of selfhood or grouphood arising from it – is a social construction. Of course, these kinds of essentialist claims, whether or not they are couched in the language of identity, may (like any other truth-claims) be fallible, both in the reduction of social features to 'natural' ones, and in the construal of certain features as essential when they are only in fact accidental to the entity. I discuss these points in more detail in Chapter 4, as part of a more general discussion about the nature of essentialism, and what it means to make essentialist claims.

CONCLUSION

What Williams wrote of his first and most difficult keyword, culture, now applies to identity:

> Within this complex argument there are fundamentally opposed as well as effectively overlapping positions; there are also, understandably, many unresolved questions and confused answers. But these arguments and questions cannot be resolved by reducing the complexity of actual use … These variations, of whatever kind, necessarily involve alternative views of the activities, relationships and processes which this complex word indicates. The complexity, that is to say, is not finally in the word but in the problems which its variations of use significantly indicate. (Williams, 1983: 91–2)

Williams's approach is comfortable with linguistic complexity, seeing in it both 'unresolved questions' and potential insights into 'the problems which its variations of use significantly indicate'. It is these variations of use, specifically in a capitalist context, that will be explored over the remainder of this book. In doing so, the keyword analysis just conducted will be of great significance. As Blunden points out, just as 'learning about the background and history of a friend often adds new nuances to our understanding of them, particularly what may have been inexplicable contradictions in their character ... discovering where a word has come from, its past lives, relations and transformations, often sheds light on current problems in ways that can be quite unexpected' (2005: 2). So far, what this keyword analysis has revealed is that identity is an old word that has taken on very new senses, and specifically senses which represent a move from the notion of identity as a formal quality (sameness) of all entities, to a substantive property of individuals and groups. It has also shown that 'identity' operates as a classificatory device, and in the process, offers a particular essentialist way of construing personhood and grouphood. Treating identity as a contemporary keyword thus enables us to recognise and then explore the use of the idea of identity as a particular, historically specific way of framing and shaping concerns about the self, the social and their inter-relation. Whereas this chapter has been concerned with the operation and status of identity as a word (and a particular kind of word at that), the chapters to come will consider its use in practice, as an active device with real effects. That is, they will look beyond the meanings of the term to its variations of use in particular social and material contexts, in order to explain why identity emerged as a keyword when it did, and what this has to do with the changing shape of capitalist societies. The analysis of this chapter thus requires further grounding in a broader framework that has the capacity to explain, firstly, how ideas relate to and impact upon the material context of their expression; and secondly, how certain ideas, manifest in and driving particular practices, norms and actions may work to reproduce or challenge the social and political relations of capitalist societies. Here we move into the realm of what is sometimes called 'cultural political economy'. These issues are addressed as part of a more general development of a framework appropriate to the analysis of the relationship of the contemporary salience of identity to capitalism in the next chapter.

Notes

1. In the introduction to *New Keywords*, Bennett et al. (2005) make it quite clear that they do intend the project in the spirit of the original, and in doing so, emphasise many of the significant features of a keyword that I have just outlined. However, many of the individual entries do not quite manage to reproduce the spirit and style of the original, with the entry on identity reading more like an academic history of the concept.

2. Since carrying out the research for this book, the OED has begun to publish a digital version of the third edition, which remains as yet a work-in-progress (the estimated date of completion is 2037). In what follows, I draw primarily on the second edition, which was originally printed in 1989, and made available online in 2000. Where relevant, I will note changes that are currently being made to the online edition. Since the editors decided to begin work on the third edition at the letter M, and to proceed alphabetically from there, changes to the entry for 'identity' are incomplete. However, the entry for identity *has* been updated somewhat since the 2000 edition, in line with the editorial decision in 2008, to alternate each quarter between moving forward in the alphabet as before and updating 'key English words from across the alphabet'. As a result, the entry for identity was partially updated in November 2010.

3. There are other examples in both novels, as well as continued evidence of use of the *older* sense of identity, as in the line 'My first most vivid and broad impression of the identity of things seems to me to have been gained on a memorable raw afternoon towards evening', in *Great Expectations*, which refers to some basic unity of or correspondence between certain (important) things.

4. These latter two are miscategorised under the second compound, 'belonging or relating to personal or individual identity'.

5. There is much anecdotal evidence to support this, including a popular 2010 British television series called *Identity*, which, over the course of six episodes played precisely on these connections between the illegal appropriation of another's official identity, and the hazardous psychological impact of this on the lives of those involved.

6. The extent to which these are universally available 'choices' is something I discuss further in Chapter 6.

7. See, for example, the journal *Identities*, which has a curiously disparate and wide-ranging subject matter, as it addresses topics related to any given 'identity'.

8. Iris Marion Young's work on the concept of *seriality* as she develops it from Sartre, offers a potentially more useful way of considering these kinds of issues in relation to the characterisation of a social group (1995).

9. This point will be explained in further detail in Chapter 4, in the section, 'Making Sense of Essentialism'.

3

Cultural Materialism and the Social Logic of Capitalism

INTRODUCTION

As the last chapters showed, the idea of identity emerged in western societies in the late 1950s and 1960s, gathering pace over the intervening decades to become a key component of cultural and political discourse and practice today. This period of history has also seen a change in the organisation and structures of capitalism. The 1950s and 1960s were, in the West at least, characterised by an accord between capital and labour, evident in relatively robust labour laws and workers' wages, high levels of employment in a regime of standardised mass production, a restraint of private capital accumulation via substantial corporate regulation and taxation, and a consolidation of the social protectionist role of welfare states. This period has since been referred to as 'organised capitalism' (McGuigan, 2009), or, within the Regulation School of theory, the 'Fordist–Keynesian' phase of capitalism (Harvey, 1989; Lipietz, 1992; Amin, 1994).

Since then we have seen an intensification of capitalist processes, and the dismantling of many of these social democratic structures that had mitigated the social inequalities inherent in the capitalist system. Contemporary capitalism is arguably now characterised by the triumph of capital over labour, evident in wage suppression, a huge expansion of corporate profit and a roll-back of the welfare state (Glyn, 2006). Regulation School theorists argue that western capitalist societies have entered a 'post-Fordist' phase, characterised by new or intensified processes of globalisation, financialisation and consumption and a new regime of capitalist accumulation, which they call 'flexible accumulation'. Other sociologists and historians of capitalism, too, have claimed to identify a significant transformation of capitalism from approximately the 1970s onwards, referring variously to the contemporary phase as 'post-industrial capitalism' (Bell, 1973), 'disorganised capitalism' (Lash and Urry, 1987) and 'informational capitalism' (Castells, 1996). While there have certainly been some changes, Regulation School theorists, along with some of these others, have been criticised for theorising a definitive break in capitalism. Evidentially, there are as many continuities and intensifications of already existing capitalist processes between the mid-twentieth century and now as there are differences.

And yet there is something new happening. While the monetisation of human labour and social life has always been a constituent component of capitalism, processes of financialisation have expanded greatly, and have infiltrated and saturated new domains, leading Ingham (2008) to refer to the contemporary stage of capitalism as 'finance capitalism'. Capitalism has always had a global impetus and ambition, as many earlier critics of capitalism including Marx and Luxemburg identified, but globalisation now more accurately refers to the *actually existing* systemic interconnection of the world's markets – where these markets are themselves relentlessly expanding into ever newer social, financial and geographical terrain – rather than a driving, but in many respects unrealised, aim. Relatedly, consumption has always been a necessary feature of capitalism, as consumers are by definition required to sustain the production of commodities that capitalism depends upon. Yet there has no doubt been an acceleration of consumerism, fuelled in no small degree by the much wider availability and accessibility of credit on a mass scale since the 1970s. The state has also been significantly repositioned within the global capitalist nexus – while capitalism has always required a state to survive and prosper, via the creation of legal institutions to protect private property 'rights' and competitive market relations, and the legitimisation of the money supply required for the flow and pursuit of capital, the regulatory and social roles of nation-states have been seriously undermined. The regulation – or rather, the *de*regulation and liberation – of capital is now increasingly managed on an international scale by the international financial institutions of the World Bank, World Trade Organisation and International Monetary Fund (IMF), and the social protectionist role of nation-states has been hollowed out, as states increasingly seek to position themselves as attractive to capital and investment rather than to redistribute the resources and wealth created within their increasingly permeable borders. Finally, there has been an emergence of a new political-economic paradigm, 'neoliberalism', which, as Harvey explains it, proposes that 'human well-being can be best advanced by liberating individual entrepreneurial freedom and skills within an institutional framework characterized by strong property rights, free markets, and free trade' (2005: 2). Although again, as the name itself even suggests, neoliberalism has its roots in and continues to exhibit affinities with classical liberal economics, and indeed, developed out of a number of think tanks and foundations including the famous Mont Pelerin Society from the 1940s (Mirowski, 2009), its dominance and force in shaping economic decision-making at state and corporate level since the 1970s and 1980s has led many contemporary theorists – and especially, critics – of capitalism to refer to the contemporary era as that of 'neoliberal capitalism'. Indeed, this is the term that I shall deploy in this book to refer to contemporary capitalism, while also borrowing from the Fordist/post-Fordist method of periodisation where useful.

What is interesting from the perspective of this book is that many of those accounts which argue that we have entered a new 'stage' of capitalism have linked it to the new salience of identity that has been traced in Chapters 1 and 2. For example, in his influential account of the 'network society' that has apparently co-evolved with this new stage of 'informational capitalism', Castells argues that 'our world, and our lives, are being shaped by the conflicting trends of globalization and identity' (2004: 1–2). Theorists of the 'post-industrial' age have argued that 'identity politics' rather than traditional class politics are the most appropriate political response to the social problems generated by contemporary post-industrial capitalism (Kumar, 1995), while critics of neoliberal capitalism tend to view the emergence of identity politics as a sorry displacement of the relatively more vigorous class politics associated with the earlier, less aggressive stage of capitalism. Fraser, meanwhile, diagnoses the current 'post-socialist condition' as one characterised by three intertwined characteristics: a resurgent economic liberalism, a shift from class politics to identity politics, and the absence of any credible vision of an alternative to the present capitalist order (1997b). All of these accounts thus directly link the contemporary prominence of identity – and particularly identity *politics* – to the new social order accompanying the recent structural transformation of capitalism.

But these narratives are misleading. Firstly, they fail to recognise the novelty of the idea of identity itself, assuming instead simply a new *prioritisation* of identity in the political landscape of contemporary capitalist societies. Secondly – and relatedly – none of these accounts recognises what the last chapters have shown, which is that identity became a salient cultural and political idea during the period of 'organised' or 'Fordist' capitalism of the 1950s and 1960s; that is, *prior* to the contemporary post-Fordist, network or neoliberal 'stage' of capitalist development with which they fundamentally associate a new political and cultural prominence of identity concerns. The tendency to theorise in concrete 'blocks' of capitalist history – the 'pre-s' and the 'post-s' – is here problematic, for against the grain of such definitive periodisation, what this book has so far shown is that the emergence and consolidation of the idea of identity spans both, ostensibly distinct, periods. The perspective of this book – that there are as many continuities as breaks in the development of capitalism, and that what we have witnessed, more than anything, is an intensification of capitalist processes – allows us to look more directly at the evolution of the idea of identity in a capitalist context, without being misled by an unhelpful periodisation. But how should we do this? The central task of this chapter is to provide a means of doing so.

In what follows, I will attempt to establish a framework for exploring how the idea of identity relates to the capitalist societies in which it has emerged and consolidated, and ultimately, how this idea has been used and continues to be used to either reproduce or challenge the social and political relations of capitalist societies. There are, in fact, two questions here. The first is the more abstract, theoretical question of how an idea can have any causal force at all, or, to put it another way, how an idea relates to the material context of its expression. The second is the more empirical question of how a *particular* idea – in this case, identity – relates to a *particular* context – in this case, the cultural political economy of capitalist societies, as these societies themselves are undergoing change and capitalist restructuring.

In the literature, these two questions – the abstract and the empirical – are often treated together, or the former subsumed to the latter. In particular, there is a wide range of work which considers the connection between particular dominant ideologies, discourses or cultural formations and the workings of capitalism (or a particular 'stage' or phase of capitalism), which relies implicitly or otherwise on a theoretical model of how ideas relate to the material context of their expression (Marx, 1973 [1939], 1994 [1859]; Weber, 1976 [1930]; Abercrombie and Turner, 1978; Harvey, 1989; Jameson, 1991; Amin, 1994; Morley and Chen, 1996; Boltanski and Chiapello, 2005a; McGuigan, 2009). Given the purposive focus of this book on the *idea* of identity itself, rather than more broadly on an epochal set of cultural or political formations, this chapter addresses both questions separately, and does not subsume the former to the latter. Specifically, the first part of this chapter draws on and develops Raymond Williams's cultural materialist paradigm in order to explain how ideas are related to – either generated by or capable of impacting upon – the social and material conditions and circumstances of their expression.[1] As Stuart Hall puts it, this,

> has especially to do with the concepts and the languages of practical thought which stabilize a particular form of power and domination; or which reconcile and accommodate the mass of the people to their subordinate place in the social formation. It has also to do with the processes by which new forms of consciousness, new conceptions of the world, arise, which move the masses of people into historical action against the prevailing system. (1996: 26)

The particular value of Williams's approach in addressing these issues is that it allows us to attribute causal power to ideas while remaining within a materialist framework – that is, one that remains resolutely attentive to the real conditions, opportunities and structural constraints of people's lives.

The second part of the chapter looks more directly at the capitalist context itself, again from a cultural materialist perspective. The focus here switches from the power of ideas to the power of capitalism – not at the level of its structural economic features, but rather as a 'civilisation', or as a way of living, with the power to generate its own ideologies, norms and habituated behaviours. It offers the cultural materialist notion of a 'social logic of capitalism' as a means of exploring the constitutive power of the capitalist system and the articulation of various cultural and political practices to a capitalist logic without returning economically determinist answers. The social logic of capitalism offers an alternative to the currently popular 'spirit of capitalism' approaches, by encouraging consideration of how certain ideas associated with a capitalist way of life are reproduced in ordinary routine practices, and may not derive from acquiescence to, or persuasion by, capitalist values. While the focus in the second half of this chapter is therefore on the social logic of capitalism, the ultimate aim, nonetheless, remains to articulate a framework that will provide the basis for the remainder of this book, and the particular, historically specific question it asks of the relation of the idea of identity to the political economic contexts of its emergence and consolidation. Specifically, it is argued, this cultural materialist framework will allow us to explore how the idea of identity might work to promote integration into a capitalist way of life, or alternatively, how or where it might offer resistance to the social logic of capitalism.

CULTURAL MATERIALISM AND THE PRACTICAL POWER OF IDEAS

There exists no fully worked out account of 'cultural materialism' in Williams's work – indeed, Williams only once defined it precisely as 'the analysis of all forms of signification, including quite centrally writing, within the actual means and conditions of their production' (1981b: 64–5). His project went beyond stressing the materiality of signs, however, towards the development of an alternative materialist paradigm that could adequately account for the role of ideas, signification, language and communications – broadly, 'culture' – in social reproduction and transformation as a whole. Although Williams's work has been criticised for being incomplete (Gallagher, 1992), and 'intuitive' rather than coherent in its theoretical development (Eagleton, 1976), its overall significant contribution, to my mind, is that it opens the way for a new conceptualisation and appreciation of the productive power of ideas from a materialist perspective. In this respect, Williams, perhaps more than any other cultural Marxist, did most to rescue orthodox Marxism from economic determinism. While remaining largely within a Marxist frame of analysis, he nonetheless reshaped a Marxist cultural theory in line with what he saw as Marx's own original intent and orientation – in the process developing cultural materialism as a deliberate foil to historical economism. That is, instead of emphasising a teleological unfolding of economic history via the evolving forces of material production, Williams's cultural materialism emphasises the centrality of ideas, and the 'cultural' more generally, in what remains nonetheless a materialist account of social change,

that is properly attentive to the real conditions of people's lives and the structural constraints of a capitalist system.[2]

In developing this 'cultural materialist' paradigm, the central meta-theoretical
problem exercising Williams was the opposition of materialism to idealism, typified for him in the tension between Marxist cultural theory and English literary
criticism (1977). At its most basic, this tension can be reduced to the question
of whether social change arises from the material conditions and structures
of societal development – the 'brute forces' of history – or from the collective ideas, knowledge and meaningful intentions of humankind. For Williams,
social change always involves both, but the two traditions which for him best
articulated the causal power of 'the material' and 'the ideal' – 'Marxism' and
'Literature', respectively – did so at the expense of an adequate understanding
of the power of the other.

Overcoming the idealism–materialism divide finds repeated expression – in
more and less explicit terms – throughout the corpus of his work (Williams,
1958, 1961, 1973, 1974, 1976, 1977, 1981a). On the one hand, Williams consistently and methodically challenged idealist accounts which construed culture as
an ideational realm of values, aesthetics and intellect, dissociated from the mundane and earthly world of things. In doing so, he developed a broad notion of
'culture' that pays heed to Marx's materialist supplication that we must analyse
ideas, values and cultural forms in the social conditions of their production and
circulation. Williams thereby transcends the idealism of the 'culturalist' position
associated with the literary theory that he took issue with for failing to appreciate how ideas are located in the practical, material conditions and circumstances
by which they are also inevitably shaped. We can thus identify clear affinities
between Williams's materialist orientation towards the cultural field, broadly
understood, and long-standing Marxist conceptions of culture, ideology and
superstructure which were also based on a forthright rejection of idealist
historiography.

On the other hand, however, Williams did not wholly accept traditional
Marxist accounts of culture, for two key reasons. Firstly, and on the face of it
counter-intuitively, Williams took Marxism to task for exhibiting in its conceptions of culture and ideology 'not so much ... an excess but ... a *deficit* of
materialism' (1979: 350). While Williams supported the Marxist refusal to view
ideas, language and communication in abstraction from the social and material
conditions of their production, he was critical of how this alternative perspective was subsequently developed within the Marxist tradition. 'Instead of
making cultural history material, which was the next radical move', he argued,

> it was made dependent, secondary, 'superstructural': a realm of 'mere' ideas,
> beliefs, arts, customs, determined by the basic material history. What matters
> here is not only the element of reduction; it is the reproduction, in an altered
> form, of the separation of 'culture' from material social life, which had been
> the dominant tendency in idealist cultural thought. (1977: 18–19)

Williams complained that by failing to recognise the *materiality of cultural forms themselves*, rather than simply their reproduction in a material context, materialist accounts ended up with a weak conception of culture as dependent and derivative: ideas, language and communication were once more, in effect, banished to a materially inconsequential realm. The results of such a move were, for Williams, disastrous, as what it meant was that a 'whole body of activities … have to be isolated as "the realm of art and ideas"', and, in consequence, are not recognised for what they are, namely: 'real practices, elements of a whole material social process; not a realm or a world or a superstructure, but many and variable productive practices, with specific conditions and intentions' (Williams, 1977: 94).

Secondly, and as a logical corollary to this first objection, Williams was also critical of the materialist 'realism' in Marxism, which undermines the 'controlling power of ideas' (Williams, 1977: 59). Thus in his materialisation of culture, Williams is unwilling to relinquish a key aspect of idealist accounts; namely, recognition of the causal or productive power of ideas themselves. This, after all, was precisely the value of the literary or 'culturalist' approach for Williams. However, the problem remained of how to attribute causal powers to ideas while remaining *within* a materialist framework. Hall has subsequently identified this general problem as 'the problem of ideology', which concerns how 'to give an account, within a materialist theory, of how social ideas arise … the problem of ideology, therefore, concerns the ways in which ideas of different kinds grip the minds of the masses, and thereby become a "material force"' (1996: 26–7). By ideology, Hall specifies that he means to refer to 'the mental frameworks – the languages, the concepts, categories, imagery of thought and systems of representation – which different classes and social groups deploy in order to make sense of, define, figure out and render intelligible the way society works' (1996: 26). The problem of ideology has, he points out, an objective basis in the enormous growth and power of the 'cultural industries', and their capacity to shape and transform 'mass consciousness'; and in 'the troubling questions of the "consent" of the mass of the working class to the system in advanced capitalist societies in Europe and thus their partial stabilization, against all expectations' (1996: 25). But it is also a problem that is intrinsic to Marxist cultural theory itself. If all ideas are the expression of capitalist class relations, and ultimately of the historical material development of capitalism itself, how are we to explain the emergence of ideas or forms of mass consciousness that challenge the social relations of capitalism, or that otherwise subvert the logic of the prevailing capitalist system?

I suggest that Williams's cultural materialist approach provides a way of resolving this problem. In the course of his work, Williams in effect consistently replaces what we may call 'the materialist premise' – the notion that ideas arise from and reflect the material conditions and circumstances in which they are generated – with what we can usefully refer to as the *cultural materialist premise*. The cultural materialist premise does not challenge the materialist proposition that material forces drive history but instead reconsiders that which may legitimately be considered a material force by construing 'culture' – language, ideas, values, beliefs, stories, discourses and so on – as itself a form of material production. Williams argues that the central notion of historical materialism, that 'man [*sic*] makes his own history', had been up to now interpreted primarily in terms of man's capacity to labour when, for Williams, an equally constitutive activity in making one's own history is our 'practical consciousness'. Developing key aspects of Marxist thought, Williams argues that 'consciousness [must be] seen from the beginning as part of the human material social process, and its products in "ideas" ... as much part of this process as material products themselves' (1977: 59–60). In making this case, Williams refers to a proposition of Marx in Volume I of *Capital* where he writes:

> We presuppose labour in a form that stamps it as exclusively human ... What distinguishes the worst architect from the best of bees is this, that the architect raises his structure in imagination before he erects it in reality. At the end of every labour process, we get a result that already existed in the imagination of the labourer at its commencement. (Marx, 1976 [1867]: 185–6)

Signification – 'the social creation of meanings through the use of formal signs' – is a special form of this practical consciousness and should be recognised as a practical material activity; 'it is indeed', Williams asserts, 'literally, a means of production' (1977: 38). Rather than simply express social material reality, signification 'is ... at once a distinctive material process – the making of signs – and, in the central quality of its distinctiveness as practical consciousness, is involved from the beginning in all other human social and material activity'. This reconsideration of signification as a form of practical consciousness allowed Williams to reject idealist accounts of language which saw it as a spirit unburdened by material conditions or physical form, or as the product of individual internal meaning-making. In its place he emphasised not only the social and material conditions for language production and development, but also the operation of language as constitutive material activity itself. He writes, 'it is precisely the sense of language as an *indissoluble* element of human self-creation that gives any acceptable meaning to its description as "constitutive"' (1977: 29).

Williams's cultural materialist conceptualisation of the cultural order, then, does not relegate language, ideas, values, beliefs or other cultural forms to some ideal sphere but construes them as intrinsically material and productive. These cultural forms are material in the sense that they are necessarily embodied, embedded, animate and realised in human behaviour, practices and institutions; and they are productive in the sense that they have causal power which cannot be separated from, nor reduced to, this material embodment. Furthermore, reconsideration of the materialist premise in terms of cultural materialism means that the human productive powers that Marx prioritises are understood to be not purely material in the old sense but also as *cultural* in the sense of being shot through with meaning. What makes us human is twofold: not simply our ability to labour and thereby transform the world but also our consciousness, and our ability to think about, plan and reflect on this world communicatively, that is socially, in tandem with the active labouring capacity.

This insistence on the material and productive nature of cultural forms – and correlatively, the 'cultural' character of 'the material world' – means that Williams, in effect, resolves Hall's 'problem of ideology'. The questioning of how ideas can 'become' a material force reveals an allegiance to a conception of social reality that distinguishes sharply between the 'cultural' realm of ideas, languages, values and beliefs, and the material world, thereby rendering sensible the very question of how ideas – previously non-material – can *become* material and exert a causal force. This question is simply not sensible in Williams's terms, for he defines culture – Hall's 'languages, concepts, categories, imagery of thought and systems of representation' – as intrinsically material. By providing an account of culture which, from the outset, demonstrates its materiality, its productiveness, its embeddedness in practices, Williams does not have to 'explain' how it is that ideas can have an effect or drive change. Culture is, in Williams's memorable phrase, 'built into our living' (1973: 9). Thus culture can be a material, causal force, and ideas grip the minds of people in the cultural field precisely because culture is not some idealised sphere but exists as ideas made manifest in everyday practice: a '*realized signifying system*' (Williams, 1981a: 207).

Williams's cultural materialist thesis fleshes out and theoretically substantiates his concept of a keyword, which is so central to this investigation. Arguing against instrumental accounts of language which see signs as fixed products in an '"always-given" language system', Williams argues that 'usable signs' are 'living evidence of a continuing social process, into which individuals are born and within which they are shaped, but to which then they actively contribute, in a continuing process' (1977: 37). We see here clearly the articulation of language as both symbolic and material, and as a constitutive human process. On the basis of this cultural materialist understanding, Williams argues for recognition of 'an active *social language*' (1977: 37). This should neither be understood in purely idealist terms, '[n]or (to glance back at positivist and orthodox materialist theory) is this language a simple "reflection" or "expression" of "material reality"'. He continues:

> What we have, rather, is a grasping of this reality through language, which as practical consciousness is saturated by and saturates all social activity, including productive activity. And since this grasping is social and continuous ... it occurs within an active and changing society ... Or to put it more directly, language is the articulation of this active and changing experience; a dynamic and articulated social presence in the world. (1977: 37–8)

Importantly, for Williams, agency here is *social* rather than simply discursive – the emphasis remains consistently on people's active use of language in actual social relations, even as the limits of social thought are themselves set by the language and ideas in currency. This is quite unlike 'postmodern' and idealist conceptions of language which view the linguistic realm as coterminous with – and constructive of – the social, an idea (crudely) reducible to the notion that there is 'nothing beyond the text' (cf. Torfing, 1999).

Williams's emphasis on language as action has definite political implications as it refigures people as creative meaning-makers with the capacity to describe, interpret and therefore change their world. Far from being the passive dupes of a commercial culture, or the uneducated and 'unthinking' masses as cultural elitists would have it, ordinary people are creative actors, and ordinary culture and language the site for real struggle. As Williams argues in *The Long Revolution*, 'If man [*sic*] is essentially a learning, creating and communicating being, the only social organization adequate to his nature is a participating democracy, in which all of us, as unique individuals, learn, communicate and control' (1961: 118). Thus knowledge, language and communication are considered by Williams to be central elements of social change – though crucially, the institutional and political context must enable and facilitate this, or be changed to do so. It is in this context of a rethinking of culture as collective meaning-making practices that Williams's project of identifying certain words as keywords had a definite political character as it refers us to the democratic possibilities for people to participate in the discussion of those things that matter to them in their everyday lives and, in the process, to change them. In his own appraisal of the political potential of a keywords perspective, Williams writes:

> This is not a neutral review of meanings. It is an exploration of the vocabulary of a crucial area of social and cultural discussion, which has been inherited within precise historical and social conditions and which has to be made at once conscious and critical – subject to change as well as to continuity – if the millions of people in whom it is active are to see it as active: not a tradition to be learned, nor a consensus to be accepted, nor a set of meanings which, because it is 'our language', has a natural authority; but as a shaping and reshaping, in real circumstances and from profoundly different and important points of view: a vocabulary to use, to find our ways in, to change as we find it necessary to change it, as we go on making our own language and history. (1983: 24–5)

While in one sense, the salience of a particular (key)word is to be understood as a *product* of some of the prominent social evaluations, beliefs, interests and struggles of a given historical moment, in another important sense Williams wants us to see that actively using and changing particular vocabularies – creating keywords – can impact upon the very struggles they are used to discuss. This constitutes the unique cultural materialist perspective on the relation of ideas and language to social change. And in this way, Williams's 'historical semantics forms part of a more general materialist history in which thought and language are integral elements of social reflection and action' (Durant, 2006: 9).

THE SOCIAL LOGIC OF CAPITALISM

This cultural materialist framework which allows us to understand the relation of ideas to the material contexts of their expression provides the basis for the empirical question of this study, namely, the relation of a particular idea – identity – to a particular context – the cultural political economy of capitalist societies. This framework suggests that rather than simply *situate* the 'turn to identity' within the cultural political economy of advanced capitalist societies, we must examine changes in the social relations and material conditions that have provided the context and motivation for these political and social expressions of 'identity'; and how these in turn may have given rise to new perspectives and behaviours which may 'act back' on that capitalist context.

Studies which address the relation of a particular idea to capitalism often frame this abstractly in terms of the relation of 'culture' to 'economy'. But the cultural materialist perspective of this study suggests that this is not a useful way to proceed. Firstly, as the last section has shown, the idea of identity cannot be relegated to some isolated cultural sphere, but as Williams has shown, is 'built into our living', and thereby may be practically deployed across multiple spaces in capitalist societies, including what we think of heuristically as 'culture', 'politics', and indeed, 'the economy'. Secondly, it is not helpful to construe capitalism simply in terms of 'the economy'. While capitalism has an obvious and constitutive set of economic features, it is also sustained and perpetuated socio-culturally, in belief systems, habituated practices and social values; and socio-politically, in terms of power and its unequal distribution, particularly as these are manifest in the relations of social class. It is these socio-cultural and socio-political features of capitalism that make it sensible to speak of a capitalist *society* at all, and which indeed differentiate it from other qualitatively different societies, whether agrarian, feudal or communist. Significantly, when we ask about the relation of an idea – in this case, identity – to capitalism, it is primarily these socio-cultural and socio-political spaces of capitalist societies that must necessarily concern us. It is only from such a perspective that we can usefully address what are, in fact, the key questions of this study: namely, how could the pressures and motivations associated with living in a capitalist society contribute to either the emergence of the idea of identity, or exert a formative influence upon the particular ways in which it has come to be used today? And conversely, how could the idea of identity in any way impact upon capitalist processes, and enable either accommodation or resistance to a capitalist way of life?

Big questions

In order to address these questions over the remainder of the book, I want to here set out the notion of a social logic of capitalism, as a means of exploring how capitalism encourages a particular way of life, or what Ferdinand Braudel (1973) has called a 'civilisation'. The focus is not how capitalism organises the economic relations of society, but rather how it generates particular ways of doing things, normalises certain practices and encourages distinctive evaluations. As a conceptual device, the social logic of capitalism allows us to make sense of capitalist societies generally, rather than capitalist economies specifically, and to see how capitalistic motivations and rationales can operate across the whole social space, and not just the economic. It allows us to theorise the *constitutive* power of capitalist and class relations in forming and influencing language, ideas and communication, as well as, more broadly, behaviours, practices and institutions. As such, it offers an account of social reproduction and transformation that is compatible with the orientation of Marxist and Regulation School approaches, which, as Webster explains, are distinctive for their provision of a 'holistic explanation of social relations which attempts to grasp the overall character of particular periods', emphasising 'the ways in which a range of features interconnect to enable a society to perpetuate itself' (2006: 63). A clear advantage to this kind of approach is that our attention is usefully directed towards the way in which the economic structures of capitalism are sustained or legitimised by the social and cultural order, from which 'the economy', in common sense terms, often seems to be dissociated. However, the conceptual device of a social logic of capitalism allows us to avoid the totalising tenor of many Marxist or Regulation School analyses, as it enables us to see how many spaces in capitalist societies are not (or not yet) colonised or dominated by capitalistic processes or rationales, and how there may exist a range of ideas and practices that challenge or subvert this logic. It is at this level of understanding and analysis, and not in terms of the abstract relation of 'culture' to 'economy', that we will properly grasp how the idea of identity relates to the capitalist context of its emergence and consolidation, and specifically, how it may either support the reproduction of capitalist relations or, alternatively, offer forms of resistance to them.

By way of contrast, and in order to emphasise what especially distinguishes this cultural materialist approach, I will begin by providing an outline and appreciation of a recent, valuable attempt to explain how people 'acquiesce to capitalism', in terms of a 'spirit of capitalism' (Boltanski and Chiapello, 2005a). Boltanski and Chiapello have primarily worked within a Weberian rather than a Marxist tradition, and in updating Weber's original concept of a Spirit of Capitalism, stipulate that they 'draw above all from Weber's approach the idea that people need powerful moral reasons for rallying to capitalism' (2005a: 9). Boltanski and Chiapello then define the spirit of capitalism as:

> precisely the set of beliefs associated with the capitalist order that helps justify this order and, by legitimating them, to sustain the forms of action and

predispositions compatible with it. These justifications, whether general or practical, local or global, expressed in terms of virtue or justice, support the performance of more or less unpleasant tasks and, more generally, adhesion to a lifestyle conducive to the capitalist order. (2005a: 10–11)

Boltanski and Chiapello essentially take issue with the types of economic arguments typically put forward in support of capitalism, concerning technological progress, the efficiency of competition-driven production and the supposedly auspicious relationship between capitalism and individual liberties. They say that these are not and have never been enough to convince ordinary people to fully embrace capitalism, nor the particular way of life it requires. Instead the spirit of capitalism must be 'concretized' for ordinary people by situating them within three everyday 'dimensions', which offer either 'excitement', 'security' or 'fairness' for capitalist involvement (Boltanski and Chiapello, 2005b: 164). Thus the spirit of capitalism serves to 'furnish it with precisely what capitalism lacks: reasons for participating in the accumulation process that are rooted in quotidian reality, and attuned to the values and concerns of those who need to be actively involved' (2005a: 21). According to Boltanski and Chiapello, capitalism is successful because the spirit of capitalism has justified people's commitment to capitalism, and then rendered this commitment attractive. Boltanski and Chiapello thus take the power of the capitalist system as *evidence* of a general acceptance of and attachment to the system.

However, we need to ask, what would happen if the justifications of capitalism, in its current or previous stage of development, were weak or absent? Are justifications and critiques really as influential in determining the course of capitalist development as they say?[3] Arguably, Boltanski and Chiapello's emphasis on the *spirit* of capitalism is overly cognitivist and tends towards idealism. That is, it understates the importance of practice and actual lived relationships relative to 'arguments', 'justifications' and discourses. From a cultural materialist perspective, it detaches these arguments and ideas from the real material conditions and social relations with which they are inextricably bound up. In doing so, it operates an overly rationalistic view of behaviour and of the formation of commitments, as if people first need motives and justifications *before* they can act. Boltanski and Chiapello fail to take into account two key alternative reasons why people may 'acquiesce' to capitalism. Firstly, it may be the case that people acquiesce to capitalism, not because they are rationally convinced or even excited by it, but because it now forms part of their 'economic imaginaries' – how they assume 'the economy' must work, and how they behave on that basis. It may also be the case that people acquiesce to capitalism because they simply have no choice: people may very conceivably be overwhelmed by the sheer force and extent of the capitalist system, such that living outside it might be unimaginable (and have immediate implications for one's survival and well-being).

As an alternative to this notion of a spirit of capitalism, let us now consider in more detail the notion of a 'social logic of capitalism'. The notion of a 'social logic' is an intrinsically cultural materialist concept, as it refers us to a set of ideas made sensible and animate in practices, processes and social relations, but specifies that these are organised around a particular principle or rationale. A given 'social logic', in the specified cultural material sense, has causal power as a way of thinking, organising and acting, because it governs people's social interactions and therefore creates a whole range of expectations, motives, costs and benefits that can encourage or even force them to extend that logic to other interactions. It is a personally habituated and structurally institutionalised way of operating, that does not only make sensible but also generates a whole range of practices. Furthermore, a social logic does not refer to a problematic or contentious idea or set of ideas and practices but instead a very well-established, largely (or apparently) coherent and functional idea or set of related ideas and practices. Importantly, a social logic can engender social change as well as social reproduction in the fields in which it operates – it can disrupt older, more established practices in some fields, and reinforce or entrench certain practices, or introduce new ones, in others. Finally, a social logic is not necessarily con- fined to the social field of the corresponding character. So, for example, a social logic that is religious in character – premised today, perhaps, on the notion of 'Christian charity', or in mediaeval times, 'the great chain of being' – does not necessarily just shape and inform religious practices, but economic or political practices too.

What, then, of the social logic *of capitalism* specifically? The social logic of capitalism does not refer to an abstract economic law, nor the preordained unfolding of history according to some 'historical material' principle, but to an active, living and meaningful logic, expressed in and confirmed by the actions and practices of individual, state and corporate actors. Specifically, *the social logic of capitalism refers us to how individuals or collectivities act in a way that manifests, embodies, rationalises or normalises the principle of capital accumulation.*[4] The notion of a social logic of capitalism emphasises the meaningful social practices that people engage in, that serve not only to reproduce the 'abstract' logic of capital accumulation, but also the social institutions of markets, private property, com- petition, wage labour and monetary exchange themselves. Thus the social logic of capitalism helps explain the *social and cultural* reproduction of the economic features of the capitalist system. Furthermore, it allows us to explore how *other* social practices, ideas and institutions associated with or apparently accom- panying capitalism – such as, for example, individualism, the heterosexual nuclear family, conceptions of liberal equality – may be related to capitalism, by examining how the social logic of capitalism operates across a range of non-economic contexts too, shaping and influencing practices, behaviours and beliefs in what we think of as 'culture', 'politics' and 'society' more generally. In all of these cases, what is at stake is more than a belief which guides action, but a particular way of *doing things*, institutionalised in practices, institutions,

structures and systems of belief. Attention to the social logic of capitalism further emphasises, as suggested above, that people may acquiesce to capitalism,
not because they are rationally convinced or even excited by it, but precisely
because it saturates their everyday lives, or, to use Williams's words, is built into
their living. None of this, however, is to diminish or deny the power of corporate, financial and state entities – or individuals – to protect, institutionalise
or enforce capitalist structures and systems – this is obviously the main way in
which capitalism is and has always been sustained. But this is not the concern
here. The concern, rather, is how capitalistic ways of being and knowing are
reproduced both within and beyond what we think of as 'the economy', with
the effect, therefore, that they at once socialise people into a capitalist way of
life, and influence a range of social, political and cultural practices and decisions
in a capitalist society.

The social logic of capitalism in practice

Let us now look at the social logic of capitalism in practice, focusing in particular,
for illustrative purposes, on the naturalisation and social reproduction of capitalist
markets. Against the argument that people must be first convinced, securitised
or excited by capitalist markets in order to willingly participate in them, this
approach emphasises that people may have no other real choice, and that their
apparent endorsement or support of capitalist market relations may not arise from
any prior allegiance to a spirit of capitalism but rather from the way in which
capitalist markets have become integrated into their lives in practical ways. At the
same time, people may be convinced by a market logic because of its power and
presence, and because of the evolution of scientific and everyday narratives that
point to its 'natural' existence, and its compatibility with 'human nature'. There
is a mutually reinforcing interplay between the practical and discursive legitimation of the capitalist market system – the fact that people engage in market
transactions on a near daily basis seems to confirm its natural or inevitable existence, while the common sense acceptance of its apparently natural status further
facilitates the organisation of society according to market principles. Similarly we
can see how, in a capitalist market context, people are practically incentivised to
act competitively, because competition has been built into everyday life in such
a way that one must compete or lose out: it is not necessary for 'competition' in
itself to be viewed auspiciously by the actors in question. Furthermore, while
it is capitalism itself that rewards competition, this has been refigured as part of
'human nature'. The competitive, capitalist market system is then, by definition,
deemed the most appropriate system for managing social and economic relations.
    This practical legitimation of the capitalist market has implications for the
evolution of other key social values too. For example, Hall (1996) points out
that by construing 'profiteering' – 'excessive' profit taking – as the only kind
of exploitation that may take place in a market, the fundamental exploitation of workers' labour that constitutes and underpins *all* market exchange

is concealed. Additionally, 'freedom' is construed in this context as 'unforced' entry into the labour market and the 'free' exchange of goods for money – and not in terms of the freedom to step outside capitalist market relations, and opt for a different way of life or alternative set of social relations.

The notion of 'possessive individualism' is here particularly significant. Possessive individualism refers to a 'conception of the individual as essentially the proprietor of his own person or capacities, owing nothing to society for them' (Macpherson, 1964: 2). Originally an element of seventeenth-century political liberal thought, possessive individualism has come increasingly to describe the self-perceptions of people living in capitalist societies, as the types of practices in which they must engage encourage behaviours that seem to confirm this kind of self-perception. The individual-*qua*-owner is ostensibly 'free' from dependence upon others, and at liberty to enter only those relations that suit his/her interests. Although interdependency is a constitutive feature of the human condition, at the very least in infancy and old age, a significant proportion of the social relations people *do* enter into in capitalist societies are mediated and contained by the capitalist market, which does indeed treat the individual – and requires the individual to act – as an independent, self-interested actor, free to make those rational choices best suited to realise his/her subjectively defined preferences. This 'homo economicus' is thus faced with a wide range of market decisions across most facets of his/her life, from earning a wage, to acquiring food and housing, and – increasingly – accessing education and healthcare. This requirement to engage in market activity across so many areas of life may in itself be enough to convince people that possessive individualism, and not mutual dependence and moral obligation to wider society, is the natural state of affairs. As Macpherson explains, '[t]he relation of ownership, having become for more and more men the critically important relation determining their actual freedom and actual prospect of realizing their full potentialities, was read back into the nature of the individual' (1964: 3). In this context, 'freedom is a function of possession' (1964: 3). But this cannot be taken as evidence of the truth of possessive individualism, nor, it must be said, as evidence of some kind of 'false consciousness' or simple acceptance of capitalist ideology. For it is the case that in capitalist societies, a certain kind of freedom *does* arise from possessive individualism, for when someone acts as though they depend on nobody and owe society nothing, as long as they are sufficiently endowed with wealth, they can realise the promises of the capitalist system. But this, as Kaufman expresses it, is 'a peculiar kind of freedom. It includes the freedom to buy what we want, if we have the money; the freedom to try to become capitalist entrepreneurs, if we can; the freedom to buy and sell labour; and the freedom to do what we want with our property' (2003: 55). Expanding upon the same point, Tormey argues that '[c]apitalism celebrates such freedom as the essence of its own creation. Without freedom those essential constituents of the capitalist "space" are lost: wage labour, new ideas, innovation' (2004: 27).

It is important to recognise that these ideas about what constitutes human nature, exploitation and freedom are not necessarily explicitly articulated or defended by people living in a capitalist society – though they may be in overtly political discussions – but rather are routinised in unexceptional daily market practices. In this way, argues Hall, the key 'bourgeois' political themes of equality, freedom, property and individualism 'may derive from the categories we use in our practical, commonsense thinking about the market economy. This is how there arises, out of daily mundane experience the powerful categories of bourgeois legal, political, social and philosophical thought' (1996: 34). This is the social logic of capitalism in practice.

How does the social logic of capitalism operate across society more broadly, and relate to other cultural and social, rather than obviously economic practices, in capitalist societies? Indeed, while there is broad enough consensus over the economic features of capitalism, such as markets, private property and wage labour, theorists have long argued over what constitutes the essential or necessary cultural and political features of the system. In his call for the disaggregation of capitalism, Wrong (1992) is critical of attempts to pin down the 'constitutive' cultural and political features of capitalism. Against such an approach, he claims that 'the changing historical context of capitalism necessitates continual consideration of which non-economic values and institutions are compatible with it, which limit or even threaten it, and which constitute necessary or sufficient conditions for its birth, growth and survival' (1992: 149–50). The conceptual device of the social logic of capitalism allows us to explore precisely these important questions. It encourages us to explore how capitalistic ways of being and knowing work in or through a range of fields (not only economic), motivating and shaping a wide range of practices (again, not only economic), and generating, shaping or sustaining the institutions, social norms and belief systems central to its operation in a given historical juncture. These social institutions may include political democracy, marriage, family care arrangements, 'green politics', 'race'-relations and any other prominent or emergent 'cultural' or political formations. Any and all of these will be likely to be found to relate to the social logic of capitalism in partial, contingent, negotiated and historically specific ways. Indeed, a number of important studies have already shown this to be the case. For example, Ellen Meiksins Wood (1995) has analysed the way in which capitalism and democracy have related to and impacted on each other in an incomplete and historically specific fashion. Heidi Hartmann (1979), Sylvia Walby (1990) and other feminists have demonstrated the interlinked nature of capitalism and patriarchy, showing how they operate together in complex and intertwined ways, without either system fully 'determining' the other. And John D'Emilio (1983) and David T. Evans (1993) have traced the co-evolution of sexual norms with the development of capitalism. These analyses are valuable and even groundbreaking, offering important ways of exploring how the capitalist system does not exist independently in some economic realm, but actively uses and works through various other social, cultural and political formations. At the same time, they show how these other 'non-economic' formations can impact upon the development of capitalism, either offering points of resistance or emphasising a particular trajectory in its development.

The notion of a social logic of capitalism likewise does not rest on the assumption that the capitalist economy is separate from these social institutions, but enables us to see how each may depend on and in part create the other, often in contingent ways that cannot be predicted by a determinist theory in an *a priori* fashion. In addition, rather than remain at the level of structural analysis, it particularly emphasises the practical ways in which people themselves are integrated into a capitalist way of life that, in the process, shapes these other social institutions, such as marriage or political democracy. In effect, then, the social logic of capitalism provides us with a means of exploring how other cultural and social formations are articulated to, or linked with, the political economy of capitalism. Of particular relevance to this study, it offers a means of exploring how different ideas and practices can either promote or challenge a logic of capitalist accumulation and social class division, even where these are not, on the face of it, explicitly pro-capitalist or even 'economic' ideas or practices.

The social logic of capitalism in neoliberal societies

Let us now look at some of the features of the current stage of 'post-Fordist' or neoliberal capitalism through the lens of the social logic of capitalism. Key features of this new stage of capitalism include 'consumerism', 'financialisation', 'globalisation' and the political-economic paradigm of neoliberalism (Bello, 2008; Harvey, 2010), though as discussed earlier, none of these represent entirely new processes but rather an intensification of already existing ones. The social logic of capitalism draws our attention to the ways in which people may act habitually, often without actively choosing to, in a way that sustains the abstract logic of capital accumulation as it manifests in these historically prominent features, while in the process reinforcing the ideas that themselves animate and justify these practices.

Let us begin with the phenomenon of consumerism. Under capitalism constant reinvestment in order to create further capital requires consumers who will 'realise' that value by buying the commodities produced. But since the worker is not paid enough to consume the goods s/he produces (in aggregate), the corollary of this logic of capitalism is that more and more consumers must be found, or called into the circuit, so that this value is realised, and so capital can be freed up for further investment. Both orthodox and heterodox economists have explored the ways in which capitalism overcomes this limit of 'insufficient demand'. Two key 'resolutions' are typically identified, namely, the creation of new needs and wants in the existing consumer population, and the creation of new consumers by pulling new populations into the capitalist relationship (the increased and intensive targeting of children as 'consumers', for example, clearly exemplifies this strategy).

These resolutions have created the 'consumer society' that has prevailed in the Global North since the 1950s. Indeed, consumption has been elevated to one of the primary purposes or foci of people living in western capitalist societies today. The political subject of liberal societies has in many ways been reconstituted as the sovereign consumer, who is encouraged to believe that her/his consumer choices will sustain the economy and foster growth. This is refigured as an end in itself, without very much attention to what is consumed (with pornography and handguns as valuable as locally grown vegetables or books on political democracy). When western societies enter crisis citizens are told it is their patriotic duty to go out and shop. And boy, do they shop. As will be further elaborated in Chapter 6, individuals are encouraged – and more, themselves actively try – to be different and to stand out, not through their social contributions, but through their displays of personal acquisitions. In this context, social class differences come to operate on the terrain of culture, even as the reality of social class continues to be premised on a deeply unequal distribution of income and wealth. Via the social logic of capitalism, individuals see themselves and behave as consumers in a way that perpetuates the accumulation of capital – though not necessarily in a way that renders them beneficiaries of the wealth produced.

As many theorists have noted, neither 'resolution' of the problem of insufficient demand – creating new consumer 'needs' or targeting new consumers – can actually *fully* resolve the problem, as the need for profit ensures that labour costs are kept lower than the total value of the goods and services produced by the workers in aggregate. The problem of insufficient demand is simply reproduced on a larger scale. This is particularly emphasised in a neoliberal context, which has been characterised by a repression of real wages, to the extent that these have not even kept pace with the rate of inflation (Glyn, 2006). Thus this period of neoliberalism called forth a *third* 'resolution', which has recently been captured forcefully by Mellor (2010), Ingham (2004, 2008) and Harvey (2010). This is the unrestrained creation of private credit, via mortgages, credit cards and bank loans, in order to allow for the continued sustenance and growth of consumer 'demand' and spending. As Harvey puts it, 'the gap between what labour was earning and what it could spend was covered by the rise of the credit card industry and increasing indebtedness' (2010: 17). The significance of this resolution is starkly revealed by the statistics – in the last generation in the US, household income has risen by 1%, while household debt has risen by 1000% (Scurlock, 2007: 5).

This is a key aspect of the processes of financialisation that have come to characterise the current capitalist system, though consumer debt, large as it is, is really the tip of the iceberg that is the excessive amount of credit and debt circulating in the corporate financial sector. As Mellor (2010: 25) explains, debt-based money issued by banks creates a growth imperative in the economy, as the original sum must be paid back with interest – and *systemically*, this interest can only be achieved through the creation of further debt-based money. 'Capitalist market economies are [therefore] dependent on these circuits of debt-based money' (Mellor, 2010: 25). Ingham argues that it is capitalism's capacity to create limitless credit as debt that best explains 'its capacity for dynamic innovation and rapid growth' (2003: 298). The constant production of money quite literally facilitates the (hypothetically) limitless process of capital accumulation, though, as Bello points out, this creates profit, but not value, as this can only be achieved by industry, agriculture, trade and services. 'The result', he says, 'is an increased bifurcation between a hyperactive financial economy and a stagnant real economy' (2008: unpaginated). This is particularly evident today in the massive explosion of new instruments of 'financial innovation' – derivatives, debt-credit swaps, asset-backed securities and so on – that has allowed the level of credit sloshing around the corporate financial banking and shadow-banking sectors to reach stratospheric levels. As Harvey puts it in his account of the intensification of financialisation that characterised the latter decades of the twentieth century, 'It was almost as if the banking community had retired into the penthouse of capitalism where they manufactured oodles of money by trading and leveraging among themselves without any mind whatsoever for what the working people living in the basement were doing' (2010: 30). And as Mellor astutely points out, with particular relevance today, '[i]t is not without irony that the market claims the monopoly of wealth creation and describes this as making money. Through the banking sector this is what it quite literally does' (2010: 33).

Attention to the social logic of capitalism illuminates these trends towards personal indebtedness and debt-fuelled consumption on *an everyday level*, and again demonstrates that people may often acquiesce to this new 'finance capitalism', not because they are convinced or excited by it, but because it now forms part of their 'economic imaginaries' – how they assume 'the economy' works (or *must* work), and how they behave on that basis. Mellor's account of what she calls the 'people's capitalism' illustrates this notion of an economic imaginary wonderfully (2010: Ch. 3). It suggests that rather than document a new managerialist 'spirit', or moral ethos of thrift or profligacy, we should look at the *practical ways* in which ordinary people have been integrated into capitalism through credit cards, mortgages, home ownership and pensions. For example, convinced that homes are 'assets', that future security lies in 'investment' rather than savings, and that personal debt is unremarkable if not a sign of social status (via credit cards, 'creditworthiness' and enhanced consumption), the ordinary people of the world's affluent nations have acquiesced to – and more, embraced in their everyday choices, actions and life decisions – the practices, beliefs and institutions that constitute what the theorists of capitalism call 'financialisation'. Indeed, as Lapavistas (2014: unpaginated) argues, while the term itself reflects the ascendancy of the financial sector, '[e]ven more important, it conveys the penetration of the financial system into every nook and cranny of society ... The penetration of finance into the everyday life of households has not only created a range of dependencies on financial services, but also changed the outlook, mentality and morality of daily life.' Through financialisation, the social logic of capitalism is hard at work.

This expansionary drive of capitalism does not just pertain to its insatiable need for increasing demand and raising consumption levels, but also to its requirements for new sources of capital or new spaces to 'capitalise'. The requirement is clearly at the root of processes of 'globalisation' prominent today. The phenomenon of economic globalisation is transformed – at least in the Global North – via the social logic of capitalism into what *appears* to be a popular cultural phenomenon. The wearing of garments produced by transnational corporations, the following of television shows and films produced by a global entertainment industry, the use and celebration of the internet and other new information technologies, the accessing of national bank accounts far beyond state jurisdictions, the demand for cultural and culinary products from opposite sides of the world and the increased participation in leisure-based or work-driven travel, migration and relocation are all processes in which people seemingly – for the most part – willingly participate, and which are promoted as part of the wonderful new world of globalisation. The (cultural) part obscures the (economic) whole, and the social logic of capitalism ensures this obfuscation as people habitually or apparently by choice engage in these practices – thereby ensuring that the logic of capital accumulation under globalisation proceeds apace. However, it must be noted here that processes of globalisation are experienced very differently in the Global South, as forced migration, economic exploitation and the spread of sweat-shops constitute its main features. The social logic of capitalism is less relevant here, as people are not so much socialised into a capitalist way of life as forced by economic necessity and the power of global capitalism to participate in these processes.

A second well-recognised way in which capitalism overcomes the problem of insufficient supply is through the capitalisation of social, as opposed to natural, resources. This is neoliberalism in action. As Jessop (2002: 29) notes in his account of the 'ecological dominance' of capitalism,[5] we see this in 'the commodification of political, educational, health, scientific and many other activities, so that they come to be primarily and directly oriented to opportunities for profit'. These processes are ideologically sustained, as this vast wave of privatisation that has swept around the world since the 1970s has been 'carried on the backs of the dogma that state-run enterprises are by definition inefficient and lax and that the only way to improve their performance is to pass them over to the private sector' (Harvey, 2010: 28). Attention to the social logic of capitalism demonstrates how these neoliberal policies and ideas are integrated into people's lives in very practical ways. Many people have come to conflate discourses of moral with fiscal responsibility in a manner which not only casts the state as wasteful and profligate, but even relieves the state of the provision of social protections, transferring the costs of education and healthcare to the individual consumer. In this context, citizens come to see themselves, and act, as 'consumers of government, expecting the best return for the price paid in taxes, rather than as citizens supporting an expansive array of broadly accessible public agencies and institutions' (Duggan, 2003: 38). Private schools and private healthcare arrangements are defended by many people on the grounds that they want, and will do, 'what is best for their children', a powerful social motivation that has been distorted by the consistent rhetorical and substantive attacks on public institutions, which leave them hollowed out and lacking in resources. This is a clear case of neoliberal policies appearing to prove what they have in fact created, but sustained by classed mechanisms and the actions of even under-resourced citizens who may feel they have no other choice.

These processes have intensified in the context of the current economic recession, as across the western world citizens have bought into narratives that equate the running of 'the economy' with the running of the house-hold, thereby accepting as a matter of fact – if not preference – the need for 'thrift' and 'belt-tightening'. This is a powerful analogy, inevitably prefaced by politicians and economic commentators with the claim that the state can-not spend more than its income – and that 'everyone who runs a household knows this basic truth'. Well, everybody *does* know that, but not necessarily that this is a false comparison. Unlike households, states may indeed increase the money supply, though this is invariably cast as the wilful and irresponsi-ble 'printing' of money, and thus economically dangerous (while as we saw, the widely under-acknowledged privileges of private financial institutions to create money is just business-as-usual). Across the western world it has been the case that citizens have voted in national legislatures promising to 'reduce wasteful public expenditure' as a way out of recession, and while public resist-ance to this has been at times vigorous, it has on the whole been disjointed if not confused. What is more, as corporations use the language of recession to further justify low tax regimes and outsourcing, citizens continue to exhibit 'gratefulness' for the relatively few jobs created in their jurisdictions by mul-tinationals, without much recognition of the vampirisation of state resources that paid for the health and education of the workers employed – not to men-tion the physical and legal infrastructure of the state relied on, but not paid for, by corporations (Iversen and Armstrong, 2006).[6] While the massive power of corporate and political elites, both ideologically and in terms of setting policy, cannot be underestimated, what these examples show is that capitalist ways of being and knowing may be sustained, justified and even perpetuated, not because people are convinced or excited by the capitalist ideologies ped-dled by these elites, but because capitalist practices have infiltrated the very fabric of their everyday lives.

CONCLUSION

People who live in a society organised according to a capitalist logic will come to think and behave in a way that legitimates this logic and ensuing structure – not always and inevitably, but *habitually*, as they reinforce and reproduce this logic in their everyday actions. It is entirely possible that people may not believe or rationally accept capitalism's promises but instead may resent living in and under capitalism, yet continue to perpetuate this social logic in their ordinary lives. They may recognise its exploitative nature and uneven distribution of wealth, 'success', poverty and 'failure', but remain structurally positioned so as to be unable to do anything much about it. What people can do in capitalism depends primarily on what they have, not on their justifications. Contrary to Boltanski and Chiapello's claim that 'capitalism needs a spirit in order to engage the people required for production and the functioning of business' because 'these people cannot be set to work and kept working by force' (2005a: 485), it seems that 'these people' may just have no other choice, at least as they see it, or because it has been integrated into their lives in such a practical, common sense way, that it does not even appear to be a choice. Against accounts of the spirit of capitalism, I suggest that the assumption that capitalism works and is sustained by the degree to which people believe and invest in the promises of capitalism (security, excitement, justice) misses something about the power of capitalism, which is located in its institutionalised, habituated logic, rather than a rational belief in its promises. Rather than see the 'spirit' of capitalism as the primary causal force within capitalism, we should instead recognise that these narratives and justifications are *themselves* activated by the social logic of capitalism. At the same time we need to recognise that many of these discourses and justifications are deliberately perpetuated and mobilised by powerful actors who stand to benefit from legitimation and intensification of capitalistic processes.

Finally, the notion of a 'social logic' generally, and the 'social logic of capitalism' specifically, is not meant to emphasise a disembodied force at the expense of individual or group actions and human agency, as some conceptualisations of a capitalist 'logic' have tended towards. From a cultural materialist perspective, it is important to conceptualise human agency as *part* of this social logic, in order to understand how individuals and groups actively negotiate these discourses and practices for what they perceive to be their own interests; and how individuals have varying degrees of power in this respect. What is important is that we recognise that people use this social logic, but are also vulnerable to its effects, as their everyday and long-term options are shaped in accordance with it.

This concept of a 'social logic of capitalism' underpins the analysis to come in the rest of this book, rather than being central to it, providing a framework for assessing how the idea of identity relates to capitalist societies in an intrinsically cultural materialist way; that is to say, one which is attentive to both the causal and practical power of the idea of identity, and the formative capacity of capitalism to integrate people into a capitalist way of life. As we will see, the idea of identity is itself complicated, because it is sometimes used in ways that conform to this capitalised way of living, and at other times, in ways that explicitly challenge it. This challenging is not necessarily at the level of overt anti-capitalist politics – but that, after all, is itself obvious, and has in part provided the grounds for the social versus cultural left debate, and accusations that identity politics ignore or legitimate capitalist inequalities. However, as we will see, it is not as simple as this. The idea of identity is actively used by many people in a range of economic, popular cultural and political settings. It is an empirical question as to whether it will reinforce other capitalist ideologies, or challenge them; and whether it works to socialise people into a capitalist way of life, or not. This is a political issue as much as a cultural one, as it has to do with the differential power people have to act in particular ways, on the basis of different practical ideas, as these people are themselves structurally positioned in unequal relation to one another in capitalist societies.

Notes

1. See also McGuigan and Moran (2014) for a further development of this framework.
2. In this respect, the project of cultural materialism has important affinities with the work of Antonio Gramsci, particularly in relation to his conception of hegemony; the Frankfurt School; the Birmingham School of Cultural Studies under the direction of Stuart Hall; Pierre Bourdieu; materialist feminism, which has its own complicated history; and certain strands of post-structuralism. Indeed, Milner (1993: 9) has suggested that we may helpfully think of this whole body of cultural theory as cultural materialism – and insofar as we define 'cultural materialism' as the attempt to develop a materialist theory which is attentive to the huge significance of cultural processes, then this is true.
3. With thanks to Andrew Sayer for raising these questions, and the general point in this section about the disproportionate weighting of moral 'justifications' to practical concerns in Boltanski and Chiapello's work (from personal correspondence with Andrew Sayer).
4. The 'principle of capital accumulation' is sometimes discussed in terms of a more general, economic logic of capitalism, which derives from the 'abstract' nature of capital itself, as for example, in the work of Heilbroner (1985) and Harvey (2010). In some hands (though by no means all), the notion of a 'logic of capitalism' has been used in a rigidly universalising and ahistorical manner, as Wallerstein (1983) has argued in his criticism of traditional leftist histories of capitalism for identifying a pure logic of capitalism as a series of abstract laws, and then attempting to trace those laws at work in specific historical examples. Although the notion of a social logic of capitalism also depends on the 'principle of capital accumulation', it is to be explicitly distinguished from these accounts by virtue of its emphasis on the meaningful and contingent social practices by which the principle of capital accumulation is justified or enacted.

5. Jessop uses an analogy from the natural sciences to explain how one system exerts an over-riding influence upon the other species in a given ecological community.

6. The database Nexis identifies 233 English-language newspaper articles with the words 'grateful' or 'thankful' for jobs in the title alone, from 2003 to 2013. These are not simply admonitions from economic 'experts' that people *should* be grateful, but many are opinion pieces or contain interviews with workers, who declare themselves to be grateful, as in the case of Ben Atkins, a graduate working for £7 an hour for Amazon, who says he and his co-workers are 'grateful for the work — any work'.

4

A Pre-history of the Idea of Identity in Capitalist Societies

INTRODUCTION

A keyword, Raymond Williams tells us, is a complex yet familiar word, such that the 'problems of its meanings [are] inextricably bound up with the problems it [is] used to discuss' (1983: 15). Engaging in a keyword analysis, Chapter 2 traced the changing meanings and uses of the *term* identity historically, and showed how our contemporary senses of the term have evolved in complex ways from earlier meanings and uses, culminating in an explosion of new uses in popular, political and academic discourse from roughly the 1960s. The transition is from a very narrow philosophical sense of 'identity' meaning the sameness of an entity – *any* entity – to itself, to the senses with which we are familiar today, namely 'personal identity' and 'social identity'. This analysis also showed that these two main contemporary senses of the word identity are historically very recent, which suggests therefore that the very possibility of construing oneself as 'having an identity' – whether personal or social – is a historically novel formulation. At stake here is more than a simple popularisation of a word and concept, but rather a new way of framing and shaping historically persistent concerns about selfhood, others and the relations between them. And what this book has shown so far is that, despite being routinely treated as a substantive property of individuals and groups, identity in fact functions lexically as a device that classifies according to what is considered essential to a particular person, type of person or group. What remains now is to explore these new uses and meanings – these expressions of 'personal' and 'social' 'identity', and this essentialist mode of social classification – as part of, and in relation to, the social relations which give rise to and which are in turn affected by them.

The last chapter set out a cultural materialist framework with the ability to account for the evolution of ideas in the material conditions of their production and circulation – both in terms of the generative power of the social context, and the causal power of ideas themselves to inform and guide a range of social practices. Via the notion of a 'social logic of capitalism', the chapter also offered a way of explaining how certain historically specific ideas achieve prominence in or are otherwise related to a capitalist context, in a way that recognises the immense formative power of capitalism itself to shape ideas, norms, institutions and social action. This framework thus enables consideration of how the use of identity as a keyword – in the specified cultural materialist sense – relates to the social logic of capitalism across a number of fields in contemporary societies. This relationship is the subject of the remainder of this book, as it investigates the emergence of the idea of identity in twentieth-century capitalist societies: its naturalisation, the uses to which it is put and the work it currently does. Why did the word identity undergo these changes? How could the pressures and motivations of living in a capitalist society have contributed to the emergence of the idea of identity as we know it today, or have exerted a particular formative influence on the senses that have come to prominence? And how was the social and political landscape of capitalist societies itself altered as a consequence of this explosion of use?

This chapter begins this analysis by tracing the historical and practical evolution of the ideas that would *eventually* be captured by the word identity, and specifically, tracking the various social forces that would make these ideas so important in the cultural political economy of capitalist societies. Against popular histories of identity which trace the origins of contemporary uses of the term directly to Erikson's work in the field of psychology in the 1950s, this chapter demonstrates that the notion of identity has a far deeper history than that, involving conceptualisations of self- and grouphood that can be traced back to the Enlightenment. What is important is that these other ideas about selfhood and groups pre-existed their ultimate articulation as 'identity', but were eventually consolidated and more, shaped, by the choice of the very word 'identity' – as it carried with it its own history of meanings – to capture them. Furthermore, against histories that trace a recent 'diffusion' of the supposedly 'original' psychological sense of identity into a range of more obviously social contexts, this chapter shows how the ideas which make up the 'pre-history' of identity themselves had a distinctively social character, as they developed as a largely politically motivated way of thinking about selves, groups and their relationship to others in the context of unequal capitalist societies. As this chapter will show, the pre-history of the idea of identity is also, in important ways, the pre-history of 'identity politics'.

IDENTITY BEFORE IDENTITY POLITICS?

The now familiar story of identity politics tells us that identity politics emerged suddenly onto the political scene in the 1960s, challenging both the older, ostensibly universal, but in reality exclusive, politics of class, and the organisation of society in ways which systematically favoured some groups on account of their identities and stigmatised and disenfranchised others. There are two main problems with this narrative. Firstly, as this story is often told, identity politics have only a shallow history in the civil rights and freedom movements of the 1960s. This perspective has been challenged and remedied by a number of 'historians of identity' who have uncovered a far deeper history to identity politics, tracing its motivations and aims to the nineteenth century if not earlier (Hall, 1992; Calhoun, 1993; Kellner, 1995; Bauman, 2004; Nicholson, 2008). Nicholson, in particular, provides a particularly strong example of this kind of revision. In *Identity Before Identity Politics,* she explores the ideational pre-history of identity politics, and argues that though the movements themselves were not new, their aims and emphases shifted during the 1960s, to focus directly on 'identity issues' (2008: 5). She opens her history of identity politics with the following passage:

> During the late 1960s, certain political phenomena appeared on the US land-scape that altered the terms of the debate about social justice. The political movements on behalf of African Americans and women took a distinctive turn. Both of these movements had been a force in United States politics prior to the late 1960s, most visibly in the earlier civil rights and women's rights movements. In these earlier incarnations, these movements had fought for legislation aimed at expanding the access black people and women had to opportunities long denied them for reasons of race and sex. But in the late 1960s, a new kind of emphasis emerged within both movements. While many within these movements continued to work for the above goals, others, particularly those who were younger and angrier, began to articulate different kinds of aims. Those who started calling their movement 'Black Power,' instead of 'Civil Rights,' and 'Women's Liberation,' as distinct from 'Women's Rights,' created a politics that went beyond issues of access and focused more explicitly on issues of identity than had these earlier movements. Other activists, such as those who replaced 'Gay Rights' with 'Gay Liberation,' made a similar kind of turn. The more explicit focus of these groups on issues of identity caused many to describe this new politics as 'identity politics'. (2008: 1)

This account supports the argument of this book, insofar as it also challenges the anachronistic argument that social movements organised around race, gender and so on were always concerned with 'identity'. As Nicholson's narrative also makes clear, these earlier gender- and race-based social movements could not be said to be 'about' identity in any meaningful sense, but were instead concerned with questions of universal access and equality. In order to understand *why* these social movements became explicitly concerned with 'identity issues', Nicholson proposes to undertake a 'history of ideas' approach, to 'illuminate the historicity of some of the ideas about social identity that have organised the lives of women and black people in the history of the United States and that motivated activists to challenge those forms of organisation and the ideas behind them' (2008: 5). Only this, she tells us, will help us grasp 'why identity politics emerged when it did', and give us 'insight into some of the conundrums about social identity that we still face today' (2008: 8). So far, so good.

However, despite proposing such a deeply historicising approach, it is not clear that Nicholson avoids the second, more serious problem which dogs both the shallower and the more historically attentive accounts of the emergence of identity politics. This is the assumption that the category of identity itself, as we now know it, significantly preceded the identity politics of the 1960s, by several centuries if not longer. This is evident even in the title of Nicholson's book, 'Identity *Before* Identity Politics'. It is also evident in the tendency of Nicholson and the other historians of identity to refer to nineteenth- and twentieth-century conceptualisations of race and gender as *identities* themselves, even though this, as Chapter 2 showed, is also a historically recent conceptual shift. The implication of this kind of assumption is that, in effect, the activists of the social movements of the 1800s and early 1900s *could* have chosen to mobilise around identity had they wanted to, or had certain other contextual features been in place. In contrast to this, this book makes the case that the category of identity as we now know it was just not available to them, nor was it meaningful in any way that would have made it sensible for them to organise their claims around it. The category of identity only emerged as a meaningful way of organising and framing certain political positions and demands as part of a longer historical development of ways of thinking about the self and social categories, in specifically essentialising terms. And importantly, it was only at a relatively advanced stage in the development of this kind of thinking that the idea of identity came into play, scientifically and popularly, to capture and consolidate essentialist understandings of personhood and grouphood. Contrary to what Nicholson and the others claim, there *was* no identity before identity politics.

With these clarifications and caveats in mind, this chapter draws on these prominent historicisations of 'identity' in setting out its own 'history of ideas' approach to understanding the contemporary salience of identity. But as should now be clear, this is a history of ideas with a difference. Firstly, whereas other historians of identity distinguish between what they see as two or three distinct instantiations or conceptions of 'identity' in different historical periods, tracing, for example, successive 'modern' and 'postmodern' notions and formations of identity (Hall, 1992; Kellner, 1995; Bauman, 2004; Nicholson, 2008), this chapter argues that our contemporary notions of identity developed *out of* historically distinct sets of ideas, which in themselves were *not* specific views on or instantiations of 'identity', but instead different ways of thinking about self and its relation to others. There *were* no eighteenth- or nineteenth-century conceptions or instantiations of 'identity', as we now understand the concept, but rather only particular (and changing) conceptions of selfhood and grouphood, which, for a variety of reasons, crystallised into the category of identity in the second half of the twentieth century. What this approach emphasises, then, unlike these other 'history of ideas' accounts, is that the concept of identity did not pre-exist its contemporary popularity and salience, but emerged as part of the general development of a political position that was concerned with the unequal relations between different groups – and indeed, different 'types' of person. Secondly, in contrast to the implicit idealism of some of the 'history of ideas' accounts, which explain social history in terms of a series of unfolding ideas, this approach offers a specifically cultural *materialist* account, which deliberately emphasises the material conditions and social relations with which the evolution and emergence of the idea of identity is bound up.

In what follows, I trace the development of a series of essentialist ideas about personhood and grouphood from the eighteenth to the twentieth century that eventually came to be captured in the concept of identity as we now know it. To anticipate the argument of the next chapter somewhat, what I will suggest is that our current concept of identity only emerged when those pre-existing essentialist ideas about self- and grouphood themselves became problematic. This was to occur in two ways. The first was when essentialist arguments about self- and grouphood were actively mobilised to challenge discrimination and gain political power. It was the politicisation of the previously taken-for-granted 'knowledge' that selves and groups were of particular kinds, identifiable according to some shared biological, psychological or cultural characteristics, that at least in part created the need for this ordinary 'feature' of individuals and groups to be explicitly named and articulated – in the event, as 'identity'. The second way in which notions about the essential nature of self and groups became problematic was when they were directly challenged and destabilised – experientially, by a series of structural shifts in advanced capitalist societies, and epistemically, by a sustained social scientific attack on the possibility of essentialism itself. These experiential and epistemic challenges are now commonly referred to together as 'the crisis of identity'. Thus against dominant understandings, I will suggest that the emergence of identity as a keyword was bound up with both the evolution of the 'identity politics' and the 'crisis of identity' it is popularly imagined to have preceded, and to have been politicised by. But this is to jump ahead somewhat, as this story cannot be told in full until we have traced the pre-history of ideas that come to consolidate and be captured in the contemporary sense of identity. It is to this cultural materialist history of ideas that I now turn.

SCIENCE, NATURE AND THE ENLIGHTENMENT SUBJECT

Many prominent historians of identity argue that identity was '*born as a problem*' with the advent of modernity itself (Bauman, 1996: 18–19). In these accounts, modernity is typically used to refer to a post-mediaeval historical period in the West from about the sixteenth century onwards, though it should be noted that this notoriously slippery periodising term has been the subject of much dispute.[1] Kellner, nonetheless, captures the typical narrative when he writes that '[a]ccording to anthropological and sociological folklore, in traditional societies, one's identity was fixed, solid and stable ... it was unproblematical and not subject to reflection or discussion' (1995: 231). In these 'pre-modern' societies, he tells us, 'identity was a function of pre-defined social roles and a traditional system of myths', and was derivative of one's clan or a 'fixed kinship system' (1995: 231). As Bauman further explains, in this pre-modern era, 'premodern estates ... determined identity by birth and hence provided few if any occasions for the question of "who am I?" to arise' (2004: 49). However, the onset of modernity – so the story goes – disrupted these traditional patterns of life, and in the process, affected 'identity' itself. The argument continues that beginning with the Enlightenment, with which we may associate the early period of modernity (cf. note 1), this unproblematic conception and experience of identity began to change, becoming more 'mobile, multiple, personal, self-reflexive, and subject to change and innovation' (Kellner, 1995: 231) as modernity advanced, ultimately disintegrating altogether with the advent of 'postmodernity' in the late twentieth century.

While these histories claim to trace changing conceptions of 'identity' itself, what in fact is at stake here is actually *changing conceptions of the subject*, and how that subject is progressively defined and redefined over time in relation to the social order in which it exists. Analytically, therefore, it is a mistake to attempt to follow 'changing conceptions of identity' as Bauman, Hall and others would have it. Instead we must follow changing conceptions of subjecthood within the framework of modernity, as the Enlightenment notion of a sovereign individual, rooted in nature, is progressively challenged: firstly with the emergence of more social and psychological conceptions of the subject, whose sense of self is created in the interaction between the self and an increasingly complex society; and subsequently with the total 'postmodern' rejection of *any* 'essentialist' understanding of the self at all. It is precisely this movement from the idea of an autonomous self, created by nature, to a social person, created by the environment or 'culture', that eventually gives rise to the notion of identity as we now know it. But in order to understand this properly, we must start at the beginning and follow the evolution of those early notions of autonomous individuals and natural differences, up to their eventual displacement in the twentieth century.

A key claim of Kellner, Hall and other theorists of modernity including Giddens, Calhoun and Beck is that modernity brought into being the moral and political paradigm of individualism, which is premised on a conception of the individual subject as rational, autonomous, sovereign, indivisible and unique. As Stuart Hall discusses, several major movements in western thought and culture, now associated with the transition to modernity, heralded and enabled this new conception of the human subject, including:

> Renaissance humanism, which placed Man [sic] at the centre of the universe; the scientific revolutions, which endowed Man with the faculty and capacities to inquire into, investigate and unravel the mysteries of Nature; and the Enlightenment, centred on the image of rational, scientific Man, freed from dogma and intolerance, before whom the whole of human history was laid out for understanding and mastery. (Hall, 1992: 282)

The new scientific orientation of the time in particular had implications for understanding the human subject, and indeed, for making sense of the social order more generally. No longer was humanity's social order understood to be stratified according to some divine plan, as set out in the hierarchical 'great chain of being'. Instead, the relation between subjects was understood to be a function of biology and evolution – social differences had become 'natural' differences, governed by nature and observable through science.

According to Hall, we may associate a particular 'conception of identity' with this (and indeed each) historically instantiated interpretation of the human subject. In this instance, he argues that the 'identity' of 'the Enlightenment subject' is to be found in a unified and continuous core of that self. He elaborates:

> The Enlightenment subject was based on a conception of the human person as a fully centred, unified individual, endowed with the capacities of reason, consciousness and action, whose 'centre' consisted of an inner core which first emerged when the subject was born, and unfolded with it, while remaining essentially the same – continuous or 'identical' with itself – throughout the individual's existence. The essential centre of the self was a person's identity. (Hall, 1992: 275)

In reality, this accurately describes the Enlightenment conception of the *subject* – but not of anything that could be called 'an Enlightenment conception of identity' in the sense we mean it today. Remember that identity at this time referred to the persistence of an entity – whether human or inanimate – over time, and crucially *not* to a sense of self or of self-understanding as it has come to mean. In this context, it means the *quality of self-sameness*, or the exact sameness of an entity to itself, and not a substantive (and historically variable) *sense* of self, possessed by a particular individual or group. This meaning is also apparent in discussions of the so-called 'problem of personal identity' which animated philosophy around this time. Also referred to as the problem of 'numerical identity' (a term I prefer for the clarity it brings to the distinction), this was the problem of how a particular self could be understood to persist as that same self, despite transformations of its bodily form. Crucially, the 'problem of personal identity' did not mean then what it means now. These discussions of what is called 'personal identity' continue today within analytical philosophy, as philosophers continue to puzzle over 'the relation each thing has to itself and no other thing', and to explore this issue specifically in relation to the problem of the persistence of the human person despite changes to its qualitative state. But, as Noonan (2009) points out, these philosophical debates or problems do not even *require* the language of identity – as we now know it. 'For example', he writes,

> it is a puzzle, an aspect of the so-called 'problem of personal identity', whether the *same* person can have different bodies at different times. But this is just the puzzle whether *a* person can have different bodies at different times. So since it can be stated without the language of personal 'identity', it is not a problem about identity, but about personhood. (2009: unpaginated)

Despite these equivocations in usage of the category of identity, it is nonetheless quite clear that the Enlightenment marked a new conception of the *subject*, as an autonomous, rational, sovereign individual, whose status and rank were no longer divinely ordained, but instead determined according to a 'natural' order of things. Both science and nature offered a means not only of explaining the existence of the subject, but of differences between individual persons too. Over the eighteenth and nineteenth centuries, as Nicholson (2008) demonstrates, nature became a credible source of explanation for social differences, generating physical categories that were superimposed onto already existing hierarchies of inferior and superior types. 'At this point in time', she writes, '"race" came to mean a division of the human species into a small number of groups distinguished from each other by observable physical differences' (2008: 11). These distinctions were mapped onto the previously existing quasi-religious distinctions between 'heathen', 'primitive' and 'savage' on the one hand, and 'Christian' or 'European' on the other. At the same time, the category of sex distinguished between men and women on the grounds of observable bodily differences, in particular, differences in reproductive systems. Both categorisations worked on the basis of identifying physical differences, 'firstly, as criteria for differentiating groups, and then later, particularly by the mid nineteenth century, as signals of the deep-seated nature of such differentiations' (2008: 12). Thus, these understandings reinforced a conception of human nature as itself grounded in biology.

Significantly, however, there was some conflict between these biologically constituted categories which grouped people according to some original physical type, and the autonomous, rational notion of the sovereign individual with which they coexisted. This was because the notion of a biologically ordained racial or sex-specific nature seemed to deny to these autonomous individuals the possibility of free will. Furthermore, in practice, this understanding of a rational, autonomous self was *not* actually extended to all people, but was reserved in the main for white men, and only infrequently understood as an accurate depiction of women or non-whites. Nicholson shows how these tensions between the notion of a biologically ascribed nature and the existence of a free-thinking, choosing, autonomous individual were in fact 'resolved' by mapping them onto the 'racial' differences between whites and non-whites, and the sexual differences between men and women. In this way women and non-whites could be *biologically* defined in more naturalistic terms, and as 'closer to nature' than others, while men and whites could again be biologically defined as rational, independent and more amenable to civilisation. This way of thinking effectively revived the notion of the 'great chain of being', and reproduced the idea that humans of different types could be hierarchically ordered according to their position within this chain, though this time, as destined by nature rather than divinity. 'This is how the idea of the great chain of being functioned within nineteenth century racial science', writes Nicholson.

> Whites, because at the top of the chain, were understood as both a part of nature and as not part of it. While sharing certain bodily features with other types of human beings, whites also displayed attributes that allowed for rationality, individuality and choice. Non-whites, on the other hand, and Africans in particular, were portrayed as a human type midway between whites and those forms of animal just below humans, specifically, apes and monkeys. (Nicholson, 2008: 16)

A similar move was made with the category of sex, as women were assigned to a sexual category that more intensively associated them with their reproductive nature than was the case for men. The particular character of a woman's supposed reproductive nature marked her out as more fit for 'mothering' activities, and thus as closer to nature by definition. In contrast, men were understood – again as a biological category – to be relatively undefined by their reproductive status, and so to be further from nature and defined primarily by their cognitive, rational capacities. This meant that with the category of sex too, biology came to determine who was 'naturally' a rational, autonomous individual, and who was not. This strategy thus effectively dealt with what was a major problem for the powerful groups in society in relying on nature to explain group differences, which, as Nicholson points out, was that 'such uses end up denying the individuality of white men as much as they deny the individuality of blacks and women' (2008: 24). However, as she explains, 'By claiming that nature itself is the cause of the greater individuality of white men, one gains the authority of nature without assuming the liabilities that appeals to nature impart' (2008: 24).

These biologically essentialist understandings of social categories and group formation play an important role in the development of the idea of identity as we *now* know it – they arguably make 'identity', with its original signification of sameness, an appropriate and helpful choice of word to capture and express this view of group membership. However, although these early biological understandings of selves and groups came under attack in the late nineteenth and early twentieth centuries – as we will see later in this chapter – the underlying notion of essentialism did not. Instead, the new understandings which replaced these biological understandings simply *relocated* the essentialism, and identified the source of being a particular person, of a particular kind, and thus a member of a particular group, elsewhere – specifically in the individual environment, in individual psychology, and in 'culture'. But in order to trace this development properly, we need first to be clear about what essentialism is.

MAKING SENSE OF ESSENTIALISM

Essentialism is today a much maligned philosophical device, and is the subject of substantial critique within the social sciences – particularly in debates over the nature of identity, as we saw in Chapter 2. However, at least some of this critique rests on a poor understanding of what it means to make an essentialist claim. This is what O'Neill (1998: 8) argues when he claims that 'essentialism is rejected variously for being incompatible with the recognition of "difference", [and] for entailing a reduction of social categories to non-social natural categories'. He suggests that this rejection is based on an inaccurate understanding of essentialism, and as a result, 'what is criticized in recent anti-essentialism is in fact a caricature which is defended by nobody' (1998: 9). He makes the case that while essentialist arguments can be flawed (essentialist claims are fallible, as are any and all other knowledge claims), this cannot be taken to mean that essentialism is flawed by definition. Furthermore, against the postmodern treatment of essentialism as a 'term of abuse', he argues that essentialist claims are both philosophically defensible and often indispensable in making sense of the world. The 'minimal essentialist position', he writes, is that '[t]he essential properties of an entity of a particular kind are those properties of the object that it must have if it is to be an object of that kind. Accidental properties of an entity of a particular kind are those properties it has, but could lack and still be an entity of that kind' (1998: 9). He then uses this basic proposition to demonstrate the falsity of many of the assumptions of 'anti-essentialist' philosophers. For example, it is regularly assumed that essentialist claims presuppose 'inner principles that produce "necessary effects" by the mere fact of their presence' (1998: 10). Against this, O'Neill argues that because 'many essential properties of objects are dispositional properties that are actualised only in certain circumstances' (1998: 9), essentialism is instead concerned with the 'capacities and power of objects to produce certain effects' (1998: 10). This means that it is a mistake to believe that an essence *always* gives rise to certain properties, as these may depend on the context for activation, and thus entities that share a common essence may differ in their attributes. To take an example, aggression may be considered an essential property of wildcats, but this does not mean that all wildcats are always aggressive – rather that they have the capacity for aggression, and that its activation depends on the context and a range of other contingent factors such as the appearance of a threat, learned behaviour from the pack and the experience of hunger.

O'Neill is also exercised by the assumption that essentialism does not allow 'variation in the properties of different instances of some kind of entity', and claims that the idea of accidental properties demonstrates that an object can possess certain features which are not required in order to be an object of a particular kind, and yet remain an object of that particular kind. One of the main assumptions of anti-essentialists is that to make the claim that people – or particular 'kinds' of people, such as women – have an essential nature is to deny the possibility of differences among them. This type of argument is particularly what is at stake in the disputes about essentialism that I am concerned with in relation to the question of identity. However, O'Neill shows that one *can* make essential claims about particular people or groups without claiming that there can be no differences at all between them, or that these essential properties must always be exhibited. Thus while the kinds of biological argument I have just considered *do* make essentialist claims insofar as they attribute to particular kinds the essential properties they must have in order to be an entity (or person) of that kind, we need not assume that in doing so they are also positing that there can be no differences at all between entities of a particular kind, or that their essential properties are always exhibited.

Nevertheless, proponents of essentialist arguments often end up making these kinds of faulty extrapolation. Thus O'Neill points out that there is a certain 'danger associated with essentialism of taking properties of one particular variant of a species of being to be essential properties of all' (1998: 12). He recognises this to be a specific concern of feminists who are critical of the attribution of particular culturally and historically specific characteristics to all women. However, once again, he reiterates that this should be recognised as an argument against false essentialist *claims*, rather than the falsity of essentialism per se. A second common basis for suspicion of essentialist claims that he entertains is the fear, again held by feminists, that essentialist accounts 'entail biological reductionism, and a commitment to a purely biological explanation of gender differences and power relations' (1998: 13). Again, he contends, if this were inevitably the case, then we would have reason to be concerned. However, he unpicks this objection too, arguing that:

essentialism need not involve any such failure to recognize the differences in the nature of objects of the human sciences and those of the natural sciences. More specifically, the essentialist can accept that institutions like markets are not natural objects: in particular essentialism is consistent with the claim that social objects are constituted by relationships and acts which have social meanings whereas natural objects are not. (1998: 13)

This is a particularly important point for our purposes here, and returns us to the issue which led into this discussion of essentialism: this is that essentialist claims need not be overtly concerned with biological phenomena, nor implicitly involve biological reductionism, but can function as an accurate description of the properties of social phenomena and entities too.[2] To anticipate the development of the argument somewhat, this means that conceptions of the self and group that depend on psychological or cultural explanations can operate essentialist arguments *qua* psychological or cultural explanations, without automatically ending up as *biologically* essentialist arguments. A clearer understanding of essentialism enables us to see that the explanatory accounts which make up the 'pre-history' of identity can all be said to make essentialising claims, insofar as they identify features of persons which make them a particular kind of person, and then a member of a group made up of that kind of person. However, these claims need not always be biological in nature, nor always reduce cultural and psychological essential features to natural ones. Further, they need not rule out difference – given the legitimate existence of accidental properties and the fact that the essential features need not always be actualised – though in practice it is often the case that they do.

What is significant for the story I am telling here is that when the biological accounts of group differences discussed here were challenged, the underlying essentialism was not, and so the psychological and cultural explanations which replaced them continued to make essentialist claims about the nature of the self and social groups. These essentialist understandings would come to provide a strong motivation for using the term identity to capture these understandings, given the original sense of identity as the sameness of an entity to itself. But what this discussion has shown is that the notion of identity enables slippage between what are acceptable and *unacceptable* essentialist claims. What becomes important to work out is whether the claim is unacceptable because of an inaccurate application of essentialism (i.e. that that which is claimed to be essential to a particular group via the concept of identity in fact is *not* essential), or because of an invalid inference from what is otherwise an acceptable essentialist claim (e.g. when the accurate claim that a group has a number of features – represented by its 'identity' – is falsely taken to imply that there can be no differences between members of that group, and/or that these shared features have a biological source). However, none of these issues would arise until some other important contextual features were in place, so let us now return to the pre-history of identity, and continue to follow its development.

THE MODERN SUBJECT AS THE SOCIOLOGICAL SELF

The second major transition marked by historians of modernity is that from the Enlightenment to the fully modern subject. However, this too is regularly presented in terms of shifting conceptions of 'identity'. Thus in what he presents as the history of the concept of identity in modernity, Hall identifies a transition from the Enlightenment subject to the 'sociological subject', which he argues gives rise to a conception of identity as arising out of and mediating the space between a 'core' self and a value-laden, socially complex society – in this period, according to Hall, 'identity thus stitches the subject into the structure' (1992: 276). Hall's classification is broad and expansive, and refers us to 'the rise of the new social sciences' – modern economics, psychology and sociology – for explication (1992. 284). Hall characteristically links the emergence of these new social sciences to changes in 'modern societies', which, as they 'grew more complex … acquired a more collective and social form' (1992: 283). He describes how this came about:

> Classical liberal theories of government based on individual rights and consent were obliged to come to terms with the structures of the nation state and the great masses which make up a modern democracy. The classic laws of political economy, property, contract and exchange had to operate, after industrialization, amidst the great class formations of modern capitalism. The individual entrepreneur of Adam Smith's *Wealth of Nations* or even of Marx's *Capital* was transformed into the corporate conglomerates of the modern economy. The individual citizen became enmeshed in the bureaucratic administrative machineries of the modern state. A more social conception of the subject then emerged. The individual came to be seen as more located and placed within these great supporting structures and formations of modern society. (1992: 283–4)

Hall convincingly shows how large-scale social changes impacted upon the nineteenth-century conceptualisation of the subject, as the notion of the autonomous, sovereign individual became harder to sustain in a society where everyone clearly depended in more and more complex ways on everyone else; and where that relationship must have made a far greater impact on one's sense of self than any abstract notion of individual sovereignty. Similar claims are made by Calhoun (1994: 10–12), who sees the discourse of and concern with identity as 'distinctively modern' and relatedly, 'distinctively problematic', as the opportunities for self-definition multiplied exponentially in the complex societies of the nineteenth-century onwards. Bauman offers a specifically class-based analysis as he argues that during this period, the 'human identity of a person was determined primarily by the productive role played in the social division of labour' (2004: 45), which was itself becoming increasingly differentiated. These accounts variously reproduce the familiar narratives of identity moving from the pre-modern state of being solid, stable and predetermined to its modern state of being mobile and socially contingent. Yet as Kellner claims,

> the forms of identity in modernity are also relatively substantial and fixed; identity still comes from a circumscribed set of roles and norms: one is a mother, a son, a Texan, a Scot, a professor, a socialist, a Catholic, a lesbian – or rather, a combination of these social roles and possibilities. Identities are thus still relatively fixed and limited, though the boundaries of possible identities, of new identities, are continually expanding. (1995: 231)

Leaving aside for a moment the (misleading) claims these theorists make about 'identity' specifically, what these accounts nonetheless convincingly tell us is that this period of modernity oversaw a significant shift in conceptions of *selfhood*, such that one's position in society was determined increasingly by socially defined norms and roles, including one's position in the social division of labour, rather than by nature or myth, as was the case in the Enlightenment and pre-modern eras respectively. It is worth noting also the immense formative power and role of capitalism – and what I have been calling the social logic of capitalism – and not just modernity, in these shifts (Meiksins Wood, 1997). It was primarily the logic of capitalist development, both social and structural, that entailed the closure of the commons, the mass movement of people together into large urban spaces and the structural segmentation of people according to social class – crudely, distinctions between capitalists and workers, and within that, between productive (male) and reproductive (female) workers. In England in particular, the 'birthplace' of industrial capitalism, this was all harnessed by the capitalist 'ideology of "improvement"'. As Meiksins Wood remarks, this was 'not the Enlightenment idea of the improvement of *humanity* but the improvement of *property*, the ethic – and indeed the science – of *productivity* and profit, the commitment to increasing the productivity of labour, the ethic of enclosure and dispossession' (1997: 548).

While these analyses of the social impacts of the shift from the Enlightenment to a period of capitalist modernity are illuminating, linking the structural changes and emergence of the new social sciences directly to a 'new' conception of identity is problematic. It was not a new sense of *identity* that these structural shifts gave rise to, or that were documented and analysed by these new social sciences, but rather a new sense of the *subject* and its relation to others in a complex, capitalist society. These structural changes, and these new social sciences which accompanied them, did not change an already existing conception of identity but in fact contributed to its emergence as we now know it. This occurred at least in part as a result of the necessary rethinking and resituating of the old biologically essentialist notions in the context of a complex society, so that the essential core of self was no longer understood to be provided by 'biology', but instead by culture, environment and psychology. Indeed, it was this new emphasis on culture, environment and psychology, as opposed to biology, which formed the bases of the new disciplines of the burgeoning enterprise of the social sciences, as they sought to explain the relationship between the self and society.

The psychological self

In her more detailed history of 'identity before identity politics', Nicholson charts a shift in the history of ideas about 'identity', from one which saw the difference between various social categories as constituted by nature to one which saw these differences in more individualist terms, driven by personal history, growth and 'psychology'. Through the general emergence of psychology as a social scientific discipline, the idea that a person's make-up was determined by their individual histories and personal experiences began to achieve significant explanatory power in setting out what it is that makes a person uniquely that person and no other. These new psychological models of 'human character' challenged the older naturalistic models which differentiated according to some biological type, replacing this with the notion of a responsive human who was shaped according to his/her environmental influences. On the one hand, these psychological models saw all humans as equivalent insofar as they shared the same psychological structures, biological instincts and capacities to respond. On the other hand, since what differentiated humans from each other was their particular developmental experience as a function of their environment, these new psychological models came to explain difference in more individualistic terms.

By the late nineteenth century, Freud had become particularly important in giving a theoretical grounding to these understandings. His theory was founded on the premise that humans were universally united by instincts, drives and desires. Yet, as Nicholson points out, Freud 'abandon[ed] nature as a differentiating force even when nature remain[ed] for him a causal element' (2008: 42). In other words, Freud was attentive to how these natural drives manifested and were dealt with *differently* by each individual. This individual response solidified as the individual 'character', which, once formed, was understood to be relatively fixed, and definitive of that person. Thus Freud's contribution to understandings of self was to go beyond naturalistic or biological categorisations, yet to articulate what was nonetheless a psychologically essentialist account of the self. Specifically, while this is an essentialist account in that 'minimal' sense of setting out the essential properties an entity (in this case, a person) must have in order to be that person, it also seems to make that extra and unwarranted step sometimes associated with essentialist accounts, which is to presuppose 'inner principles that produce "necessary effects" by the mere fact of their presence' (O'Neill, 1998: 10). Thus we can see how, even though the term identity was not at the time used, its original sense of the persistence of an entity over time meant it would eventually come to be seen as a sensible term to use to capture or describe this psychological property of humans too.

Indeed, as we saw in Chapter 2, one of the first psychologists to use the term identity in order to describe these issues was Erik Erikson. In 'The Problem of Ego Identity' Erikson claims the term identity 'connotes both a persistent sameness within oneself (selfsameness) and a persistent sharing of some kind of essential character with others' (1959: 109). As Zaretsky (1994: 204) describes it, 'Erikson defined identity as "the ability to maintain inner sameness and continuity," and explained it as the outcome of "the selective repudiation and mutual assimilation of childhood identifications, and their absorption in a new configuration".' Here we see Erikson explicitly promote an essentialist under-standing of personal development through the concept of identity. However, there was an extra dimension to this too, as Zaretsky (1994: 204) points out, say-ing that 'Erikson's aim was to "add" a social dimension to psychoanalysis. Thus he defined identity as the product of an interaction between self and society.' Thus it is only in the 1950s – as charted in detail in Chapters 5 and 6 – that the concept of identity is finally used to explicitly connect the self to the complex society of which it forms a part. The term identity did not, until this point, have the meanings which Hall, Calhoun and others attribute to it over the course of modernity.

While it is true, however, that Erikson was among the first to have used the term in the sense we now easily recognise, it is misguided to credit him with the invention of the idea, as many (implicitly or otherwise) do. Rather, Erikson settled on the term 'ego–identity' to capture a way of understanding the human subject that had a long and developing history in psychological and social thought prior to this. Though he shortened the term to identity, and arguably added to contemporary understandings of the relationship between the self and the social via his particular delineation of the concept, he cannot be said to have introduced the idea itself into the popular and social scientific imagina-tion. Rather, he captured, named and promoted an already existing 'zeitgeist' or what Williams (1961) might have called a 'structure of feeling'. Williams gradu-ally developed this term to refer us to a shared, though not fully articulated, sense of a particular experience of life (cf. Matthews, 2001 for a comprehensive overview of the concept). He further elucidated this concept by explaining that a structure of feeling 'was a structure in the sense that you could perceive it operating in one work after another which weren't otherwise connected – people weren't learning it from each other; yet it was one of feeling much more than of thought – a pattern of impulses, restraints, tones' (1979: 159). This con-cept captures perfectly what is at stake here, and what we must seek to firmly

grasp when reviewing this history of ideas: that the idea of identity existed in
the collective imagination even before it was explicitly named as such. While
the word may have been first articulated in psychology – though as Chapter 2
has shown, this is difficult, if not impossible, to fully ascertain – its significant
pre-history concerns a substantial unfolding of a set of *social* ideas about types
of selves and their differences from others. Thus, it was not that the word was
somehow magically transported from psychology into seemingly unconnected
domains, but that the ideas identity came to capture had a long pre-history
in society and politics, making the later, widespread use of the word not only
eminently sensible but deeply useful too. The history of the emergence of the
psychosocial sense of identity does not, then, begin with Erikson, but rather
he arrives somewhere in the middle of the story, offering a new lexical vehicle
for the expression of already developing modes of understanding. Indeed, even
before the notion of identity was explicitly utilised to capture this new sense
of self, we see a strong correspondence between the individualistic understandings of particular selves promoted within the emergent field of psychology, in
the works of Freud, as well as significant others such as Adler, Horney, Maslow,
Rogers and, finally, Erikson, and the notions of individuality, personality and
character that are today discussed as a function or property of one's 'identity'.[3]

To the extent that these psychological accounts of personhood emphasised
individual variability, they offered an attractive alternative in particular for those
who found themselves negatively defined by natural or biological classifica-
tions. Nicholson also notes this when she points to the 'liberatory consequences
of the introduction of dynamic psychology into popular discourse', arguing
that these new models 'made possible the theorization of human behaviour
in new kinds of ways, ways that were particularly liberating for women, the
racially stigmatized, and those who experienced same-sex desire' (2008: 63).
While this emergent notion of identity had moved from psychological textbooks into popular discourse by the late 1950s, significantly it did not find
a place in contemporary forms of politics until the 1960s, as the next chapter discusses in detail. Furthermore, this more psychological sense of identity
remained in a certain tension with older naturalistic categorisations, which had
not been wholly displaced, as well as with the more 'cultural' and 'anthropological' understandings of the self as a member of a particular group, to which I now
turn. As we will see in) Chapter 5, it is the coexistence of these competing sets
of understandings about the self and its relations to others, and to society more
generally, that provided the grounds for the emergence of the social sense of
identity in the field of politics, in the particular context of the advanced capitalist societies of the world in the 1960s.

Culture and the appreciation of difference

Important new 'cultural' understandings of selfhood and groups can be traced
to the work of Margaret Mead, Franz Boas and other anthropologists who, in

the early twentieth century, started to explain social differences in terms of cultural constraints and influences. These cultural understandings differed from the psychological accounts of difference, for rather than emphasise individual differences, they emphasised group differences, and in the process, ended up emphasising *similarities* among the group members. But these accounts also challenged the biologically essentialist view of selves and groups, for though these culturally demarcated groups often mapped onto the older biologically demarcated groups, this time it was shared 'cultural' experiences, traditions, ways of living and ways of being that marked people out as members of a particular group, rather than 'hereditary' type, bodily function or skin colour. Even as these accounts did not rely on biological markers, they can none-theless be considered essentialist in the sense of attributing to all members of the group certain properties which *make* them, by virtue of those prop-erties, members of that group. Again, we can see here how the concept of identity, with its original connotations of sameness and oneness, would finally emerge as a useful way of capturing this experience of being part of such a culturally formed group. Discussing these same authors, Mackenzie posits, 'I do not think the cultural anthropologists used the word "identity" in a tech-nical sense until Erikson made it popular: but perhaps it is fair to foist it on them … because one of their primary methodological assumptions was that a culture was unique, consistent and binding' (1978: 41). Furthermore, Erikson himself acknowledges his reliance on the insights of these cultural anthro-pologists, stating in *Childhood and Society* that 'it would be impossible for me to itemize my over-all indebtedness to Margaret Mead' (1950: 13). Indeed, as Gleason carefully observes, 'Erikson knew and admired Margaret Mead's work on the American character', and even figured out his ideas on the relationship between 'ego identity' and 'group identity' during his time working alongside her (1983: 925). This further demonstrates the co-evolution of the psycho-logical and cultural conceptions of self- and grouphood that would ultimately culminate in the concept of identity.

Once again, even before the explicit emergence of the concept of identity to capture these ideas, we can see how these culturalist ideas of self- and group-hood might have offered a more positive alternative for self-conceptualisation than the biological accounts they displaced – and even the psychological accounts they coexisted with. The trajectory of development of the category of culture over the course of the twentieth century – as traced by Williams (1981a, 1983, 1989 [1958]), who saw in this conceptual evolution a key insight into broader social shifts taking place in democratic societies[4] – was such that it moved away from elitist conceptions of 'civilisation' and 'high culture', to signify the meaningful practices of everyday life. This understand-ing of 'culture' persisted in and animated the notion of individual 'cultures', where it involved an exposition and validation of the traditions, values and practices associated with a particular way of life, or a particular group of peo-ple. These conceptions of culture were deliberately non-evaluative (in intent at least), and thus less susceptible to judgements of superiority and inferiority. In fact, 'cultural diversity' became increasingly construed over the course of the twentieth century as something to be valued; and even as exotic, 'cosmopolitan' and sophisticated. Nicholson draws similar conclusions when she argues that:

> The new popular use of 'culture' reflected not only an attitude of tolerance towards those practices which differentiated communities within the United States, but also a sense of appreciation for these differentiating practices. Those practices associated with 'culture' – such as dress, mannerisms, forms of worship, etc. – were seen as 'private' matters. This enabled many Americans to view such aspects more in aesthetic rather than moral terms. It contributed to the sense that diversity in such aspects of life made the United States more 'interesting', more aesthetically complex. (2008: 85–6)

This appreciation of different 'cultures' was thus not restricted to academic or 'literary' fields, but achieved a remarkable level of general popularity and acceptance. As Nicholson points out, Ruth Benedict's *Patterns of Culture* (1934) was one of the best-selling non-fiction books of the twentieth century in the United States. Williams similarly notes in the mid-1940s a huge shift and popularisation of the term 'culture' beyond its 'tea shop' use, to refer instead to a *particular way of life* – "American culture", "Japanese culture"' (1983: 12). It was this conception of culture which came to provide an important alternative to race in particular, as a means of social classification, in mid-twentieth-century America. It received added impetus from the widespread suspicion of the use of racial categories in the aftermath of German Nazism, and the perceived need for an alternative way to capture social differences (Weigert et al., 1986). As Gleason notes, although 'the belief that different human groups are marked by distinctive characteristics is at least as old as Herodotus, it had fallen into disrepute in the 1930s as a result of its association with racialism' (1983: 924). In this respect, '"culture", with its implication of tolerance towards these non-political differences, became an important tool for social acceptance' (Nicholson, 2008: 88). This was even institutionalised in the United Nations Educational, Scientific and Cultural Organisation's (UNESCO) 'postwar Tensions Project', which deployed the concept of culture in an effort to resolve 'tensions affecting international understanding' (cited in Gleason, 1983: 924). This, then, was the route by which 'culture' came to provide a means for different groups to emphasise their ethnic or religious differences without denying them their status as citizens. No longer an 'either-or' situation, 'culture' allowed groups to be proud of that which made them different, while at the same time eschewing any of the dangerous biological or political (nationalistic) categorisations that would have marked them as non-American.

How does this understanding of culture connect to identity? What Nicholson claims is that these culturalist ideas about 'identity' were subsequently used by those who went on to engage in 'identity politics'. While it is true that these culturalist understandings would be key in the emergence and evolution of identity politics, it is not true that they were, prior to this, understood in terms of the idiom of identity. As previewed at the start of this chapter, it was not until these essentialising claims were politicised that they came to be explicitly framed in terms of 'identity'. This overt politicisation of both psychologically and culturally essentialist understandings of selfhood and groups, in what would come to be known as identity politics, is addressed in the next chapter. In addition, the connections between 'culture' as a way of life, 'lifestyle', the psychological sense of self and the emergence of the notion of 'personal identity' specifically are discussed in detail in Chapter 6.

CONCLUSION

By the mid-twentieth century, psychological and cultural anthropological perspectives on self- and grouphood were in common currency, and had seriously challenged the earlier conceptions of selves and groups that were based on natural differences. Both perspectives remained essentialist nonetheless, even as they replaced the 'naturalistic' understandings that are perhaps more widely *regarded* as 'essentialist'. Against simple histories, then, which associate 'essentialist' accounts of identity with biology, locating the genesis of both to the Enlightenment period of early modern history, what this chapter has shown is that all three evolving notions of selves and groups ('natural', psychological and cultural) – though not yet captured by the term 'identity' – were, and continue to be, essentialist, and furthermore, that they cannot be contained within an Enlightenment or early modern period of history. Importantly, however, the explicit articulation of these essentialist understandings as 'identity' only came with their overt politicisation in a new form of politics in the mid-twentieth century: identity politics. This is the subject of the next chapter.

Notes

1. Chronological conceptions of modernity typically distinguish between 'early' (1500–1789), 'classical' (1789–1900) and 'late' (1900 onwards) modernity (cf. Berman, 1983, cited in Osborne, 1992: 25). However, as Osborne complains, this does not take account of how 'modernity' itself ushered in a new way of periodising history, which was premised on a *qualitative* categorisation of what was 'new' – 'it is precisely this ... idea of a *differential* temporality which is associated, classically, with the idea of modernity itself' (1992: 25). While acknowledging the acuity of this

insight, for the purposes of the narrative of this chapter I accept the chronological distinction between 'phases', as indeed do most of the authors I discuss herein.

2. For example, Christians are essentially defined by their belief in a Christian god – this is clearly an essential characteristic of the group, for without this, they could not be defined as Christians. But Christians are also regularly defined as charitable people, or as socially conservative. These are not essential characteristics, as someone may be a Christian in that they believe in a Christian god, yet be neither charitable nor socially conservative. Thus 'belief in a Christian god' is an essential feature of Christians, whereas 'charitableness' is not. But both 'belief in a Christian god' and 'charitableness' are clearly both social rather than natural or biological phenomena or characteristics. And it is perfectly sensible to discuss and distinguish between accurate essentialising claims (clearly, that all Christians believe in a Christian god; if they do not, they are not Christians) and flawed ones (one may believe in a Christian god yet may not be charitable) in relation to the identity of this group.

3. I postpone further discussion of *these* links until the Chapter 6, which deals more directly with the notion of personal as opposed to social identity, though we will see there, as we see here, how both ideas are, of course, indelibly linked in terms of their historical evolution, though ultimately put to different uses.

4. Indeed, 'culture' was Williams's 'original keyword'. In the introduction to *Keywords*, Williams recalls returning to Cambridge in the postwar years to find himself unnerved by the sense that the world he had left behind had changed, in some significant though as yet intangible way. While the particular character of that change was not immediately apparent, it was clear to him that it was bound up with changes in social outlook and understandings, valuations and interests; it was a change which, for the moment, he felt could only be expressed through the frustratingly commonplace, though fitting assertion that the new generation 'just don't speak the same language' (1983: 11). The word that particularly caught his attention for manifesting not only a semantic shift, but also for representing some more fundamental change in how people understand the broadly social aspects of life, was 'culture'.

5

Identity Politics, Globalising Capitalism and the Crisis of Identity

INTRODUCTION

Chapter 4 documented the pre-history of the idea of identity, tracing changing conceptions of the subject through modernity that would eventually culminate in the idea of identity as we know it today. But why did the notion of identity – which had such a rich pre-history – emerge when it did, exploding across multiple domains of practice from the 1960s? Of particular relevance to this chapter, why did 'identity' become a central mobilising force and factor in the new social movements around race, gender and sexuality, as well as the (re)assertion of various cultural and ethnic claims for recognition in the latter decades of the twentieth century? From a cultural materialist perspective, this emergence of the idea of identity cannot be understood as a simple popularisation of an already existing term, but must be situated within the changing cultural political economy of capitalist societies, to which it is inevitably related in substantive, material ways. Contrary to other 'histories' of identity politics, what this chapter will show is that the idea of 'social identity' did not pre-exist the arrival of identity politics, but emerged as part of them.

THE DISPLACEMENT OF CLASS POLITICS?

The emergence of identity politics is often explained in terms of a displacement of class politics, most particularly by analysts of a broadly Marxist orientation. The argument, which has a certain weight to it, is that the conditions for the emergence and development of identity politics were provided by a consolidation and restructuring of capitalism and attendant refiguring of social relations over the latter half of the twentieth century. At local or national levels, these changes are argued to have led to the weakening of organised labour and working class politics, aided by overt political suppression of unions in many cases. At an international or global level, and as we will see later in the chapter, the restructuring of capitalism in the form of 'globalisation' is argued to have created the dislocation of peoples and workers on a vast scale. The consequent reconfiguration of social relations and political foci along identitarian rather than class-bound lines is seen to have been facilitated by a more or less deliberate suppression of political alternatives or challenges to global capitalism, and reinforced by a series of justificatory ideological narratives and strategies.

Beginning their history in the mid-twentieth century, in what Chapter 3 identified as the 'organised' or 'Fordist' phase of capitalism, Marxist analysts have emphasised how Cold War repression and the mainstreaming of trade union and social democratic politics combined to create the conditions for a political and theoretical shift away from issues of class to issues of identity. In the US there was an active and deliberate suppression of left-wing politics via a clamp-down on socialist and communist parties and institutions, and the expulsion of suspected communist sympathisers from trade unions. Aronowitz (1992) argues that the passing of the 1947 Taft–Hartley Act, which criminalised various labour tactics and created obstacles to organising, brought about a 'complete capitulation' of unions to a capitalist state, a surrender reinforced in the expulsion of many leftist unions from the CIO (Congress of Industrial Organizations) in 1949 (1992: 227). Although union membership in the US grew through the 1950s, the political elite were able, in the context of the 'Soviet threat', to characterise explicit class politics as socialist and thus as anti-American. Elsewhere in the world many trade union movements fragmented along Cold War lines: Aronowitz describes the emergence of '"free" labour movements' that, in contrast to older labour movements, 'align[ed] themselves willingly with the Western ideological, political and military objectives, which henceforth serve[d] as the overall framework for political and economic action, including the demands for wage increases and welfare measures' (Aronowitz, 1992: 227).

For most of the first three decades after the Second World War in many western societies, trade union movements and social democratic parties who had made their peace with capitalism were indeed able to deliver on wage and welfare demands. Harvey identifies a careful balance of power and interests across advanced capitalist societies in the postwar years, where a certain union power and presence were 'grudgingly accepted' by corporations so long as they guaranteed a relatively docile labour force, whose wage gains stimulated demand for increased production of consumer goods (1989: 134–5). This change of role and purpose of the trade unions can be read as the incorporation of the labour movement into the management of capitalist economies; its deradicalisation removed much of the basis for the articulation of a politics based on class position and opposition to capitalism. While this balance was to prove relatively short-lived, its political discourses meant that the language of class politics had been weakened even before it endured the full-on assault of neoliberalism. The perception in the Cold War US that the expression of social grievances in class terms was un-American gave rise even on the political left to a 'shift in political discourse from class to "oppressed minority"' (Aronowitz, 1995: 116). But more than simply a question of language and labels, Aronowitz argues, this was also about real prospects for political identification with others. Whereas once communism and socialism offered universal and counter-hegemonic prospects for political allegiances, this was no longer the case. Instead, the only readily available 'political' positions were those that were constructed around different, ostensibly non-class-based groups, where the political impetus was to name grievances in particularistic terms.

A second important feature of 1950s America identified in these accounts was an 'extraordinary economic boom' and an accompanying rise in living standards (Gitlin, 1995: 61). Gitlin documents the sudden wave of commodities and domestic possessions rapidly made available to the new 'middle class'. 'The sense of having arrived (in the suburbs, in a car) was extraordinary. The majority felt comfortable. Who needed a popular front?' (1995: 163). The combination of anti-communist sentiment with this apparent fulfilment of the 'good life' through capitalism provided the basis for the consolidation of the (now iconic) 1950s individualistic, consumerist American outlook. The growing affluence of middle class families, and the associated fostering of the ideals − and practices − of possessive individualism, reinforced the idea that capitalism was a progressive force; and that the problems people would come up against would not be the unequal distribution of resources, wealth and power, but the individual failure to realise the capitalist promise that 'you can have it all'. As Gitlin puts it,

> What did inequality of income and the far greater inequality of wealth matter? The majority of Americans were willing to overlook inequality as long as the opportunities for improvement abounded. Through the 1960s, enough upward mobility took place among a middle-class person's middle-class acquaintances and relations that those who failed to ascend apparently only had themselves or their spouses to blame for not being up to snuff ... For the majority, any class resentment yielded to gratitude for a system that delivered the goods. (1995: 65)

Thus the demise of class politics is linked in these accounts, not only to the attack on communism by the political elite, but also to its *de facto* rejection by the US majority who saw capitalism as better able to answer their (increasingly individualised and consumer-oriented) needs. Certainly, at this time, in the 'Fordist' societies of 1950s and 1960s America in particular, participation in the social logic of capitalism seemed to be paying dividends.

Although these broadly Marxist analyses have offered a convincing account of how the restructuring of capitalism reduced the opportunities for class mobilisation and made it likely a new, non-class-based form of politics would emerge, they nonetheless provide only a *partial* explanation for the emergence of identity politics. Unable to explain why this alternative political logic was expressly an 'identity'-based one, Marxist analyses have tended to resort to functionalist-type arguments: the 'reason' for this alternative logic to be expressed in identitarian terms, they are forced to argue, is that this must somehow service capitalism – identity politics must be useful to capitalism. These Marxist accounts thereby fail to recognise what this chapter will demonstrate, which is that this 'new' politics emerged specifically as identity politics because traditional political fora and strategies did not address the demands or oppressions experienced by groups who *rightly* perceived their oppression in identitarian terms, and who – for a range of reasons which cannot be reduced to 'false consciousness' – saw in the notion of identity an opportunity to resist. This is not to say that the oppression they experienced was not connected either structurally or residually to capitalism, only that how it emerged and how it was experienced and structured was in terms of the particular social categories or groups of which they formed a part – groups and categories which were primed at this point in time to be understood as particular 'identities'.

THE EMERGENCE OF IDENTITY POLITICS

Why identity politics emerged when they did has to do not just with the suppression and sidelining of class politics, but with the failure more generally of universalistic democratic principles. A central point in the narrative of Chapter 4 was that the Enlightenment understanding of a rational, autonomous self, upon which all legal and political principles and entitlements were premised, was *not* actually extended to all people in western societies. As Nicholson has pointed out, certain groups were defined in alternative, even oppositional terms, notably women and non-whites, and differences of 'biology' were mobilised to sustain this differentiation.[1] A central aim of many of the early social movements of women and black people was to defeat accounts of biological difference, and assert a fundamental equivalence with the white men against whom they were defined. These earlier movements depended on breaking down rather than emphasising group-based differences, on the grounds that it was these group-based differences that legitimated unequal treatment. Such equivalence-based campaigning was central, for example, in relation to voting rights for women in the suffragette movement of the early 1900s.

By the 1960s, however, it had become apparent that political strategies based on claims of universal citizenship and the denial of difference were not achieving their hoped-for ends insofar as significant groups of people continued to experience substantive oppression, discrimination and inequality. And what could not be denied was that these forms of oppression and discrimination continued to be experienced in explicitly group-based terms – perhaps most visibly, by women and non-whites. This ongoing form of group-based oppression was thrown into sharp relief in the period of relative affluence characterising Fordist societies, the benefits of which were not equally distributed. It was during this time that there emerged a series of 'new' political struggles organised around specific group-based constituencies, most notably black people, women and students, in what have come to be known as the 'new social movements', so-called to differentiate them from the supposed 'old' social movements of class. Though these are sometimes portrayed monolithically as 'identity politics', I suggest this is to misrepresent the substance and focus of many of these movements. In fact, there are grounds for distinguishing between three phases (and types) of 'new' social movement: the 'civil rights' movements, the 'freedom struggles' and, only then, 'identity politics'. And although not all these phases were concerned with questions of identity, the issues at stake in the earlier phases (civil rights and the freedom struggles) were to prove absolutely crucial in the transition to identity politics, and indeed the very emergence of the term identity as we now know it.

The first phase of these 'new' forms of political struggle was the civil rights phase. In many ways this developed and intensified the forms of struggle that were already ongoing. However it was not until the late 1950s and 1960s, with the emergence of new vibrant forms of (often church-led) community activism and an organised, angry student body, that the African American civil rights struggle achieved the status of a mass movement, even garnering support from white Americans. Its success was marked, achieving in 1964 the Civil Rights Act, and then in 1965 the Voting Rights Act, which together outlawed discrimination on the basis of race and guaranteed the full range of political and civil rights to African Americans. Although it was framed in terms of civil rights, many of the groups involved, such as the NAACP (National Association for the Advancement of Colored People), SNCC (Student Non-violent Coordinating Committee), CORE (Congress of Racial Equality) and SCLC (Southern Christian Leadership Conference), saw their struggle as about far more than simply equality before the law – they were also concerned with the broader egalitarian ideals of respect, dignity and political, educational, social and economic equality. While the movement and individual organisations deployed a range of political and symbolic strategies and actions in achieving their goals, the political framework underpinning each was, in this period, nonetheless one which continued to assert the fundamentally equal status of black people with white. At play here was the conception of the individual *qua* individual, and the rejection of biological 'racial' characteristics which legitimated the unequal treatment of African Americans. The civil rights movement thus achieved for African Americans what Nicholson argued would be required to overcome the construction of black people as a particular biological kind; that is, it provided a means for black people to '"de-racialize" themselves … [and] to minimize that view of who they were that linked physiology with a distinctive grouping of mental and behavioural traits. They had to become "individuals" in the same kind of ways that white people were' (2008: 20). However, whether this (largely legalistic) achievement was enough to meet their demands for racial equality was not yet clear.

In the years just following these African American civil rights campaigns, the nascent women's movement also began to mobilise around the issue of women's rights. In the US, Betty Friedan, who had just published the highly successful *The Feminine Mystique* (1963), founded with a number of other activists the National Organization for Women (NOW) in 1966. The founding statement of purpose of the organisation declared:

> We, men and women who hereby constitute ourselves as the National Organization for Women, believe that the time has come for a new move-ment toward true equality for all women in America, and toward a fully equal partnership of the sexes, as part of the world-wide revolution of human rights now taking place within and beyond our national borders.
>
> The purpose of NOW is to take action to bring women into full participation in the mainstream of American society now, exercising all the privileges and responsibilities thereof in truly equal partnership with men. (NOW, 1966)

Thus there was a clear component of civil rights activism within 'second wave feminism', which saw a surge in women's activism more generally, as movements emphasising equal rights for women sprang up in the UK, mainland Europe, Australia and Ireland. Indeed, the civil rights movements of this period extended beyond the struggles of African Americans and women, and by the mid-1960s, a whole range of civil rights movements were underway across many of the industrialised nations of the West, including the Northern Ireland civil rights movement, aspects of the gay and lesbian rights movement and the American Indian movement (AIM), amongst others.

At the same time, though in many ways connected to and inspired by these civil rights movements, there emerged another kind of movement, which was premised primarily on ideals of freedom, autonomy, anti-statism and anti-authoritarianism. These were the student, peace and anti-war movements of the 1960s, most visible in the anti-Vietnam War protests which swept America in the late 1960s; the student and worker revolts of Paris in May 1968; and the counter-cultural 'hippie' movement of 1967–9, typified in the so-called 'Summer of Love' of 1967. The Vietnam War seemed to highlight to many Americans the hypocrisy of a nation premised on equal rights and liberty, and to demonstrate its deeply ingrained racist and imperialist impulses. Yet in some accounts, the emergence of *this* New Left was by definition anti-solidaristic. For example, Gitlin claims that 'from the start, by contrast with earlier American Lefts, the New Left had been unimpressed by the common man' (1995: 72). He argues that suspicious of majorities (white, privileged, genocidal), repelled by the American nationalism represented in the Vietnam War, and deeply wary of the 'very language of commonality' (1995: 100), the New Left gravitated away from the creation of a popular front towards an engagement with a range of particularist struggles. By the later 1960s, '[p]eople lived, felt, desired and revolted as members of identity categories … For the most part, divisions of race, then gender, then sexual orientation proved far too deep to be overcome by universalist rhetoric' (1995: 101).

These anti-war and student movements are often characterised as being concerned with the expression of identity, not only in Gitlin's account above, but also in more standard 'new social movement theories' (cf. McAdam, 1986; Johnston et al., 1994). However, there is little evidence that this is in fact the case. Very few of the slogans or documents associated with these movements emphasised or even mentioned identity (cf. Ali and Watkins, 1998) and it seems more accurate to say that they were far more explicitly concerned with the values of freedom, autonomy and peace than with 'identity'. These movements are relevant for understanding the emergence of identity politics, however, for the manner in which they contributed to the sense of possibility and urgency of political activism and engagement outside the traditional channels of politics.

As for traditional class politics, though the 1968 uprising in Paris had heavy union involvement and leadership, and questions of class remained central in its early days, this was soon to change. At the height of the agitation in Paris in May 1968, French Prime Minister Georges Pompidou struck a deal with the trade union leaders, with significant pay increases promised in return for an end to the strikes. However, the striking workers rejected the deal: 'They don't just want the money. Their protest is about more than that' (Ali and Watkins, 1998: 104). Nonetheless, by the end of that year, the striking workers returned to work – this time, with the help of the Communist Party. 'Just as students and workers stood on the verge of overthrowing the Gaullist state, the French Communist party supported De Gaulle's call for new elections and a return to normalcy, a conformist policy that helped return the president to power and restore the status quo, thus dashing the hopes of revolution' (Best and Kellner, 1997: 5). For those convinced of the progressive potential of class and labour politics alone, this capitulation of the unions to the demands of a capitalist state heightened a sense of disillusionment with the forms of politics that began with and succeeded the freedom and peace movements of 1968. Either way, though, it seemed as though the social logic of capitalism – that is, the social motivations and pressures of living in a hegemonically capitalist society – had given rise to a political context in which solidaristic and class-based forms of politics appeared unfeasible and even irrelevant. But, at the same time, the limitations of other forms of politics were also apparent.

By the end of the 1960s, the civil rights movements had achieved at least some of their aims, and the freedom struggles of various 'counter-cultural' student and peace movements were in full swing. However, these politics, and the achievements of the civil rights movements, came to be perceived as limited – and not just by disillusioned 'Lefties'. It became increasingly apparent that social, political and economic inequality would *not* disappear in the aftermath of the institution of the civil rights legislation, but would continue to be experienced in group-based ways. Furthermore, the counter-cultural freedom movements were increasingly perceived to be highly class-based in themselves, the expression of a disaffected, white, middle class youth, rebelling against what they saw as unacceptable authoritarian restrictions on their personal and sexual freedoms, rather than a challenge to entrenched forms of social and economic inequality (Storey, 1998). A widespread group-based resentment towards the unfulfilled promises of the American dream of prosperity grew rapidly during this period. Harvey refers to the deep dissatisfaction felt by African Americans and women in particular, at their exclusion from the new affluence supposedly characterising America. Specifically, he argues that the benefits of Fordism were in fact confined to certain sectors of the economy, thereby creating massive discontent in those groups who were exposed to the promise of consumption but denied the means to achieve it.

> The resultant inequalities produced serious social tensions and strong social movements on the part of the excluded – movements that were compounded by the way in which race, gender, and ethnicity often determined who had access to privileged employment and who did not … Denied access to privileged work in mass production, large segments of the work-force were equally denied access to the much-touted joys of consumption. This was a sure formula for discontent. (Harvey, 1989: 138)

Harvey argues that it was this discontent that led to the explosion of the earlier, peaceful civil rights movement into 'a revolutionary rage that shook the inner cities', and to an 'equally vigorous feminist movement' populated by women angry with the lack of possibilities for consumption afforded to them by their 'low-paying jobs' (1989: 138). But, given the levels of discontent, exclusion, misrecognition and social inequality experienced by these groups, why did they mobilise around *identity* specifically?

'Naturalistic' understandings of groups clearly did not offer a useful basis for mobilisation against ongoing forms of oppression – after all, it was precisely the legitimation of unequal treatment on the grounds of a 'naturally' inferior status that was successfully challenged in the civil rights movements. And the problem was that despite these successes, group-based oppression persisted. Some other approach, based on some other conceptualisation of groups, was required. And it is at this point that a particularly potent conceptualisation and approach presented itself via the emergent notion of 'identity'. This notion of 'identity' must have seemed in many ways to have resolved the conundrum facing these groups. It offered a way of naming the formation of self through group cultural experiences, but in drawing on Freudian and Eriksonian understandings of 'individual psychology', did not reject the notion of the autonomous individual so important to the civil rights campaigns. 'Identity' also provided a way of reclaiming group-specific understandings, and of using them personally, politically and with pride. 'Identity' thus clearly had explanatory purchase as well as political clout, and it is arguably for these reasons that it came to be used explicitly in the self-understandings and political proclamations of groups fighting for change. Thus here we arrive at the third distinct phase or type of the 'new' social movements: an identity politics that replaced black civil rights with the notion of 'Black Power'; that replaced 'women's rights' with 'Women's Liberation'; and that saw the emergence of other groups that organised themselves around specifically politicised understandings of their 'identity', such as 'The Grey Panthers' and the 'Gay Pride' movement.

Crucially, all these movements *explicitly* used the term identity in articulating their self-understandings, their explanations for the forms of oppression they endured, and the grounds for a new form of resistance and struggle. So, for example, while Martin Luther King, associated primarily with the black civil rights movement, did not refer to identity *once* in a range of 15 major speeches, spanning the years from the mid-1950s till the mid-1960s, Malcolm X, who was associated with the 'Black Power' movement, began to refer to identity with some consistency from 1963 onwards. In a speech entitled 'God's Judgement of White America', given on 4 December 1963, Malcolm X proclaims that 'The Honorable Elijah Muhammad has restored our cultural roots, our racial identity, our racial pride, and our racial confidence. He has given us the incentive and energy to stand on our own feet and walk for ourselves.' In the same speech he also criticises the 'black bourgeoisie', whom he defines as 'the brainwashed, whiteminded, middle-class minority who are ashamed of black, and don't want to be identified with the black masses, and are therefore seeking to lose their "black identity" by mixing, mingling, intermarrying, and integrating with the white man'. Here we see a distinctive and new combination of the biological, the cultural and the experiential in Malcolm X's delineation of 'black identity'. Although the history of these ideas (Chapter 4) indicates that there are some contradictions and tensions between them, Malcolm X powerfully deploys the language of identity in a way which overwrites these tensions, using it as a clarion call to those who have experienced oppression on account of their African heritage, and yet who seek to use this same heritage as a source of pride and political mobilisation. In particular, the notions of group history and group experience, captured by the notion of 'culture', became highly relevant for those who came to organise their politics around their exclusion from privileges and the mainstream precisely on account of 'who they were' – or what was increasingly by now referred to directly as 'identity'. The more psychological understandings of self were brought into play too. In a speech given two years later, Malcolm X uses the idea of identity to make essentialist connections between the individual and the group of which he [*sic*] forms a part, while simultaneously tapping into those psychological understandings of the formation of the self though interaction with the environment:

You show me one of these people over here who have been thoroughly brainwashed, who has a negative attitude toward Africa, and I'll show you one that has a negative attitude toward himself. You can't have a positive attitude toward yourself and a negative attitude toward Africa at the same time. To the same degree that your understanding of and attitude toward Africa becomes positive, you'll find that your understanding of and your attitude toward yourself will also become positive. And this is what the white man knows. So they very skilfully made you and me hate our African identity, our African characteristics. (Malcolm X, 1965)

These new ways of thinking about the self and its relation to groups and society via the category of identity thus challenged older, more universalistic ways of thinking, and the derivative political claims which focused on individual rights. The emphasis on individual rights was accurately recognised to have inadequately accounted for the group specificity of various forms of oppression, and even to have enabled forms of group oppression and inequality, as it disregarded what were important cultural, economic and institutional obstacles to the realisation of these rights. 'Black Power', as a new nomenclature, therefore specifically emphasised group identity and group pride as a means of achieving not only equal rights and cultural recognition, but also the political parity and economic power which continued to be denied to African Americans in American society. As Frazier (2012: 69) writes, '[c]ulturally, Black power found expression in fashion, television and film, music, naming traditions, and the celebration of body image. Socially, Black power ranged from control of school boards, independent schools, and Black studies programs in universities to community and national unity groups.' But it was '[e]conomic power, in particular [that] became a central component of Black power' (2012: 69). While 'Black capitalism' – that is, the incorporation of elite African Americans into positions of power in the capitalist system – was widely challenged by Black power activists who espoused socialism as a means of achieving economic justice for black people (Allen, 1992 [1969]), Frazier makes the case that one of the key, if less well known, successes of the Black power movement was the institution of 'community development corporations', also known as 'community capitalism', in poor Black communities. 'Utilizing federal, state, city, foundation, and corporate money,' Frazier writes, 'CDCs attempted to lift Black people out of poverty through job training, homeownership, banking access, low-interest loans and employment opportunities' (2012: 70). Though on the face of it culturally instantiated, the idea of identity underpinning and mobilizing the Black Power movement enabled the activists who worked in its name to achieve far more than group pride and cultural recognition: it enabled them to make great strides in the arena of political and economic equality too.

A story similar in many respects can be told about the transition to the 'Women's Liberation' movement. Again, whereas earlier feminist speeches and documents associated with the women's rights movement did not use the term identity, focusing instead on the principle (and language) of political equality with men, later documents associated more explicitly with the Women's Liberation movement tended to see their oppression – and also the sources for resistance to it – in terms of the idea of a specific female identity. Thus, for example, the organisation NOW did not deploy the term identity in its formative statements or aims, and none of the seven 'Task Forces' set up at its inaugural meeting in 1966 was explicitly concerned with the question of women's identity, nor sought to use it as a means of achieving their political ends. Neither was the word identity mentioned in the document *Sex and Caste* distributed by Casey Hayden and Mary King (1965) to women in the civil rights, peace and freedom movements, based on their experiences of sexism as SNCC volunteers, and widely regarded as one of the founding documents of the emerging Women's Liberation movement.

Betty Friedan's *The Feminine Mystique*, which is widely credited with having kick-started the women's rights movement in the US (and American 'second wave' feminism more generally) *did* use the term identity, even as the particular organisation she founded (NOW), and the wider movement it formed a part of at that time did not. There is even a full chapter of the book devoted to the subject, entitled 'The Crisis in Woman's Identity'. Here Friedan deploys the term identity in a very specific, individualistic way, at once drawing on Freudian understandings and writing against them. Her key claim is that an idealised version of femininity, 'the feminine mystique', has led women to define themselves in terms of their homes, their husbands and their children. Forsaking career, external interests and intellectual development, the woman is denied the opportunity to develop her own 'individual identity' or 'personal identity', as she variously referred to it (Friedan, 1963: Ch. 5). While this is significant in terms of the evolution of the personal sense of identity, there is yet no evidence here that identity is understood in any group-bound sense. This is still, for Friedan and her readers, a world of individuals – individual choices, chances, opinions and behaviours – that women have been excluded from. Salvation will not come in the form of recognition of feminine specificity but instead, it is believed, in its denial, and in the equalisation of women with men, as rational, autonomous choosers, with the capacity to define their own lives through their interaction with the world, and to acquire – in Friedan's terms – a full and meaningful 'identity' as a result. Thus while Friedan's work put the concept of identity on the map for the women's movement, widespread emergence and explicit use of the term 'identity' within the women's movement was to arrive through another channel – and, when it did, it was not in the individualistic Freudian sense Friedan had championed, but on the back of more group-based, 'cultural' understandings, which emphasised shared female experience.

The key concept in this development of the women's movement, and its transition from political mobilisation around rights-based claims to political mobilisation around identity-based claims, was the notion of 'gender'. As Ann Oakley put it in her famous 1972 tract, *The Difference between Sex and Gender*, '"sex" is a biological term;"gender" is a psychological and cultural one' (2005: 7). Here again we see the explicit displacement of naturalistic understandings of groups and individuals with more psychological and cultural ones. This conception of gender provided the means for the notion of a 'female identity' to emerge, as it offered alternative ways of thinking about what it means to be a woman, without relying on – and indeed, explicitly rejecting – discredited and dangerous notions of biological essentialism. And it was this notion of identity as the definitive product of a common cultural or psychological experience that came to play a very important role in the women's movement of the late 1960s and 1970s. In 1968, the national US newsletter, the *Voice of the Women's Liberation Movement*, ran a series of reports on how different radical women's groups were formed and what they were doing, in the explicit hope that these would provide some organising ideas for other women who would like to form similar groups. The first of these, from 'The Women's Radical Action Project' in Chicago, reported that although initial group discussions were tentative and exploratory,

> as we gained a group identity and common understanding we could probe more deeply into such questions as the role of women in the radical movement, the conflict between an identity as a woman and as a person, and the relationship between issues of women's liberation and radical action and education. (Carol, 1968)

Around the same time, a group calling themselves 'Radicalesbians' wrote and distributed an influential manifesto which deployed the notion of identity in its explanation of 'the rage of all women' and its argument for lesbianism as a political position. They wrote:

> As the source of self-hate and the lack of real self are rooted in our male-given identity, we must create a new sense of self ... It is very difficult to realize and accept that being 'feminine' and being a whole person are irreconcilable. Only women can give to each other a new sense of self. That identity we have to develop with reference to ourselves, and not in relation to men. (Radicalesbians, 1970: unpaginated)

A few years later, in one of the first explicit references to identity *politics*, the Combahee Women's Collective, in its famous 1977 'Black Feminist Statement', asserted:

> We realize that the only people who care enough about us to work consistently for our liberation is us ... This focusing on our own oppression is embodied in the concept of identity politics. We believe that the most profound and potentially the most radical politics come directly out of our own identity, as opposed to working to end somebody else's oppression. (1979 [1977]: 365)

Thus with the emergence of the notion of identity, there also emerged a new type of politics within the women's movement. As was the case with Black Power, the Women's Liberation Movement was not content with equal rights before the law, nor indeed with simple cultural recognition of their specificity, as the label 'identity politics' is now sometimes taken to imply. Instead, they used the idea of a shared identity to organise vigorously for substantive political, social and economic equality too. In her memoir of her time in the movement, Fraad Baxandall writes

> We expressed individual rage, but on behalf of a more communal political and economic radicalism than is imaginable now. The aim was to challenge the systems through which the classifications of 'masculine' and 'feminine' are constructed and maintained. We saw structures of race, class and gender as interconnected and we knew that social deformations had to be corrected through radical institutional transformation. (2007: 211)

Thus we see that both the Women's Liberation Movement and the Black Power movement mobilised women and African Americans to resist forms of oppression experienced on account of their collective 'identity', while at the same time using this notion of identity as a source of strength and pride. *This* was identity politics, with its mobilisation around the very idea of identity distinguishing it from other group-based politics. Arriving on the scene a little later than, though sometimes overlapping with, the earlier civil rights and freedom movements,[2] these first instances of 'identity politics' proper appeared in the late 1960s, gathering considerable pace over the 1970s. Thus from our historical vantage point, we see that the notion of identity emerged as a key political concept at precisely that point in time when other forms of political activism appeared to have failed specific groups, *and* when certain ideas about individuals and groups, which had been in circulation for decades and even centuries, achieved a critical mass and were drawn together to name and newly articulate the issues which were of immediate political importance. The idea of social identity, as we now know it, is born – crucially in, through and as part of the 'identity politics' it gave life to.

To finish here, let us place this discussion of the emergence of the idea of identity in historical perspective. Until roughly the 1960s, general essentialist understandings of the self and the formation of the self and groups were so normal and unremarkable that they did not even warrant special naming as a *particular* way of understanding the self or groups. What, by the 1960s, made them remarkable was that historically disenfranchised groups, disillusioned with the politics of formal equality that centred on claims of universal sameness, began to actively rely upon notions of cultural and psychological essentialism to more fully understand the oppression they experienced, and how they could challenge it. Essentialism – a formerly unspectacular notion in thinking about the constitution of groups – suddenly became an issue when used to disruptive political effect to struggle against a broad range of previously unacknowledged and unarticulated forms of oppression. This was identity politics. Contrary to dominant belief, the emergence of identity politics does not represent a brand new set of political aims but rather the 'watershed moment' of an older form of politics – an attempt to realise the unfulfilled promises of equality and freedom of modernity, but in a way which utilised to significant political effect a range of broadly 'essentialist' notions of selves and groups also associated with modernity. Although the concept of social identity is very recent, it nonetheless relies on an older essentialist way of thinking, deploying this to subversive and counter-hegemonic effect in a new political model – identity politics.

Thus we see that the emergence of the idea of identity, and the politics which crystallised around it, came as the *crux* or culmination of a range of processes already in train (Chapter 4). This is in contrast to what is usually presented as the case: that the emergence of identity politics marks the starting point of the (late) modern concern with identity, expressed in the common claim that the 1960s saw the 'birth' of identity politics, and that they in effect emerged out of nowhere, with only a shallow history in 1960s civil rights politics. In fact, identity politics emerged as an *end*-point, expressing politically (and often dramatically) a series of understandings about the self and groups that had a long history prior to that. Nicholson, Hall and other historians of the idea of identity and identity politics are therefore quite right to view their development as the culmination of a long series of shifts and events, against the mainstream view. However, we need to go further and appreciate how the *very idea* of identity as we now know it, and not just the politics activated in its name, emerged at a point of, and as a part of, structural change and social upheaval in mid-twentieth-century capitalist societies.

While the forms of identity politics documented in this first half of the chapter came about through a *positive* process – that is, as a way of framing and packaging certain understandings of self and social difference in order to make certain political claims, in the process in part creating the very 'identities' they seemed only to mobilise around – there was at the time another set of forces gathering that gave rise to the process of 'identity' creation in a more *negative* way. These emerged as part of a process of defending particular 'cultural' ways of being and knowing against destruction – ways which also came to be articulated as particular 'identities' in and through this defensive political process. While this 'defensive' form of identity politics was also in many ways bound up with the emergence and consolidation of the very notion of identity I have been here discussing, its defensive and resistant impetus highlights the extent to which the very essentialist understandings and experiences represented by the notion of identity were themselves starting to come under threat. This has been routinely captured in the notion of a 'crisis of identity', and it is to this that I now turn.

FROM IDENTITY POLITICS TO THE 'CRISIS OF IDENTITY'

The 1960s to the 1980s are widely regarded as the heyday of identity politics, as groups mobilised politically around their gendered, sexual, racial, ethnic, cultural and 'disabled' identities, and identity-based areas of study such as 'women's studies', 'black studies', 'disability studies' and 'queer studies' achieved institutional recognition in universities across North America and Europe (Gitlin, 1995; Fraser, 1997a; Phillips, 1997; Duggan, 2003; Bernstein, 2005). Curiously, however, this same period of political history is regarded by many, especially in its latter years, to have coexisted with a serious 'crisis of identity' (Hall, 1992; Calhoun, 1994; Nicholson and Seidman, 1995; Rajchman, 1995; Bendle, 2002). This is not meant in the Eriksonian sense of an 'identity crisis' to refer to a developmental stage of adolescence, or a personal crisis deriving from a loss of meaning or direction in life, but rather is meant in the sense of a fundamental challenge to the very concept and experience of identity itself. This 'crisis of identity' is imagined to have arisen from two key sources – firstly, as a fall-out from an intense restructuring of capitalism under globalisation, which is argued to have seriously challenged experiences of grouphood and cultural belonging; and secondly, as a result of a direct attack on the concept of identity within the humanities and social sciences. In both cases the assumption is that the notion of identity, and, indeed, the existence of different cultural 'identities', pre-dated the ensuing crisis imagined to have unsettled both. Against this, what I argue is that the idea of 'identity' did not significantly precede its 'crisis', any more than it preceded the 'identity politics' documented in the last section – indeed, as Chapter 2 demonstrated, the notions of 'identity' and 'identity crisis' emerged in tandem. Instead, what happened was that the essentialist notions of self- and grouphood that 'identity' came to represent *themselves* came under attack, both conceptually and experientially. Crucially, these challenges to culturally essentialist understandings of grouphood provided further impetus for the use of 'identity' to describe and *defend* them. Thus, where analysts of the 'crisis of identity' see a disruption and unsettling of a historically persistent concept during this period, what we have here is in fact a further crystallisation and consolidation of the idea of identity in the political and popular imagination. Let us begin with the argument that the global restructuring of capitalism has seriously destabilised and undermined cultural and ethnic 'identities'.

Globalising capitalism and the threat to cultural identity

The first iteration of the so-called 'crisis of identity' is the argument that the forces of globalisation associated with the transition to post-Fordist and neoliberal capitalism have seriously disrupted and destabilised contemporary experiences and expressions of identity. There are two main versions of this argument, which are not entirely compatible with each other. On the one hand, some theorists of globalisation have argued that the general effect of globalising processes has been to weaken or even dismantle particular forms of 'cultural identity', most particularly ethnic, national, regional and religious 'identities'. Stuart Hall, for example, argues that 'cultural identities' are becoming increasingly unstable and fragmented as the bonds that generate place-bound and traditional 'identities' are undermined by the forces of global capitalism. He identifies several features of global capitalism as of particular relevance here, namely: the global mass media, which projects hegemonic pictures of western culture around the globe; the rise of global consumerism and the banal sameness of many of the products marketed and sold; and the phenomenon of mass migration, which means that disparate peoples come to live together in the great urban centres of the world, losing their unique ethnic and cultural traditions in the new 'melting pot' of the host city. 'The more social life becomes mediated by the global marketing of styles, places and images, by international travel, and by globally networked media images and communications systems', he tells us, 'the more *identities* become detached – disembedded – from specific times, places, histories, and traditions, and appear "free-floating"' (Hall, 1992: 303). A similar appraisal leads Morley and Robins to ask whether it is 'at all possible, in global times, to regain a coherent and integral sense of identity … [when] [c]ontinuity and historicity of identity are challenged by the immediacy and intensity of global cultural confrontations' (1995: 122). This argument has been reiterated by several others since then, who have continued to claim that the broad processes of social and cultural change associated with capitalist globalisation have made it impossible for us to experience our 'identities' as whole, coherent or stable. Detached from any stabilising group or locale, 'identities' have become insecure, ruptured and 'hybridised' (Sassatelli, 2007).

On the other hand, the case has been made that globalisation has emphasised and strengthened rather than fragmented or hybridised ethnic and cultural 'identities'. From the perspective of the 'new social movement paradigm', expressions of group identity are considered to be an active, cognisant response to a series of changes generated by the transition to a post-industrial or network society (Touraine, 1981; Melucci, 1988). These new social movement theorists reject the Marxist or functionalist notion that social life is structurally determined and instead analyse these 'new' social movements from the perspective of the actor who wants to bring about social change, and whose 'identity' is understood to play an important role in this process. Manuel Castells formulates one of the stronger versions of this argument in *The Power of Identity*, where he claims that,

> Our world, and our lives, are being shaped by the conflicting trends of globalization and identity. The information technology revolution, and the restructuring of capitalism, have induced a new form of society, the network society … This new form of social organization, in its pervasive globality, is diffusing throughout the world … shaking institutions, transforming cultures,

creating wealth and inducing poverty, spurring greed, innovation, and hope, while simultaneously imposing hardship and instilling despair. (2004: 1–2)

For Castells, however, globalisation represents only one side of the story, as alongside this structural transformation, he writes, 'we have experienced, in the past twenty-five years, the widespread surge of powerful expressions of collective identity that challenge globalization and cosmopolitanism on behalf of cultural singularity and people's control over their lives and their environment' (2004: 2). He explicitly links the 'construction of collective identity' by religious fundamentalists (Islamic and Christian), Catalan and post-Soviet nationalists, African Americans, Zapatistas, women, gays and lesbians, and 'green' environmentalists to the 'process of social change in the network society' (2004: 12). According to Castells, globalisation is the catalyst for the consolidation of these identity groups, who mobilise to defend their 'cultures', beliefs, value-systems, ways of life and ultimately 'identities' against the modernising and industrialising changes wrought by a globalising capitalism.

The argument that a global restructuring of capitalism has led to intensification of experiences and expressions of group-based identity has also been made by a number of Marxist commentators, though they have typically viewed this in a less positive light. 'The surge of identity politics', writes Francis Fox Piven (1995: 111), 'is not just the result of a collapsing central government or a receding class politics. It is also the result of the massive dislocations of people set in motion by capitalist restructuring.' According to Fox Piven (1995: 108), this capitalist restructuring under globalisation creates and aggravates forms of group conflict, 'by accelerating the migration of peoples, by intensifying competition for scarce resources, and by creating the widespread economic and social insecurity which always accompanies large-scale change'. What is key here for Fox Piven, as indeed for other Marxist-influenced accounts, is that the economic foundations of these divisions are obscured, and the mass social and economic inequalities created between these dislocated and impoverished peoples are instead interpreted in ethnic, racial or religious terms (Balibar and Wallerstein, 1991; Langman, 1994). People are encouraged to understand their disempowering circumstances in terms of the increasingly visible juxtaposition of different identity groups: identitarian differences rather than class commonalities then provide the grounds for and substance of contemporary political struggle, which is further aggravated by the fact that this economic restructuring is also 'enfeebling existing forms of working class political organization which in the past sometimes restrained particularistic conflicts in the interests of class solidarity' (Fox Piven, 1995: 108). Against the argument that these groups are mobilising to defend a valued 'identity', the Marxist reading is that these groups are misled to understand their social and economic dislocation by the forces of global capitalism in terms of their 'identitarian' status. The restructuring of capitalism on a global scale is thus understood to have given rise to a particularly conflict-ridden form of identity politics. As Fox Piven dramatically describes it:

instead of wiping out all ancient prejudices, a globalizing capital is prompting a rising tide of fractious racial, ethnic, religious and gender conflict ... We can see this most awesomely in the conflicts between Hindus and Muslims, Sikhs and Hindus, Hindus and Kashmiris in India; between Xhosa and Zulu, Christians, animists and Muslims in Africa; or between Germans and Turks, French and Algerians, Serbs and Muslims and Croats in Europe; or between Chechens, Ossetians, Abhkazians and Russians; or between Jews and Blacks, Gays and fundamentalists in the United States ... No people, no place, is immune from the tide of identity politics. (Fox Piven, 1995: 103–4)

The true consequences of globalisation are in this context, it is argued, even less likely to be understood in terms of the destructive force of capitalism, but instead in terms of clashes between identitarian groups of people, differently positioned by this global *economic* system, but unable to see it in these terms (Žižek, 1997).

These accounts all recognise the aggressive impact of capitalism on traditional ways of life, but differ in their interpretation of the impact of this on the supposed 'cultural identities' in question, and specifically whether it leads to their disintegration or consolidation. Despite these differences, they all run up against the key claim of this book – that is, they assume 'identities' to have existed unproblematically for centuries, only to run into trouble as a consequence of the dislocating forces of global capitalism. Against this I suggest that it is not that changes in the structural organisation of capitalist societies have impacted upon already existing formations of 'cultural identity', but rather that they have impacted on understandings and experiences of *grouphood*, as the links which tie individuals and groups to specific locales, traditions and customs are disrupted by the social logic of capitalism as it is embedded and reproduced in people's ordinary lives, and by the structural pressures of a globalising capitalism which moves people and products in pursuit of the accumulation of capital. Contrary to what Hall and others claim, then, this is not the point that 'cultural identity' *underwent* its major crisis, but rather this is the point at which the idea of 'cultural identity' emerged. Identity presented itself as a means of referring to social groups in core, essentialist terms at precisely that point in time when those very understandings themselves started to come under sustained pressure, as a result of economic, political and social shifts engendered by globalisation.

There is a truth in the second argument articulated by new social movement theorists and Marxists, nonetheless, which is that the very act of defence *itself* further calls forth the notion of identity (though this is not precisely how they express it). The argument set out by Castells, Fox Piven and others is, in effect, that the changes wrought by a globalising capitalism have led to the *invigoration* of particular identities – what was once simply just the local, the communal, the familiar and the traditional has now, in the face of a discombobulating globalising logic, had to be defended against destruction and change. But where this is regularly interpreted as a defence of already existing 'identities',

I argue instead that this defensive action itself leads to the very creation of these groups *as* 'identities'. I do not mean this in the 'postmodern' sense of social or textual construction, but rather in that sense I have been arguing for all along – namely that the idea of identity emerged as a means of capturing a liminal set of ideas which had not, until that point, required specific articulation. These cultural or group-based experiences and subject-positions were not explicitly articulated as 'identities' prior to the emergence of these defensive forms of 'identity politics', but only came to be named as such once those cultural and group-based ways of being and knowing came under threat. For one thing, the word was not available, but for another, the word was not *required*, as that which it subsequently was used to capture was, until this point, unexceptional and unchallenged. However, as a result of the structural and often devastating changes wrought by a dynamic, invasive and intensifying logic of capitalism on the everyday lives of particular groups of people, the notion of identity presented itself as a new and powerful way of first identifying, then claiming, and finally defending that which had come under attack. Here again we see that the political action in defence of these old ways of being is inseparable from their new articulation as 'identities'.

This is what the new social movement theories pick up on – the very act of mobilising can itself also create an 'identity'. In fact, for Melucci, 'people's propensity to become involved in collective action is tied to their capacity to define an identity in the first place' (Melucci cited in Buechler, 1995: 446). Thus we see that the shifts represented by the 'crisis of identity' both indicate a threat to, and a consolidation of, the ideas captured by the notion of identity. This explains why the seemingly contradictory notions of 'identity politics' and 'the crisis of identity' emerged together – they do not in fact contradict each other, as it seems, but are both the product of a shaking up of those essentialist ideas which, in and through these disruptive processes, were named as issues of identity.

The 'crisis of identity' in academia

The 'crisis of identity' has come about not only as a result of an unsettling of certain group and individual experiences and self-understandings by a globalising capitalism, but is also the product of a more direct challenge to essentialist ideas from the social sciences   though this is typically relayed simply as a challenge to 'identity' itself. We may identify two strands to this social scientific challenge. The first derives from analysis of some of the movements characterised as identity politics. This is the criticism that identity politics operate in deeply exclusionary ways, and typically along racialised, gendered, classed or heteronormative lines, subsuming disparate experiences and 'voices' to a single experience, and a single 'voice'. For example, much of 'second wave' feminism has been criticised for its presumption to speak for *all* women. Thus, bell hooks (1984) argues that Friedan's depiction of entrapped femininity in *The Feminine*

Mystique was a highly classed vision, and that Friedan wrote specifically for white, middle class women. For black, working class women, hooks argued, the norm was in fact to work *outside* the home – and consequently, the possibility of domestic life was construed by these women as a form of luxury rather than entrapment. Thus a key challenge to the notion of identity at the heart of identity politics comes from those who largely share and support the political impetus of identity politics, but who believe they are not represented by the singular category put forward to promote the claims of that group. Margaret Somers sums up the issues at stake when she writes:

> Among the many questions we must ask, for example, is whether the new theories of identity-politics are not creating their own new 'totalizing fictions' in which a single category of experience, say gender, will over-determine any number of cross-cutting simultaneous differences such as race and class ... Feminists of color charge that feminist identity-theories focusing exclusively on gender oversimplify their situation, because gender is just one of a number of fundamental facets of identity and difference, such as poverty, class, ethnicity, race, sexual identity and age. (1994: 610)

Similar challenges have been directed to other forms of identity politics too, including the Gay Pride movement, for excluding both the experiences of lesbians (D'Emilio, 1998) and people with disabilities (Corbett, 1994); and black identity politics, for paying insufficient attention to the experiences of black women (Mostern, 1999; Collins, 2000). And it seems all forms of identity politics have been challenged for excluding the differentiation of experiences according to social class, leading some commentators to dub identity politics a form of 'middle class radicalism' (Eder, 1993). One response to this challenge has been the development of a theoretical position which asserts the existence of 'multiple' or 'intersectional' identities, as a means of avoiding the prioritisation of a singular, unitary or 'dominant' identity category (Crenshaw, 1989). On the multiple approach, individuals and groups are argued to experience or inhabit multiple identities simultaneously, and often additively. While each identity is understood to have discrete roots, the effects of or experiences associated with each are recognised to interface and aggravate each other. But even this emphasis on the multiplicity of identity has been critiqued for failing to recognise how different identities may mutually constitute each other at the point of intersection – that is, for failing to recognise, for example, how 'being black' and 'being a woman' is not the same as 'being a black woman'. Accordingly, a more sophisticated version of intersectionality theory has been developed, which recognises – as Hancock puts it in the title of her 2007 paper on the subject – that 'multiplication doesn't [always] equal quick addition', and that qualitatively new categories and experiences of identity are created at the discursive and lived point of their intersection.

While these multiple and intersectional approaches are generally considered preferable to earlier theorisations of identity, they may nonetheless be critiqued for proffering, as Brubaker and Cooper (2000: 31) put it, a 'conceptually impoverished identitarian sociology, in which the "intersection" of race, class, gender and perhaps one or two other categories generates a set of all-purpose conceptual boxes'. Indeed, what is particularly significant from the point of view of the argument of this book is that this response to the challenge that identity politics are exclusive and restrictive has served to strengthen and reinforce the very *category* of identity, as an essentialising, classificatory device. Thus Walby (2006: 11) argues that even where people are understood to experience multiple or intersectional identities, this approach 'has a tendency towards an incipient essentialism that operates to rigidify the categories under analysis ... [and which overstates] the stability and internal coherence of the communities that are the basis of the postulated identities'. What the argument of this book demonstrates is that this is predictable – more, inevitable – once we begin to use identity to think about group membership in the first place. Thus the challenge from within identity politics has tended to have the effect of reinforcing rather than dismantling the basic essentialist logic of identity, as claims of reductionism to a single voice are met with a search for ever-finer identity categories which are imagined to more properly capture the experience of a given constituency. This 'crisis of identity' thus ironically reinforces the essentialist ideas that underpin the concept, and thus further consolidates the very notion of identity itself.

However, the second social scientific challenge pertaining to this 'crisis of identity' has had the opposite effect. This is the philosophical challenge presented by 'social constructionists', 'postmodernists', and indeed, some theorists of intersectionality, who have sought to theoretically dismantle what they see as untenably essentialist understandings of the self and groups. This attack on 'essentialist notions of identity' has become so intense that the very possibility of having a politics organised around identity categories has been deeply undermined. This philosophical challenge dovetails with the objections presented by those who believe that identity politics do not adequately account for 'different voices', insofar as they question the fixed constitution of certain identity categories – indeed, this is what McCall (2005) refers to as the 'anti-categorical' approach to intersectionality, which emphasises fluidity and change over categorical stability. Rather than introduce new identity categories, or revalue old ones, these philosophically-oriented constructivist accounts challenge the very constitution of identity categories in essentialist terms, arguing instead that there can be no fixed core or centre to individual or social identities, and further, that it is this essentialist construction of identity categories that itself leads to the form of oppression subsequently experienced. Bernstein (2005: 56) characterises this general 'postmodern' critique of identity and identity politics by saying that,

In these views, the existence of status categories constitutes a form of regulation. Therefore, any activism in the name of those categories will not alleviate inequality but will reify those categories, which will increase the use of those categories to regulate and dominate subordinate status groups. Thus, identity politics hardens rather than redefines differences in status identities that are the basis for inequality. These approaches view organizing on the basis of those identities as ultimately essentialist.

This is a valid claim. However, those who make it do not recognise that the very category of identity is precisely what engenders this 'organiz[ation] on the basis of those identities as ultimately essentialist'. Thus while they dismiss an 'essentialist' conceptualisation of identity, they contradictorily retain the use of the term identity to refer to that psychological or human substrate which they then define in 'anti-essentialist' terms.

This anti-essentialist position has been developed politically by Wendy Brown (1995), who has argued that identity politics are a form of 'wounded attachment', which must reproduce and maintain the forms of suffering they oppose in order to continue to exist. She argues that reification of the effects of suffering and victimhood emerges in the proliferation of multiple minority constituencies, each with a vested interest in maintaining its identity, and thus the form of victimhood from which it is derived. The effect of critiques like these has been the emergence of a new approach to the study of identity. As Calhoun (1994: 14) describes it, 'recent approaches to issues of identity have stressed the incompleteness, fragmentation and contradictions of both collective and personal existence. They have shown how complex is the relationship among projects of identity, social demands and personal possibilities. And in order to do so, they have commonly started with the deconstruction of "essentialist" categories and rhetorics.' bell hooks (2001) has argued that this new approach to the study of identity in postmodern theory has been developed and articulated largely by those who have a vested interest in undermining the claims for equality made by black, female and other 'minority' groups. Whether or not this is true, there is no doubt but that this philosophical attack on the notion of identity has had significant repercussions for those who would engage in identity politics, as it has undermined the legitimacy and viability of the key tool of that politics – the very essentialist notion of identity itself.

However, it is important to recognise that while this overt philosophical attack on identity has been recent, the theoretical moves used have been themselves developing for a long time prior to the actual emergence of identity politics. This is because these theories are better understood, not so much as an attack on 'identity' as is widely perceived, but on the very essentialist ideas which make it sensible, and which, as Chapter 4 showed, significantly predated the use of the concept of identity to capture them. This, then, is the basis for Hall's claim that the Enlightenment and sociological conceptions of 'identity' (or, more accurately, 'the subject') entered into crisis, resulting in the final decentring of the Cartesian subject, over the course of more or less the *whole* twentieth century. Hall attributes this to five central advances in social theory and the human sciences which he believes played a central role in the 'fragment[ing]' of 'modern identities' (1992: 285). According to Hall, the first of these is Althusser's theoretical anti-humanistic re-reading of Marx, which claimed that Marx had entirely eradicated all possibilities for human agency by replacing an abstract notion of Man with disembodied social relations at the heart of his theoretical system. The second is the psychoanalytic tradition, which posited a division between the unconscious formation of the subject and the learned narrative of a unified coherent self. According to Hall, this split has destabilised any notion of a coherent self and led to understandings of identity as always contradictory and internally conflictual. Thirdly, Hall points to the 'linguistic turn', initiated by Saussure and then developed by Lacan and Derrida, which he says has demonstrated our radical inability to fix meaning, and has shown how identity is always constrained, limited and constructed within the pre-existing sets of rules, relations and meanings which constitute a language. Fourthly, he identifies the Foucauldian genealogy of the subject, which locates the self/subject as the product of increasingly surveillant, documentary and intrusive powers of modern administrative systems. From this perspective, identity is the product of disciplinary power which reconstitutes the subject as a docile body rather than the product of a core, choosing or knowing self. And finally, he argues, feminism has directly contested rational, masculinist notions of the Cartesian subject, challenged the public/private split and exposed the socialised, gendered processes of identity formation which buttressed these notions.

The problem here is that the five theoretical genres Hall refers to do not, on the whole, directly discuss 'identity', but rather, the very idea of an essential or fixed centre to a self, or the existence of a particular 'type' of person which makes the notion of coherent social groups or categories sensible. Furthermore, these theories are heavily utilised and developed in the contemporary 'postmodern' accounts which seek to undermine contemporary conceptions of identity. Thus we see that these theories have contributed to the 'identity crisis', not by challenging 'identity', but by providing the theoretical tools for challenging the notions of essentialism on which it depends.

Hall, like many other social theorists, treats these two 'crises' of identity – that is, the global shifts which have put pressure on local, traditional and cultural identities; and the twentieth-century theoretical attack on essentialism and the Cartesian subject, culminating in the postmodern attack on identity politics – together. I believe that this is to confuse what are in fact two distinct trajectories. For as I have shown, on the one hand, within the 'defensive' identity politics discussed, the trajectory is to affirm the basic notion of an identity, in terms of an individual or group 'essence', which may be biologically, psychologically or culturally derived. However, on the other hand, within the theoretical 'identity crisis', the trajectory is largely to undermine these essentialist notions of self- and grouphood upon which the notion of 'identity' depends. The failure to properly separate these two trajectories gives rise to a common error in conceptualising identity today – which is to posit the emergence of a new form or 'type' of identity, most usually 'postmodern identity', which is at once used to capture the supposedly 'fragmented' identities produced by a discombobulating globalisation, and the 'postmodern' philosophical understandings which challenge the notion of essentialism at the heart of the category of identity. But this delineation of a 'postmodern' identity is then fundamentally contradictory, as it relies at one and the same time on the real existence of 'identity', albeit fractured or hybridised by contextual forces, and on a philosophical position which undermines the very possibility for such an identity to exist. Nonetheless, this is precisely the type of claim Hall arrives at when he argues that the 'identity crisis' in effect ushered in a new 'type' of identity. He writes:

> The subject, previously experienced as having a unified and stable identity, is becoming fragmented; composed, not of a single, but of several, sometimes contradictory or unresolved, identities. Correspondingly, the identities which composed the social landscapes 'out there' ... are breaking up as a result of structural and institutional change ... This produces the postmodern subject, conceptualized as having no fixed, essential or permanent identity. Identity becomes a 'moveable feast': formed and transformed continuously in relation to the ways we are represented or addressed in the cultural systems which surround us ...The fully unified, completed, secure and coherent identity is a fantasy. (Hall, 1992: 277)

This is a particularly confused and contradictory passage. It has since been emulated in various other accounts of a 'postmodern identity', including notably by Bauman (2004) and Kellner (1995), each of whom assert the existence of a postmodern 'identity', only to immediately argue for its inessential, fluid and shifting nature.

It should now be clear just how contradictory and nonsensical such a postmodern position on 'identity' really is. For what it asks us to do is to accept the existence of 'postmodern identities' that are understood to be devoid of precisely all those attributes that made it in any way sensible to refer to them as 'identities' to begin with. Postmodern theorists offer us a choice between 'essentialist' understandings of identity, which, they argue, attribute what it is to be that person, or a member of that group, to some central core feature or 'essence'; and 'social constructionist' understandings, which recognise that this essential core is a social fiction. The choice, they suggest, is whether or not to *believe* the essentialist understandings of identity – which they clearly do not. This is not in fact an available choice, as the very idea of identity is itself, by definition, essentialist: it is not a choice to 'believe' this.[3] Hall's reading of these events and shifts leads him to claim that the 'identity crisis' marks the *transition* from a sociological to a postmodern version of identity. Against this, I suggest that (belief in) this postmodern 'identity crisis' must mean the eschewal of the very category of identity altogether. For the logical conclusion of Hall's five theoretical shifts can *only* be that the very category of identity is not a useful way of describing or understanding the human subject, as the very notions of essentialism, fixity and permanence that it has come to capture are radically undercut. There can be *no* 'identity' in the aftermath of this challenge, and talk of postmodern identities (as anti-essential, changeable, fluid identities) is a contradiction in terms. As Kobena Mercer (1990: 43) claims, 'identity only becomes an issue when it is in crisis, when something assumed to be fixed, coherent and stable is displaced by the experience of doubt and uncertainty'. My argument is that the *very concept* of identity came into being to capture those 'fixed, coherent and stable' notions of selves and groups at the very point in time at which they were coming under threat from changes in the structures of contemporary capitalist societies, as well as from developments within western social theory itself.

CONCLUSION

This chapter has argued that the emergence of identity politics should be considered a watershed moment in the history of modernity – as an attempt to realise the unfulfilled promises of equality and freedom for all, in a way which utilised to significant political effect historically persistent 'essentialist' notions of selves and groups. Indeed, the life-span of the highly self-conscious active identity politics was relatively short, for no sooner did identity politics 'proper' emerge than they were met with a series of radical and sustained challenges, both at the level of the politics at which they were fought, and at the level of the political and philosophical theory which sustained them. It now seems to be the case that this particular, lively and powerful form of identity politics no longer exists. As Nicholson (2008: 4) writes, 'Identity politics seems now to be largely dead, or, at minimum, no longer able to command the kind of public attention that it did from the late 1960s through the late 1980s.'

However, despite the short life-span of the 'heyday' forms of identity politics, the contemporary salience of *identity* forms part of a much longer historical process. We should view identity politics as the crest of a wave, whose energy has been building long before it was visible as a wave. While like the wave, identity politics are only visible in that moment of full force – just before it breaks – we should not take this to mean that they have not been building for a long time, gathering energy and momentum. And like the wave, we will not understand identity politics, or the contemporary salience of identity today, if we look only at that moment of peak, crescendo and then break, without looking to the building forces which created the wave. However, the wave did break, and presented itself to us in the form of a 'crisis of identity'. This 'crisis of identity' should not be understood as a challenge to already existing 'identities', but as a challenge to the very ideas represented by the notion of identity – that there is an essential, definitive core to selves and groups. The so-called 'crisis of identity' occurred when these essentialist ideas and experiences were threatened, both as a result of the structural changes wrought by a globalising capitalism, and via a sustained challenge to the notion of essentialism from the humanities and social sciences. Identity politics and the crisis of identity did – and had to – coexist as the very factors and forces that led to emergence and consolidation of 'identity' also led to its crisis and collapse.

While this chapter has focused mainly on the uses of the idea of identity in the social movements of the 1960s and 1970s, as one of a number of features that significantly distinguishes them from earlier forms of group-based activism, Chapter 7 evaluates this phase and form of politics in greater detail. This more explicitly evaluative project moves beyond historicisation to directly assess the impact and progressive value of the idea of identity and identity politics in capitalist societies from an egalitarian perspective. But first, in the next chapter, I will explore the emergence and consolidation of the idea of identity in the context of the 'mass' and 'consumer' societies of twentieth-century western capitalism. Whereas the relation between the contemporary salience of identity and the social logic of capitalism in the field of identity politics is complex and often ambivalent, as we will see, there is a much clearer relationship on the field of popular culture and everyday life.

Notes

1. We could extend this to include a number of other groups, including but not limited to disabled people and gay and lesbian people.
2. In fact, different movements, depending on their own internal histories as well as specific contextual factors, took up the notion of identity at different times.
3. This argument has already been made in alternative terms, from a more purely lexical perspective, in Chapter 2.

6

Personal Identity in the Consumer Society

INTRODUCTION

Chapters 4 and 5 presented a cultural materialist account of the emergence of the idea of identity, charting its 'pre-history' across the eighteenth and nineteenth centuries, and its eventual crystallisation at a time of political and social upheaval in the mid- to late twentieth century, where it gave new shape to a set of ideas that had gradually evolved in sense and importance in response to that changing context. While so far the focus has mostly been on the 'social sense' of the idea, particularly as this has evolved in political spaces in western capitalist societies, this chapter turns its attention to the 'personal sense' of identity, particularly as this has evolved in the domain of popular culture and mass consumption. It explores other, supplementary features in the development of the idea of identity that have not yet been covered, which add new inflections and nuances that are pertinent to the 'personal' as opposed to 'social' sense of identity. As we will see, this notion of personal identity is somewhat more closely, though not wholly, articulated to the social logic of capitalism.

The starting point for this analysis is the recognition that the emergence of the idea of identity did not just coincide with political changes in the form of new social movements and 'identity politics', but also with a massive growth in consumption in western capitalist societies since the middle of the last century. This was noted rather than explored in any great depth in the last chapter. Many theorists have explored the links between identity and consumption; indeed, it is routine to find these concepts treated together in contemporary cultural studies (Featherstone, 1990; Miller, 1995; Slater, 1997; Sassatelli, 2007; Ruvio and Belk, 2013). While some argue that consumption is now an important site of identity formation, such that one's personal style and possessions rather than one's social role or job, creates one's sense of identity (Giddens, 1990; Beck, 1992; Bauman, 2005, 2007; Sassatelli, 2007), others, particularly those writing from a Marxist perspective, argue that the very processes of identity formation themselves encourage and sustain practices of consumption (Giroux, 1994; Slater, 1997; Hennessy, 2000; Fine, 2006). While it is certainly true that consumption plays a role in helping people define what they see as their identities today, and also that particular 'social identities' and 'personal identity types' are deliberately targeted and commodified, generating new and lucrative markets for identity-based consumption, neither approach offers a fully adequate account of the connections between 'identity' formation and consumption. Crucially, both miss the key point that identity, as we now know it, is a recent idea in western culture and politics. Thus where these theorists make the case that identity formation *used* to occur through one's social role, family position, employment or political affiliation, but now occurs through practice of consumption, they assume the category of identity to pre-exist the processes of identity formation via consumption that they now describe and analyse. Against this, what this chapter will show is that the idea of personal identity, as much as the very practice of defining, building or marking one's identity, did not precede the emergence of consumption as a means of doing so, but developed alongside it.

DISTINCTION, EMULATION AND FASHION: A SHORT PRE-HISTORY OF 'PERSONAL IDENTITY'

In *Consuming Life*, Bauman (2007: 28) argues that consumerism arrives 'when consumption takes over the linchpin role which was played by work in the society of producers', turning 'human wants, desires and longings into the principal propelling and operating force of society'. Campbell (1995: 100) notes that 'it has become a commonplace for people to express the view that contemporary society is a "consumer society", with a predominantly "consumer culture"', that is, 'a society organized around the consumption, rather than the production of goods and services'. Consumerism, as noted in Chapter 3, is a feature of both Fordist and post-Fordist capitalism, though there has been a clear intensification of consumerist options and pressures, and a marked acceleration of consumption of the world's resources, over the latter decades of the twentieth century and into the twenty-first. The Worldwatch Institute (2013) notes that worldwide, private consumption expenditure – that is, the amount spent on goods and services at the household level – exceeded US$20 trillion in 2000, representing a fourfold increase over 1960 (in 1995 dollars). The acceleration rather than novelty of consumerism is recognised by the theorists of the 'consumer society', who tend to see it as spanning these two ostensibly distinct periods.

Although consumption fulfils a great number of basic needs and luxury desires, theorists of this 'consumer society' tend particularly to stress the relation of consumption to identity. Two basic premises of this literature are, firstly, that identity *formation* is achieved by means of consumption in contemporary capitalist societies; and secondly, that the contemporary *salience of* identity can be linked to the exponential increase in consumption that has characterised western societies since roughly the middle of the last century, as the possibilities for self-expression have multiplied with a huge explosion in consumer choice.

These analyses draw directly on the work of a number of important theorists of consumption of the twentieth century, notably, Veblen (1925 [1899]), Simmel (1957 [1904], 1990 [1907]), the Frankfurt School (Adorno and Horkheimer, 1972 [1948]; Marcuse, 1991 [1964]), the Birmingham School (Hall and Jefferson, 1976; Hebdige, 1979) and Bourdieu (1984). Although contemporary theorists tend to see the advent of the 'consumer society' itself as a historically recent development, beginning in the 1950s, they nonetheless use the work of the earlier theorists to trace connections between identity formation and consumption back to the first decades of the twentieth century. Paterson (2006: 21) claims that 'consumption from Veblen has been about articulating a sense of identity', while Sassatelli (2007: 67) attributes to Veblen the argument that 'identity construction' is achieved through practices of 'conspicuous consumption'. Meanwhile, in his critical analysis of consumer culture, Slater (1997: 121) attributes directly to the Frankfurt School the argument that 'consumer culture … integrates people within the general system of exploitation by encouraging them to define their identities, desires and interests in terms of possessing commodities'. An implicit assumption of these and other contemporary accounts of consumption is that 'identities' pre-existed the advent of the so-called consumer society, but that with its development since the 1950s, how we form, treat and act on the basis of these identities has changed. Contemporary theorists thus tend to see the earlier theorists as remarkably prescient in their claims, as they are understood to have identified these processes of identity formation through consumption decades before they overtly came to characterise today's societies. What the analysis of identity in this book shows, however, is that although the early theorists of consumption certainly discussed issues of status, group affiliation, self-presentation and social distinction through consumption, they did not actually use the word 'identity' themselves. At the time these earlier theorists were writing, the conception of identity as we now know it was not available, nor were the theorists using it, or explicitly discussing 'identities' in their work.[1] Despite this, it is commonplace to find their work reviewed as though they *had* discussed identity as we now know the concept.

These theorists, especially Veblen, Simmel and the Frankfurt School, *were* remarkably prescient in their claims, if not precisely in the way that is regularly attributed to them. Separated from contemporary narratives which read these theorists for what they have to say about the impact of consumerism on our 'identities', what we find in these early accounts instead is an exposition of the social forces, historical shifts and economic pressures around consumption that impacted upon how individuals in a classed and capitalist society saw themselves and their relations to others. Thus what these earlier theorists were documenting was *not* a shift in how we treated or formed an 'identity', but instead, the social and economic forces that would *lead* both to the emergence of the 'consumer society' and the development of the contemporary idea of 'personal identity'. While the forces documented in Chapter 5 (specifically, the political exclusion of groups and their growing resistance to that) tended to engender *collectivist* understandings of sameness and difference that eventually emerged in the 'social' concept of identity, the forces gathering in the sphere of consumption seemed instead to give rise to a need to conceptualise and name what was important or visible or salient about *individual* personhood – about being a particular type or 'class' of person, and marking that – in consumer societies.

Thorstein Veblen is particularly illuminating on this subject. In *The Theory of the Leisure Class* (1925 [1899]), he argued that by the second half of the nineteenth century, certain groups of people – specifically the '*nouveaux riches*' – had begun to engage in what he called 'conspicuous consumption' and 'conspicuous leisure' in order to distinguish themselves from other groups and naturalise their new economic standing. Veblen's thesis was based on what he claimed was a structured principle of human history: 'that status is measured by one's distance or exemption from mundane, productive labour; consequently, the manner of consuming time and goods must demonstrate that distance' (Slater, 1997: 154). By the late nineteenth century, this mechanism of achieving status was intimately bound up with the forces of production and consumption generated by the capitalist system. 'Conspicuous consumption', as the name suggests, involves the showy display of possessions which often involve deliberately wasteful expenditure and which serve no utilitarian purpose, while 'conspicuous leisure' involves 'serviceable evidence of an unproductive expenditure of time' (Veblen, 1925 [1899]: 47). While these pastimes and objects may appear to have some intrinsic value, it is, as Slater (1997: 155) points out, 'precisely their uselessness' which is the true source of their value, as it is this which is 'necessary to demonstrate status'.

'Conspicuous consumption' and 'conspicuous leisure' served two historically specific purposes. Firstly, they enabled the new 'leisure class' to demonstrate their distance from necessity and the requirement to labour, and thus from the 'productive classes'. Secondly, they allowed this new class to 'emulate' the landed aristocracy, who displayed and justified their higher status via their 'cultivated' tastes, evident in their choice of dress, objects of art, home furnishings, cultural pastimes and cuisine. In increasingly complex industrial and urban societies, it became easier to demonstrate social status through consumption than through leisure (which people may be less likely to see), and so Veblen focused in particular on the acquisition and display of material possessions. Veblen's account has been routinely reinterpreted as one directly concerning identity, and Veblen is regularly introduced as one of the first theorists to demonstrate how identity could be constructed through consumption (Paterson, 2006; Sassatelli, 2007). This is despite the fact that Veblen did not himself ever deploy the term 'identity' in his writings. We see, then, that Veblen did not in fact document a shift in how identity was formed, but instead identified and analysed some key social shifts to do with consumption, social class and the mechanisms of social distinction that would *eventually* come to be captured, at least in part, by the idea of identity. What is key is that Veblen demonstrates how self-definition became an issue at the turn of the twentieth century, when industrialisation had created a new wealthy class who sought at once to emulate the old landed aristocracy, while distinguishing themselves from the labourers who worked for them. Paterson (2006: 19–20) thus argues that in Veblen we find an explanation for the 'dramatic birth of consumption' itself, as 'the principle of social emulation [generates] … the continual drive towards increasing consumption in general and therefore the rapid growth of consumer society'. In these terms, it is not simply that these particular processes of social emulation and distinction came to operate on the terrain of consumption, but rather that they came into being as practices that were *by definition* based around new forms of consumption. The idea of identity, though not yet in play, would come to operate in the field of popular culture and everyday life precisely as a means of legitimating and sustaining this co-evolution of practices of consumption and practices of distinction.

Why did the ideas and practices discussed by Veblen in the early twentieth century later come to be captured by the notion of *identity*, specifically? An early clue is provided by Simmel (1957 [1904]), who examined the role of 'fashion' in enabling processes of both 'imitation' and 'differentiation' as part of a larger process of maintaining and policing social class hierarchies. What Simmel (1957: 544) showed was that 'fashion … signifies union with those in the same class, the uniformity of a circle enclosed by it, and … the exclusion of all other groups', while at the same time functioning to mark a person's own (supposed) individuality. Simmel repeatedly emphasises this basic tension, between 'the need of union on the one hand, and the need of isolation on the other' (1957: 546), and between the dual expression of 'equalization and individualization' (1957: 550), that he claims are constitutive of the very possibility of 'fashion'. This is because '[u]nion and segregation are the two fundamental functions which are here inseparably united [such that] one of which, although or because it forms a logical contrast to the other, becomes the condition of its realization' (1957: 544). Simmel identifies a symbiotic relationship between the need to belong to a group, and the need to distinguish oneself from others – a

Not Convincal

[?!]

gd Arg

key, constitutive feature of the contemporary idea of identity. While Simmel does not himself deploy the notion of identity, he demonstrates how this symbiotic relationship between sameness and difference is realised in the concept of fashion, and played out on the terrain of consumption. Here then we have in the very early years of the twentieth century, on the terrain of popular culture, an important set of practices organised around the marking of sameness and difference. It is not surprising that as these processes intensified with the development of consumption over the course of the twentieth century, some popular and more accessible means of expressing them might emerge. I suggest that with its roots in psychological, anthropological and cultural notions of selves and others, and its unique connotations of both sameness and difference, the idea of identity would eventually present as a useful means of doing so. Thus we see that these developing practices around consumption are likely to have contributed to the impetus for the emergence of the term identity, and indeed the particular meanings that came to dominate certain of its uses. Nonetheless, despite these developing trends, the notion of identity did not explicitly emerge within the field of popular culture until the second half of the twentieth century, and then not in any sustained way until the late 1960s and 1970s. To understand why, we need to look at those processes which led to the extension of these consumption practices beyond the elite in society, so that far greater numbers of people were involved in precisely those practices of emulation (imitation) and distinction (differentiation) identified by Veblen and Simmel. And in order to do this, we must look at the development of capitalism itself during this period, and its relation to the consumer culture of the so-called 'mass society'.

IDENTITY, CONSUMER CAPITALISM AND THE PROBLEMS OF THE 'MASS SOCIETY'

During the 1940s a number of writers started to become concerned with what they saw as a new consolidation and resiliency of capitalism, and linked this to the phenomena of 'mass culture' and 'mass consumption' in western societies. Of particular significance is the Frankfurt School's 'culture industry thesis', which made the case that culture had been commodified in late capitalism, as film, media, fiction, drama, radio, television and art developed into enormous corporate industries, and thus sites of profit creation rather than of artistic endeavour, human creativity and critique (Adorno and Horkheimer, 1972 [1948]; Marcuse, 1991 [1964]). They argued that this extension of commodity production to the sphere of culture was the inevitable outcome of the insatiable processes of capital accumulation, forced onto ostensibly or originally non-economic terrain. Significantly, they argued that in order to generate and sustain demand within this terrain, the culture industry had created a whole set of 'false' or 'manipulated' needs, which drove the demand necessary for the levels of consumption required by the expansion of capitalist production. The 'leisure time' freed up by mechanisation and the regulation of the working day was increasingly diverted into the satisfaction of these 'false needs', which was functional to capitalism on an economic level.

However, these theorists were also concerned with the role played by mass consumption and popular culture in the *legitimation* of capitalist societies. They argued that the culture industry also functioned ideologically as a capitalist tool of domination, offering illusory gratification through mass consumption, and thereby manufacturing consent to a capitalist way of life. In this way, the culture industry thesis substantiated the theoretical claim first set out by Horkheimer in the 1930s, when he argued that the economic and ideological dimensions of capitalism could not, in fact, be separated. As Agger (1992: 63) argues, '[i]n this regard, Adorno and Horkheimer gave the lie to a dualistic-Marxist separation of base and superstructure or economics and culture', as their culture industry thesis shows how 'the commodification of culture, particularly in the realm of so-called leisure time, contributes to *both* profit and social control' (1992: 60). The 'culture industry' thesis thus expresses precisely the social logic of capitalism at work, as people are incentivised and encouraged to engage in a form of consumerist behaviour that ultimately functions to sustain the mechanisms of capital accumulation. The social logic of capitalism operates particularly powerfully in the domain of consumption because it ensures integration into a capitalist way of life in a manner which obscures the nature of this acquiescence almost entirely from those who (willingly) participate in or aspire to these processes.

While the emphasis of the Frankfurt School is on the creation of false needs in order to sustain capital accumulation, we can see how this process in itself had very real effects for how people came to understand, define and evaluate themselves. As Marcuse claims in *One-Dimensional Man*, 'people recognize themselves in their commodities; they find their soul in their automobile, hi-fi set, split-level home, kitchen equipment' (1991 [1964]: 11). Mass culture did not only enable the massive expansion of personal consumption required by capitalism, and ensure consumer compliance with its workings, but did so in a way which was to fundamentally alter people's sense of self and relation to others. Specifically, as Marcuse saw, individuals in consumer societies were increasingly encouraged to understand themselves in terms of their possessions; in terms of what they consumed and what they were seen to consume, and to derive their sense of personal value and worth from this. Such consumption was made even more attractive by promising diversity, novelty and difference, thereby enabling people to distinguish themselves from – but also associate themselves with – significant others. What is further notable about the Frankfurt School analysis is their conviction that 'diversity' in capitalist societies is a mask only, as what are in reality superficial differences conceal 'the relentless logic of the commodity', which subsumes all ways of being, issues, concerns, pleasures and desires to the logic of commodification. The promise of difference and distinction offered by consumption and reinforced in aggressive marketing and advertising in fact obscures a deep process of homogenisation.

What is crucial about the period in which the Frankfurt School theorists were writing is that it was precisely at this time that the possibilities for consumption of non-essential and luxury or leisure-based commodities were extended beyond elite groups in society, to become a real option for the majority of the population in advanced capitalist societies. This period of 'organised' or 'Fordist' capitalism, stemming from the early twentieth century but really only coming to fruition across the western world in the 1950s, was characterised by relatively high wages as workers were actually – as Henry Ford famously proclaimed – paid enough to buy the products they produced. As Harvey emphasises as part of the 'Regulation School' approach, what was special about the formative Fordist vision was 'his explicit recognition that mass production meant mass consumption, a new system of the reproduction of the management of labour power, a new politics of labour control and management, a new aesthetics and psychology, in short, a new rationalized, modernist, and popular democratic society' (1989: 125–6). Aglietta (1979) explains that this Fordist period was characterised by an accord between corporate capitalism, which kept wages high enough to sustain effective demand; organised labour power, which gave up its more radical demands and maintained workplace discipline in exchange for higher wages and near-full employment; and a Keynesian state, which managed the competing demands of labour and capital, stimulated employment and raised social welfare payments in exchange for the overall reduction in the state welfare bill brought about by high corporate employment and a living wage for workers. As we saw in Chapter 5, it was this careful balance of power that enabled a generally peaceful process of capital accumulation and economic growth, with low levels of union unrest, in the postwar 'boom'.

This stage of capitalism also generated a particular 'mode of regulation' which sustained the Fordist 'regime of accumulation', and which was premised on the possibility and hegemonic endorsement of mass consumption. Thus from this Regulation School perspective, it was the structures of 'organised capitalism' themselves in this 'Fordist–Keynesian' period that gave rise to a mass culture in the US and Europe, where most people had the means to participate in the consumption process. This was ideologically sustained via a discursive shift in emphasis from the 'saving, thrift and sacrifice' (originally noted by Weber in *The Protestant Ethic*) to the enthusiastic encouragement of unrestrained consumption (Zaretsky, 1995: 249). The Regulation School approach thus effectively historicises the Frankfurt School 'culture industry' thesis as a particular stage in the development of capitalism. Slater summarises these features of Fordism from the perspective of a consumer culture, arguing that '[c]onsumer culture constitutes a "bribe" in that workers (at any rate skilled and organized workers) are offered freedom and relative plenty in the sphere of consumption in exchange for accepting intensive rationalization, alienation and utter lack of control over their work life, and for politically accepting a "democratic" system that manages but does not fundamentally challenge capitalism' (1997: 188).

This context of mass consumption also allowed for the muting of class differences, or, as Zaretsky (1995) claims, their displacement to the 'cultural sphere'. Agger (1992: 62) captures this well when he writes:

> This mass culture enables working-class and middle-class people to attain nearly the same level of creature comforts and entertainments as their bosses. Where nearly everyone can own a VCR and vacation at Disney World, explosive class differences are muted ... Mass culture is relatively undifferentiated: poor urban clacks are exposed to the same advertising and entertainment as the preppie children of suburban Yuppies. They develop similar consumer aspirations as well as a common material worldview, dominated by individualism and consumerism. This generic culture appears to level class differences, thus protecting them. *Fucking Interesting*

The processes of social distinction via conspicuous consumption that Veblen first identified were thus, by the 1950s and 1960s, evident and encouraged on a mass scale, though somewhat dissembled as a consequence of the widespread accessibility of the new consumer products. As the tendency to sell goods to people as a way of expressing themselves became more and more central to the operation of advanced capitalist economies, and a real possibility for the working class as much as the elite groups in society, it became necessary to find a language that would allow people to articulate and make sense of these processes. Furthermore, since these shifts tended to suppress and displace class conflict, despite all the mechanisms in question continuing to be very directly related to social class and the financial ability to consume, it was likely that this language would emerge in ostensibly 'neutral' or non-class terms. I suggest that the idea of personal identity that was emerging in the field of psychology would lend itself perfectly to this purpose. Furthermore, given the ability of identity to signify both uniqueness and sameness, it would be of particular value to the capitalist classes too. After all, in the mass consumer market of the 1950s, what was important was the capacity to produce these commodities in mass quantities: in this period of Fordist mass production, it was typically not possible to produce genuinely niche products that would enable true individual differentiation. As Adorno (2005 [1938]: 280) argued, 'the same thing is offered to everybody by the standardised production of consumption goods' but this is concealed under 'the manipulation of taste and the official culture's pretense of individualism'. He continues, with echoes of Simmel's critique of 'fashion', 'the identical character of the goods that everyone must buy hides itself behind the rigor of the universally compulsory style'.

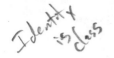

Identity would here offer itself as a very useful concept indeed, as it proffered a means of obscuring this basic sameness engendered by the relentless logic of the commodity behind a vision of 'individual', but ultimately class-based, distinction.

However, these experiences and concerns were not directly articulated in the language of 'personal identity' until the new mass society and consumer culture, which had encouraged and enabled these processes of social distinction, themselves became a source of anxiety. Again, following a similar pattern to the emergence of the social sense of identity, it was not until these ways of understanding selfhood and its relation to – or rather, distinction from – others were shaken that the concept of 'personal identity', as we now know it, explicitly emerged to capture them. As Erikson pointed out, 'we began to conceptualize matters of identity at the very time in history when they became a problem' (1950: 255). For in a context where the same social and cultural goods were, on the face of it at least, available to all, the middle classes and the elites would need to find new mechanisms for distinction. Furthermore, the Frankfurt School critique of relentless homogenisation would soon find popular expression in a widespread distaste for the 'mass society' and its uniform consumerism, as well as in a counter-cultural resistance to the 'organisation man' of corporate capitalism. Both would further render the individualistic concept of 'personal identity' an attractive mode of self-conceptualisation. However, as we shall see, the alleviation of these fears, in part via the notion of 'personal identity', would continue to work in a way that promoted rather than stymied or challenged the social logical of capitalism via personal consumption.

Beyond the mass society? Identity, counter-culture and the rebel consumer

By the time the processes of mass consumption were in full swing, there was a growing unease about the perceived experience of living in a 'mass society', and an increasing distaste towards the dull vision of the 'organisation man' of corporate capitalism. While the Fordist mode of production had given rise to a consumerist regime of accumulation in the mass society, it had also produced a whole generation of routinised assembly-line workers who were required for the efficient mass production of commodities, and an executive class of corporate managers and middle-men who exhibited perfunctory loyalty to the firm. The corporation itself had become an enormously powerful facet of American life, not just economically, but also institutionally and symbolically. 'Scientific management of all facets of corporate activity (not only production, but also personnel relations, on-the-job training, marketing, product design, pricing strategies, planned obsolescence of equipment and product) became the hallmark of bureaucratic corporate rationality' (Harvey, 1989: 134). In turn, this 'bureaucratic corporate rationality' was understood to have created the 'organisation man' – dull, conventional and robotic, the corporate complement to the conformist consumer of mass culture.

Frank (1997) makes the claim that this perception of the mass society was not – or not purely – an academic one, but was lodged in the cultural psyche. Gleason (1983) similarly argues that the key social problem facing people in the 1950s was how to survive in a mass society – this, he claimed, did not just exercise the intelligentsia, but also ordinary people. This is evidenced by the publication and widespread readership of a number of books on the topic, including the fictional bestseller *The Man in the Gray Flannel Suit* (Wilson, 1955), which was made into a film by Twentieth Century Fox in 1956, and the more academic but no less popular *The Organization Man* (Whyte, 1956) and *The Lonely Crowd* (Riesman, 1961 [1950]). Indeed, this period more generally witnessed a new authority and power of the social sciences. Convinced by their capacity to explain a range of social motivations and ills, the American public had, according to Gleason, become newly enamoured with psychologists and sociologists, looking to them to explain a whole set of personal problems in their own family, working and communal lives. It was at this point in time that Erikson began to publish on the notion of 'ego-identity', arguing that the term 'connotes both a persistent sameness within oneself (selfsameness) and a persistent sharing of some kind of essential character with others' (1959: 109). As Gleason explains, this concept of identity fitted into the broader context of a disquiet with mass society very well, as it was by definition concerned with the relationship between the individual and the society, and the formative influences of the latter on the former. Against this background, Brubaker and Cooper note that the 'prevalent individualist ethos' of American culture 'gave a particular salience and resonance to "identity" concerns, particularly in the contexts of the 1950s thematization of the "mass society" problem and the 1960s generational rebellions' (2000: 3).

Thus it was in this period that the notion of identity, in its personal sense, began to be discussed in the way with which we are now familiar, moving rapidly beyond the psychological writings of Erikson and the sociological work of Strauss and Goffman in the 1950s to gain an important place in popular discourse (Chapter 1). It would not have taken off with the speed and fluency it did without such a deep history underpinning it – this is the reason why it was then, as it is now, perceived as a deeply familiar word, as well as one that is strangely peculiar to the current time. By 1958, Lynd could already claim that the problem of identity was all-consuming for the American people, and in subsequent years, a number of books were published that started explicitly to explore questions of identity for the non-academic reader too. In 1964, *The Search for Identity* by Roger Shinn offered a range of essays discussing the 'American search for self-understanding', covering issues of religion, mass communications, politics, literature and race, while in 1972 William Glasser published the popular psychology book *The Identity Society*, which sought to characterise the malaise of that whole generation in terms of its anxious search for a stable identity. By 1970, Erik Erikson was a household name, and had appeared in a wide range of popular magazines and journals, including *Newsweek* and *The New York Times*, discussing his theories of identity and identity crisis. The idea of identity clearly seemed to have provided some answers to the problem of living in a mass society, and, where it was informed by the 'personal sense' in particular, provided a useful counter to the dull, conformist 'organisation man' of corporate capitalism.

But identity was not just useful as it supposedly captured how the individual formed his or her sense of self in relation to societal influences (which was how the sociologists and psychologists conceptualised the problem), but also because of the connotations of distinction and sameness that it carried, which were particularly relevant not just in a *mass* society, but in a *consumer* society. These patterns of consumption were as real and relevant to the everyday person on a lived and experiential basis as was the historical transition to a 'mass society'. We see then that the very existence of the word identity itself in part invited the problem it was then used to settle. That is, once people are persuaded that they 'have' an identity – in part by its very invention – they are motivated to try to find it. And in a consumer society, the psychological problem of finding an identity finds a ready solution in engagement in practices of consumption which allow for the visible marking of that identity, thereby 'finding' and 'marking' it at the same time.

Thus we see that while the notion of personal identity offered a means of asserting difference, it nonetheless encouraged participation in the practices of mass consumption which had homogenising rather than heterogenising effects. This ambivalent, even contradictory, attitude towards mass consumption is also traced by Frank (1997) in his analysis of advertising during this post-1950s period. The whole tone of this advertising was to mock and challenge the dull conformism of 1950s consumerism with a vision of the new, ironic, cynical, rebel consumer – though as he convincingly shows, this rebel consumer purchased as much as his/her conformist predecessor. Frank's argument is that the 'counter-culture' of which this 'cool consumer' formed a part was not merely *incorporated* into 'business culture', but, in reality, had developed in tandem with it from the outset. In a similar way, 'personal identity' offered a colourful alternative to the perceived greyness of the mass society: the possibility of being 'different' – of 'having an identity' – must have seemed very attractive indeed. However, the idea of identity did *not* in fact offer an alternative to mass consumer society but rather, a means of promulgating it. The 'identity' that was marketed as different was also, in fact, mass produced, and offered a way for capitalism to sell vast amounts of consumer goods to those who bought desperately into the need to stand out from the masses.

Social identity in the consumer society

What the previous discussion has shown is that the notion of personal identity took off in the arena of popular culture at more or less the same time that the notion of social identity began to inform and animate the new social movements of the 1960s and early 1970s around 'race' and gender (see Chapter 5). An interesting cross-over between senses occurs in this period, where notions of social identity – which evolved largely in political ways – began to be played out in the popular cultural spaces of these Fordist societies. As Chapter 5 noted, women, ethnic minorities, African Americans and others were not just politically marginalised, they were also excluded from full participation in the norms of consumption that had come to characterise these societies. The accord between the state, labour and capital of the postwar boom largely excluded 'minority groups', for as Slater explains, the 'whole "deal" emerge[d] from negotiations involving unionized labour: the resulting "social consumption norm" therefore [did] not apply to most women or ethnic minorities, who [were] excluded from direct participation in this process' (1997: 188). Harvey (1989) claims that it was this exclusion of 'minority groups' from consumption – while still being taunted by its consumerist dreams – that precipitated the outburst of angry mobilisations along the lines of race and gender in the 1960s.

However, there is another piece to this story. Away from the field of politics, these distinctions between 'minority groups' assumed another, less volatile form – and one that was more amenable to the social logic of capitalism. This is what Zaretsky notes when he claims that the structural shifts that led to a 'diversified proletariat' and a new centrality of consumption in capitalist societies ultimately 'gave the category of difference a new sphere in which to operate. This was the sphere of culture' (1995: 252). What Zaretsky misses, however, was the role played by the *idea of identity itself* in displacing social divisions along the lines of 'race' and gender to the 'sphere of culture'. While the social sense of identity certainly had mobilising potential in the political arena, as we have seen, there was nonetheless slippage between notions of collective belonging and resistance on the one hand, and consumerist individualism on the other, facilitated by the fact that the notion of identity could, and did, connote both. These slippages meant that the social differences created or aggravated by capitalist economic inequalities could be repackaged in a particularly invidious way, as something to be proud of, and more, as something to mark through consumption. Attached as it was to promises of pleasurable consumption, diversity and distinction, the idea of identity in its *personal* sense thus provided a key means of packaging these differences attractively, and in a way that encouraged accommodation rather than resistance to a capitalist way of life. Furthermore, it provided a means of reconstituting these different groups as target markets. So while this inviting repackaging of difference, especially racial difference, as identity surely had appeal to 'minority' consumers, it was also deeply useful to the capitalist entrepreneurs, who could target these different 'identity groups' as market segments. Indeed, as Feitz (2012) notes in her analysis of the 'corporate social responsibility' policies of the cosmetics corporation Avon in the 1970s, 'in the era of Black power, "[advertising] agency executives were increasingly told that Black consumers wanted to see unique representations that reflected knowledge of Blacks' lifestyle, culture and aspirations"' (2012: 126, citing Chambers, 2008: 206). And so the large corporations of 1970s America responded enthusiastically, with Avon in particular directly targeting African American women with parallel but different 'black' cosmetics, advertisements, models and sales-people. 'In so doing', writes Feitz, 'Avon crafted a strategy to respond to the changes Black Power had wrought while capitalizing on its most commodifiable elements' (2012: 118). However, if there is one story that catches these slippages perfectly – the volatile political differences between groups, challenged at least in part via the notion of 'social identity', and the repackaging of this difference as 'personal identity' in the field of consumption – and the value of all of this, ideologically and economically, to the capitalist class, it is the story of *Essence* magazine.

Essence magazine was founded in 1968 and began publishing in 1970. Baker (1964) noted an emergent shift in magazine publications at this time, away from the targeting of a general readership (like *Reader's Digest*) towards the targeting of more segmented groups based around demographics like 'race' and gender. 'The truth is', he wrote, 'that the wild chase to monopolize the mass mind through the magazines hasn't worked', and that 'the economics of magazine publishing [now] favors the thesis that the American mass refuse to behave itself as a mass [and] that there is more money in treating Americans as separate publics – businessmen, chemical engineers, Negroes, art lovers, camera bugs' (Baker, 1964: 93–4). In the context of this shift, *Essence* was one of a number of magazines that targeted a 'black' readership in the US. However, unlike *Ebony*, founded in 1945, and *Jet*, which began publishing in 1952, and which was famous for its coverage of the civil rights movement, *Essence* did not just address issues of concern to a black readership, but directly addressed issues of 'female black identity'.[2] The difference is evident in the name itself. While *Ebony* and *Jet* visually connote blackness, this magazine instead emphasised the notion central to the very idea of identity: essence. From its inception, *Essence* grappled with notions of both social and personal identity, with its founding editors hoping both to support and capitalise on the revolutionary black liberation movement. As a result, its editorial and substantive content was divided between coverage of the political goals of black identity politics on the one hand, and fashion, home-making and relationship advice for black women on the other. As Gumbs notes in her comprehensive critical history of the magazine:

> Though framed in the language of Black power, *Essence* actually privileged articles and advertisements that spoke to the nonrevolutionary tasks of looking good, finding a man, and keeping a house, tasks conveniently attuned to the marketing and advertising of cosmetics and household products. Readers

browsing copies of *Essence* during its forty years would note that make-up ads are prominently placed, while political and service oriented coverage is buried after page 100. (2012: 98)

Although the editorials in particular kept up a constant rhetoric of black female empowerment, the production was largely dominated by African American businessmen, who 'used the language of Black Power to legitimate their role as middlemen in a project that actually directed Black women's money away from Black businesses and communities, and into the mainstream' (2012: 104). Furthermore, if a female editor adopted an overly political stance, she was, Gumbs notes, 'attacked as "too black" or possibly even too egalitarian, too utopian, or too feminist and subsequently driven out' (2012: 98). Radical concerns about black female identity – in the 'social' sense – were consistently undermined and over-ridden by the attempt to sell to black women as a new consumer cohort, and to trade on their sense of 'personal identity' in so doing. *Essence* magazine thus ultimately contributed to the exploitation of black women consumers. 'As the advertisements transitioned from Afro-wigs and Black power fist combs to mainstream products such as McDonald's hamburgers and Maybelline makeup, the magazine's editorial philosophy also departed from promoting a separatist ideology rooted in Black cultural nationalism to an assimilative ideal of Black consumption' (Gumbs, 2012: 96). This aestheticisation of Black Power had the effect of undermining, and indeed, depoliticising, some of its transformative, solidaristic and anti-capitalist potential. Crucially, it suggested that 'certain components of Blackness were marketable, while others – the more egalitarian, visionary and collaborative notions – proved incompatible with integrating Black people into mainstream channels of capitalism' (2012: 100).

    Although Gumbs does not note this, it is clear that it was specifically the idea of *identity*, as it operated fundamentally as an essentialist classificatory device in both its social and personal senses, that facilitated the slippage between 'race'-based consumption norms for women and radical political activism around race. Furthermore, the fact that it was consumerism, and the integration of black women into a capitalist way of life, that won out seems to indicate that the idea of identity is more easily articulated to the social logic of capitalism than it is oppositional to it. This is a question to which I shall return in greater depth in Chapter 7.

POST-FORDISM AND POSTMODERN 'IDENTITY'

In the 1970s capitalism underwent a significant restructuring, such that the Fordist period of mass production, high wages and a Keynesian state was replaced by a substantial outsourcing of production to the Global South and the emer-gence of a supposed 'service economy', wage repression and a neoliberal state in the Global North (Chapter 3). The cultural face of this transition is regularly theorised in terms of a shift from modernity to 'postmodernity', such that the postmodern is considered the 'cultural logic of late capitalism' (Jameson, 1991), or the mode of regulation accompanying the regime of 'flexible accumulation' that is post-Fordism (Harvey, 1989). The postmodern is argued to be characterised by a fixation on spectacle, difference and simulation, with Baudrillard arguing that it is dominated by a 'consumerist system of signs' (1988 [1976]) – a foundationless hyper-reality, where meaning is not derived from any social determinants but from a floating network of empty signifiers. Of relevance here, this postmodern period is imagined to have significant implications for how we inhabit, experience and understand our 'identities'. While this story is told in a very particular and often abstract philosophical way in the academic narratives, there are nonetheless some 'real life' correspondences in terms of how people see – or are encouraged to see – their 'identities'.

The academic story, as we have already heard in Chapter 4, is that the 'postmodern identity' has supplanted the relatively stable modern identity as it was defined by family role, job and social status, to become fractured, transient, malleable and ultimately unsustainable. This is claimed to be the result not only of the discommoding forces of globalisation (Chapter 5), but also of the proliferation of signs and loss of referential meaning that supposedly characterise the postmodern. No longer the product of an essential core, a postmodern identity is, as Hall put it, 'formed and transformed continuously in relation to the ways we are represented or addressed in the cultural systems which surround us … [t]he fully unified, completed, secure and coherent identity is a fantasy' (1992: 277). However, it is not the supposed *existence* of a unified identity that is unsustainable as much as the concept itself. In fact, as argued in Chapter 5, the concept of a postmodern identity is a contradiction in terms: given that the very idea of identity hangs on the attribution of some essential characteristics – whether biological, cultural, psychological or experiential – to an individual or group, this postmodern conception of identity as fluid, fragmented and malleable cannot legitimately be taken as a conception of identity at all.

Partly in recognition of this, 'postmodern' theorists posit that at the same time that 'identity' is fractured, intersectional and fictive, it is also 'multiple', free-floating and detached. People, it is claimed, now 'choose' their identity – or many – from the vast array of 'identity options' open to them. This informs Giddens's work on the reflexive self (1991), and Bauman's argument that people are bricoleurs, making their biography out of a jigsaw where they do not have or know all the pieces (2004). In one of the most repeated metaphors of a postmodern identity, it is argued that in a historical period characterised by transience, impermanence and flux rather than by continuity, solidity and definiteness, where 'the world constructed of durable objects has been replaced "with disposable products designed for immediate obsolescence … identities can be adopted and discarded like a change of costume"' (Bauman, 1996: 23, citing Lasch, 1985: 1932–88). On this reading, individuals are imagined to have the capacity, and indeed, the propensity, to change their 'identity' as they like over their life-course. Ironically, we could say that that which defines – that is, the *essential* properties of – this (postmodern) self are those attributes of transience, changeability, impermanence and self-creation which are imagined to be the complete antithesis of the attributes defining the modern or Enlightenment self of earlier historical periods. This is why Madonna is often articulated as the quintessential 'postmodern' figure: always inventing and reinventing herself, likened to a chameleon, it is in the end this endless capacity for reinvention that essentially defines her.

   Despite their confusing and contradictory postulation of the existence of a postmodern identity, there is *some* truth to these narratives nonetheless – but it lies in their identification of the growing proliferation of discourses of 'choice' and 'lifestyle' that people now navigate in a world increasingly dominated by corporate branding and market segmentation. However by focusing on the putative existence of a 'postmodern identity', these accounts elide how the idea of identity *itself* works to enable this proliferation of choice, and to construct a particular understanding of the self, in a capitalist context of mass consumption and enormous social and economic inequality. For despite changing conceptions about what it means to 'have an identity', it is the case that the idea of identity continues to work in 'the postmodern society' in a way that promotes – even more aggressively than before – classed, racialised and gendered processes of distinction, and the expansion of corporate marketing and advertising. Let us see how.

Identity and corporate marketing in the postmodern society

At the level of corporate production, branding and marketing, the idea of identity continues to operate in an especially powerful way. Contemporary theorists of consumption regularly differentiate between consumption within a 'Fordist' society and consumption within a 'post-Fordist' society, such that the homogenisation and standardisation which the Frankfurt School theorists saw as a universal feature of capitalism is refigured as part only of the 'Fordist' stage of capitalism. As Slater describes these accounts, 'it is argued that the modern, Fordist mass production of standardized goods for mass consumption by homogenous consumers has given way to the postmodern, post-Fordist specialized production of goods more specifically tailored for and targeted on precise consumer groups who are defined by lifestyles rather than by broad demographic variables like class, gender or age' (Slater, 1997: 174). Mike Featherstone (1991: 83) traces a similar trajectory, from 'the designation of the 1950s as an era of grey conformism, a time of mass consumption', to the market segmentation by demographic consumer groups (as we saw with the case of *Essence* magazine), to, finally, a uniquely postmodern society 'without fixed status groups in which the adoption of styles of life (manifest in choice of clothes, leisure activities, consumer goods, bodily disposition) which are fixed to specific groups have been surpassed'. But how does this supposed new 'niche' or 'flexible' market segmentation accord with the global ambitions of many corporate enterprises today?

The problem is that where corporations seek to sell on a 'global market', they must manufacture products with universal appeal, a process requiring what global advertising agency *Saatchi and Saatchi* refer to as 'world cultural convergence', namely, 'a belief in the convergence of lifestyle, culture, and behaviour among consumer segments across the world' (Robins, 1991: 29). This world cultural convergence is accomplished by 'targeting the shared habits and tastes of particular market segments at the global level, rather than by marketing, on the basis of geographical proximity, to different national audiences' (1991: 29). This is what Hall suggests we refer to as 'the global post-modern': 'Cultural flows and global consumerism between nations create the possibilities of "shared identities" – as "customers" for the same goods, "clients" for the same services, "audiences" for the same messages and images – between people who are far removed from one another in time and space' (1992: 302). While Hall presents this in terms of the construction of 'shared identities', arguably what is in fact happening here is that corporate entities are actively deploying the very idea of identity in order to market to – and in part create – different target groups on a global scale. The underlying assumption here is presumably that individuals are less likely to respond positively to marketing based on simple demographics, such as age or location, than to marketing which targets and reinforces a 'personal identity' to which they are already attached. The notion of identity thus enables marketing to large, geographically diverse groups of people whose tastes are broadly the same, whether they identify as 'emos', 'hipsters', 'career girls', 'yummy mummies', 'surfer dudes', 'outdoor adventurers', or whatever else. But what consumers are actually invited to do is to choose a 'personal identity' from a set of pre-fabricated available identities, rather than simply to be unique individuals. That is utterly functional to mass production in a way that true individuality is not. Furthermore, in this way, one can articulate and 'construct' one's putative personal identity in complete dissociation from local and other traditional binds, in a manner that is deeply useful to corporations, as it permits the same set of products to be sold worldwide.

The same kind of argument can be made in relation to claims that contemporary capitalism promotes multiculturalism through a new valuation and celebration of cultural diversity and ethnic identities. From 'the united colors of Benetton' to celebrations of 'the global supermarket', the corporate world is awash with claims of valuing diversity (Eisenstein, 1996). And although deeply critical of the profit-seeking impetus of the 'socially responsible' corporations of the 1970s, Feitz nonetheless also notes that 'Avon's transition from a corporation built on the profitable symbolic imagery of whiteness to a racially and ethnically inclusive corporation marked the beginning of what scholars have described as an era of multiculturalism' (2012: 127). Yet while it is certainly true that one may now construct one's 'cultural identity' from a globally available range of 'traditional' cultural or ethnic fare – at least insofar as this means that one may maintain one's 'Irish identity' by frequenting Irish pubs in Dubai, or one's 'African identity' by purchasing 'Afro' hair products in East London – scratching beneath the surface reveals once again that basic sameness behind the gloss of superficial distinctions. Thus as Robins (1991: 31]) argues, while '[s]o-called world culture may reflect a new valuation of difference and particularity, … it is also very much about making a profit from it' – and this profit depends on mass consumption of mass produced commodities. In fact, the aspects of group membership that are currently conceptualised as 'identities' on the terrain of popular culture and advertising are precisely the forms of dress, cuisine and music that can be easily commodified and sold. At the same time, as Lisa Jones (1991: 36) succinctly puts it, 'brown plastic is poured into Blonde Barbie's mold', as previously 'neutral' commodities are produced in new, 'multicultural' form. As Du Cille points out, 'while Mattel and other toy manufacturers may claim to have the best interests of ethnic audiences in mind in peddling their integrated wares, one does not have to be a cynic to suggest that profit remains the motivating factor behind this merchandising of difference' (2004: 268).

Ironically, therefore, while globalisation presents as a multicultural phenomenon, this is not a necessary component of it, as the abstract logic of capitalism is necessarily indifferent to ethnic or cultural differences: what is at stake, rather, is the global movement of goods, services and labour in order to create profit. While being able to buy Japanese miso soup and Turkish coffee in the same British supermarket may appear to be about the valuation of cultural diversity, and the possibility of maintaining a valued 'cultural identity', the fact that both are packaged as 'Tesco's Own' reveals more precisely the true impetus and nature of capitalist globalisation. Furthermore, it is important to remember, as Hall (1992: 305) warns, that globalisation affects people differentially according to one's location within the global nexus: 'the proliferation of identity choices is more extensive at the "centre" of the global system than at its peripheries'. Consequently, the common claim that capitalism is 'in love with difference' should not be interpreted to mean that capitalism promotes true diversity, for it does not, but instead that it promotes and fosters difference as part of a larger logic of commodification which ultimately lends itself to far-reaching cultural homogenisation. The idea of identity is a key, though by no means the only, mechanism that enables this. Thus against celebratory accounts, the approach here suggests that although in one respect the operation of capitalism is heterogenising, as it promotes endless opportunities for the construction of different 'identities', at another, deeper level, the basic logic of capitalism is homogenising, as it turns all identity formation into the commodified process of consumption as part of an overarching process of capital accumulation. Whatever identity is 'chosen' or emphasised in the context of global corporate capitalism, whether 'personal' or 'cultural', it is one that must be bought. Contrary to the views of some of the theorists of post-Fordism, who see standardisation as specific to the Fordist period of capitalism only, the proliferation of 'identities' in contemporary capitalism masks an ultimate sameness at the heart of the logic of capitalism, which demands that all human needs and wants are met in the same way, by purchase on the market.

At the very apex of market segmentation by identity in the twenty-first century, we have the phenomenon of Facebook. Facebook does not insist on or market a particular 'cultural' or 'personal' identity, but rather provides a platform for everybody to define their own identity. This perfectly epitomises the argument of Chapter 2, where it was argued that 'identity' does not itself provide the substantive grounds on which one is categorised – 'having an identity' merely specifies that you belong to a particular group, or present as a particular 'special' individual, with identifiable 'unique' characteristics, preferences and traits, whatever they may be. Designation of an 'identity' therefore depends on *other* systems of classification, and in itself does not supply these grounds or criteria. In the world of Facebook, it is the individual who sets and provides these criteria (though the possibilities here remain constrained by the distinctively *non*-virtual patterns and relations of social class, gender, sexuality, 'race' and more). People choose and change the 'profile' they present as often as they like, yet at the same time build up a consistent, recognisable 'personal identity' as they emphasise a continuity of 'likes' and 'events', and a network of 'friends' on their personal 'page'. These 'likes' are then marketised, literally, as economic 'preferences', as Facebook sells this information to corporate marketers who target the ads that arrive into the facebooker's 'newsfeed' – in a very Orwellian sense of the word. This is not novel to Facebook: Google, Tesco and various others have successfully carried out similar forms of micro-targeting of consumers. What is significant about Facebook is the manner in which it uses the idea of identity to allow people to willingly reveal and fashion their own preferences in a highly visible, personal performance project. This is a high-maintenance project, with 1.11 billion 'monthly active users', and 665 million 'daily active users' worldwide, as of March 2013 (Facebook, 2013). As Michael Albert, the founder of the alternative social networking site ZSocial, has pointed out, Facebook is the largest spy agency in the history of the world, working not for political defence but for corporate capitalism (2011). Facebook thus perfectly captures the contradictions of the notion of a 'postmodern identity' – personally 'constructed', 'changeable', and even 'multiple', it nonetheless registers the continuity of a particular self-as-actor, and facilitates processes of distinction and emulation, all the while contributing spectacularly to the corporate capitalist accumulation of wealth.

Corporate capitalism does not just use the idea of identity to sell to different target groups – in the process, in part creating that which it peddles – it also uses the notion in order to solidify image, establish market presence and maintain customer loyalty, via the development of corporate 'brand identities' (Giroux, 1994; Van Riel and Balmer, 1997; Rowden, 2000; Schultz et al., 2000; Klein, 2002). As Chapter 1 documented, a vast industry has emerged to develop and manage brand and corporate identities: *Keen Branding*, for example, promotes its 'specialized services for brand identity development, corporate identity development [and] corporate identity design', while *Kontrapunkt* claims that 'Identity is the core of business strategy'.[3] Brand identities work like other identities – that is, by asserting a consistent, recognisable continuity of an entity, while differentiating from significant (but not that different) others. The Coca-Cola vs Pepsi and the Nike vs Adidas 'wars' are evidence of this, as they use the symbolism of the brand, rather than any very discernible difference in the basic product, to gain competitive market advantage. The particular value of promoting a specific brand identity, then, is that it enhances swift brand recognition in a field of intense competition, as well as fostering a deep, almost familial loyalty to that brand, to the extent that consumers come increasingly to associate the symbolic qualities associated with that brand with their own 'personal identities'. So, for example, while *Forbes* magazine (Kelly, 2014) reports that 'a staggering 59% [of iPhone users] admitted "blind loyalty" to the handset', the editor of *Psychology Today* perhaps said it best when she quipped, 'iPhone, therefore I am' (Perina, 2009: 5).

From the perspective of global capitalism rather than the individual consumer, however, what is of greatest significance here is the fact that, in many cases, global corporations have themselves transmogrified into global brands. Their products are no longer what they 'produce' – since at any rate, they often do not produce much anymore, as it is mainly outsourced to take advantage of low labour costs and/or possibilities for corporate tax avoidance. Rather, it is their 'identity' – their 'swoosh', their 'icon', their 'logo' – that is their source of profit. This is what was so clearly captured by Klein in *No Logo* (2002) when she documented a 'new kind of corporation' for whom 'producing goods was only an incidental part of their operations'.

> What these companies produced primarily were not things, they said, but images of their brands. Their real work lay not in manufacturing but in marketing. This formula, needless to say, has proved enormously profitable, and its success has companies competing in a race toward weightlessness: whoever owns the least, has the fewest employees on the payroll and produces the most powerful images, as opposed to products, wins the race. (2002: 4)

What the analysis of this book adds to Klein's is a recognition of the unique value of the concept of identity itself in contributing to the enhanced power of corporations in a globalised capitalist world, as they use the idea of identity to mask mass consumption behind a rhetoric of 'choice' and 'difference', and to multiply their profit-making capacities by restructuring themselves as 'weightless' brand identities.

'Because you're worth it': Personal identity and the classed mechanics of consumer choice

While the corporate world utilises the notion of personal identity to considerable and lucrative effect, personal identity also continues to operate at the level of everyday consumerist practices in contemporary classed societies – though typically in a way which serves to obscure the classed character of these processes. Across a range of popular cultural and journalistic contexts since the 1980s in particular, the concept of personal identity is regularly attached to the concept of 'lifestyle', used to refer to distinctive patterns and choices in ways of living, whether religious, career-oriented, political, or to do with fashion, music or art. As Chaney elaborates:

> While lifestyles are dependent on cultural forms, each is a style, a manner, a way of using certain goods, places and times that is characteristic of a group but is not the totality of their social experience. Lifestyles are sets of practices and attitudes that make sense in particular contexts. (1996: 5)

Where expressions and experiences of 'identity' and 'lifestyle' are considered together, as for example in television make-over and home improvement shows, and the 'Culture' supplements of middle class Sunday newspapers, they tend to refer us to a discerning, selective individual, and to emphasise practices of choice and distinction when it comes to understanding what makes people who they are. Lewis (2008: 443) argues that contemporary conceptions of identity and lifestyle give rise to a particular contemporary vision of selfhood: 'Rather than seeing selfhood as limited or constrained by one's class, race or gender, today ordinary people are held up as being able to invent (and reinvent) their own life "biographies".'

This particular conception of personal identity is not only active in popular culture and everyday life, but within academia too, as social theorists have come to rely on and reproduce such understandings in their analyses of contemporary consumer societies. Campbell (1995: 111) suggests that the whole emphasis on identity in contemporary theories of consumption arises from sociologists being convinced 'that modern industrial societies have evolved in such a way that individuals are presented, effectively for the first time, with the possibility of choosing their identity by varying their pattern of consumption'. Many of these theorists have also focused on the concept of lifestyle, and its role in a self-reflexive project of identity construction in an era of consumerism (Chaney, 1996; Bell and Hollows, 2006; Sullivan and Lane West-Newman, 2007). Perhaps the most prominent of these theorists are the 'individualisation' theorists, notably Beck and Giddens, who present us with an image of a reflexive self, engaging in a project of identity construction through a process of negotiating and choosing from a range of options in the 'risk society' of late modernity (Giddens, 1990, 1991; Beck, 1992; Beck et al., 1994; Beck and Beck-Gernsheim, 2002). Both Giddens and Beck argue that this project of constructing individual identities and life-biographies is not optional: 'we all not only follow lifestyles, but in an important sense are forced to do so – we have no choice but to choose' (Giddens, 1991: 8). In these accounts, the positive opportunities for the self-creation of these identities in late modernity – the term they prefer to postmodernity, though there are many correspondences – are provided through education, 'flexibility' in skills and labour, and importantly, acts of consumption.

These theorists arguably reproduce rather than challenge contemporary popular discourses of personal identity, by promoting the idea that in contemporary societies people are able to define their identities through personal choice and consumption, making this a wonderful era of freedom from previously ascribed identities. However, these theorists pay insufficient attention to the realities of 'self-creation' in classed societies. Although these processes of identity formation are understood to take place in nominally capitalist societies, the concept or even existence of social class is notably absent. Instead, inequalities are spread across the life-cycle, and arise from the failure to properly negotiate the risk and precarity inherent in late or postmodernity. As Atkinson (2007: 354) astutely comments, 'Western societies are still capitalist, and yes, Beck contends, inequality of income remains stable. But it is "capitalism *without* classes" … and inequality of income firmly detached from its old moorings in class categories.'

In effect, many of these accounts read the contemporary salience of identity categories, and the contemporary emphasis on 'self-creation', as *evidence* of a demise of social class. For Beck, class is a 'zombie category', which does not accurately capture the processes of individualisation that now govern life chances and economic (in)security, while for Giddens, the imperative to choose, and to construct one's own self-identity 'transcends all class differentiation, so that its "influence is more or less universal, no matter how limiting the social situations of particular individuals and groups may be"' (Loyal, 2003: 120). While there are many well-documented problems with the repositioning, or indeed, dismissal of the relevance of social class in these accounts (Savage, 2000; Skeggs, 2004), what is of particular concern to this study is the way in which Giddens and Beck fail to see how the idea of identity *itself* acts as a powerful mechanism for obscuring, displacing and even legitimising the social class inequalities that continue to structure capitalist societies.

The paucity of this analysis, which interprets the contemporary emphasis on identity categories as evidence of a demise of social class, is revealed by comparison of their work with that of Bourdieu, who clearly demonstrates how social class is reproduced precisely in the supposedly 'free choices' people make in the 'cultural' domains of education, 'lifestyle', consumption and 'identity creation'. Interestingly, although Bourdieu's analysis of the processes of 'distinction' is regularly interpreted by contemporary social theorists as an account of how 'identity' works today, Bourdieu himself rarely used the term, and it was certainly not an analytical concept that he put to any significant use. But Bourdieu's work *was* centrally concerned with social distinction, status hierarchies, social conflict and class struggle displaced onto the arena of culture. Like Veblen, Bourdieu (1984, 1986) emphasised the *symbolic* as opposed to practical uses of things, and in particular, the display of commodities, possessions and sensibilities (as resources) in order to mark distinction from others. And like Veblen, Bourdieu saw consumption as 'part of the cultural reproduction of social relations' (Slater, 1997: 148). However, while Veblen focused on the acquisition and display of material possessions as markers of status, Bourdieu also conceptualised cultural knowledges and dispositions as actual material resources, or forms of 'capital'. He argued that 'taste' and preference function as markers of cultural distinction, and accrue as 'cultural capital', which plays a key role in the perpetuation and legitimation of class divisions. Bourdieu introduced the concept of 'habitus' to explain the embodied dispositions, tastes, sensibilities and 'talents' of individuals, which *appear* biologically or naturally given, yet which in reality represent the materialisation of class differences and inequalities in the body. This explains, for example, the familiarity of some groups with elite cultural institutions, and their apparently natural ability to enjoy opera, abstract art or other 'high' cultural art forms. As Sayer (2005) explains, just as much as the unselfconscious and 'natural' swing of the racket of the proficient tennis player, who does not pause to consider the precise mechanics of the action, obscures years of learning and practice, so does the apparently 'natural' inclination to like classical music or the easy familiarity with high cultural institutions such as museums and universities obscure years of investment in time, experience, practice and networking. Bourdieu's analysis thus shows that even where social differences appear to be a product of one's education, taste, talent and lifestyle 'choices', they are in fact better understood in terms of the formative power of social class.

The apparent freedom to construct a particular 'self-identity' or lifestyle looks very different when viewed from this Bourdieusian perspective, which emphasises the extent to which 'free choices', 'taste' and 'cultural preferences' are not only constrained by the level of one's financial resources, but also shaped by the embodied mechanics of social class. Relocating contemporary discourses of identity and lifestyle to a Bourdieusian framework also sheds light on how the notion of 'identity' itself may be used to reproduce and obscure the class relations of contemporary capitalist societies. Television shows such as *How to Look Good Naked* (UK) and *What Not to Wear* (US) which emphasise, on the face of it, the building of self-esteem through the construction of a 'fashionable' personal identity are revealed to be as much about processes of social class distinction, and indeed, the policing and subjugation of the working class, as any project of self-realisation. Hearn (2008) argues that these shows promote a clear logic of 'self-branding', also expressed in the popular management literature of the late 1990s, which she argues is presented as the only viable personal response to the precarity and work/life insecurity of post-Fordist societies. Reviewing three American 'make-over' shows, she demonstrates how a series of underpaid, underemployed and generally addled women are successively mocked, humiliated and then disciplined into cultivating an acceptable and fashionable self-identity, which they are then encouraged to 'sell' in order to achieve success in this precarious world. 'Personal identity' is here reconstituted as a necessary asset which needs to be worked on and marketed in order to achieve some modicum of security and respect. The primary means of achieving this is, of course, through shopping, as participants learn to overcome their 'fear of shopping', and more importantly, *how* to shop, as each show 'emphasizes the fact that shopping *is* work, and, as such, is the key to creating an effective self-brand' (Hearn, 2008: 499). However, unlike Giddens and Beck, Hearn does not view class as a zombie category in her analysis of how people are forced to construct and sell a glossy self-identity in order to survive in a precarious economic context. 'In one particularly upsetting episode', she notes,

> Lisa, a single mother on welfare, has been given the services of a nutritionist to teach her how to eat properly. As the nutritionist goes through Lisa's food cupboards pointing out the poor food choices, Lisa, humiliated and ashamed, explains that she simply cannot afford to buy healthy food. Rather than acknowledge the class issues at work here, however, the nutritionist simply ignores them and takes Lisa out for some 'retail therapy' on the show's dime. (Hearn, 2008: 502)

The value of the concept of identity in policing social class while all the while encouraging increased consumption cannot be underestimated. 'Without exception', writes Hearn, 'the participant claims that she is more confident, has conquered her fears and insecurity, and has come to appreciate shopping as a way to express her new-found sense of self' (2008: 500). If self-branding via consumption is so consistently presented as the answer to the problem of low-paid employment and economic insecurity in contemporary capitalist societies, little wonder, then, that many people pile up credit card debt as a means of realising this 'solution'. Indeed, as noted in Chapter 3, personal indebtedness has increased exponentially in capitalist societies since the 1970s. While a large portion of this is incurred to make up the shortfall in income required to achieve a minimum standard of living, at least some of this personal indebtedness derives from the purchase of non-essential consumer goods deemed so central to creating a marketable self-identity, and indeed, a sense of self-worth. As the highly successful L'Oreal advertising campaigns for cosmetics tell us – it is 'because you're worth it'. While this, on the face of it, emphasises consumer self-esteem, as well as confirmation of status and distinction, it effectively calls up and plays upon deeply entrenched, experiential notions of social class, which as Sayer (2002), drawing on Bourdieu, argues, are bound up with what we think we are worth, and what we perceive others to believe we are worth. These, he posits, are the 'hidden injuries of class', as people struggle with processes of self-justification, combined with recognition of the undeserved advantages *and* disadvantages that social class confers. These struggles find a ready outlet in the concept of personal identity today – 'This is me! *I'm* worth it!' – thereby effectively diverting attention away from the fact that it is social class that remains the primary mechanism for attributions of worth and worthlessness in contemporary capitalist societies.

This notion of a discerning, distinctive and 'tasteful' individual who is encouraged to mark her/his identity via practices of consumption clearly fits well with the social logic of capitalism. As well as construing shopping as necessary work, and individualising – thereby obscuring – social class inequalities, it also complements neoliberal economic understandings of the market as an organic structure that responds to authentic (and rational) consumer choice via the simple mechanisms of supply and demand. This has promoted a presentation of the free market as a deeply attractive and just system, and encouraged a faith in the power of individualistic market forces to shape the good life, specifically through consumption. In this context, the idea of identity as it is embedded in other discourses of lifestyle and personal choice operates as a key tool of capitalist legitimation.

On the whole, then, theorists of identity and lifestyle in the postmodern society, such as Giddens and Beck, focus on a use of identity as a category of practice that is only substantially available to the more highly resourced individuals in contemporary societies, while suggesting that this is the norm for society as a whole. Bourdieu's work thus offers a corrective to the more optimistic accounts of identity and consumption, which see an unlimited potential for creativity and choice in the figure of the consumer, by offering a class-based analysis of what others view as 'identity formation' through consumption. Indeed, as Atkinson notes, Bourdieu repositions the self-identity projects that Giddens and Beck see as universal as very specific, middle class projects, in his identification of 'an emerging "new petite bourgeoisie" whose lifestyle is characterized by a search for identity and self-expression and a refusal to be assigned to a class – all demonstrated in the vast number of practices they undertake, from aikido to yoga, astrology to weaving, dance to transcendental meditation' (Bourdieu, 1984: 354–71, cited in Atkinson, 2007: 362). Far from evidencing the demise of class, therefore, these self-identity projects of the middle classes demonstrate and contribute to its reproduction. Thus – although he does not make this claim himself – Bourdieu's work supports the argument of this chapter, which is that the very notion of identity, as marking a distinctive, possessive individual, arose out of the increased possibilities for marking (and indeed, obscuring) such class distinctions in novel ways via consumption. While Giddens and Beck's analyses are fruitful insofar as they demonstrate how 'identities' – in the sense they intend – are often created through consumption in a context of increasing social and economic precarity, they ultimately fail insofar as they pay insufficient attention to questions of capitalism and social class, which determine who precisely is engaging in such consumption and who, therefore, has the capacity to fashion a 'self-identity' at all.

CONCLUSION

Theorists of consumption tend to claim that the period of mass consumption reviewed in this chapter saw the emergence of a new 'consumer identity', which continues to be the primary identity of people in advanced capitalist societies today. However, those who find themselves adopting these consumerist values, preferences and belief systems – either in the 1950s, 1960s or today – do not expressly understand themselves to have a 'consumer identity', indicating that the term 'consumer identity' operates as a category of analysis, but not as a category of practice. Instead it is the case that people living in 'consumer societies' see themselves as having a distinctive *personal* identity', which they display through their choice of commodities and clothes, lifestyle and 'image'. Thus rather than call into being a new kind of identity – 'a consumer identity' – what this chapter has shown is that these processes of consumption called into being and animated the very idea of 'personal identity' itself, precisely as something that one may own, cultivate and display, significantly through purchase on the market. At the same time, this very idea of personal identity fostered and encouraged a whole new set of consumption practices around the establishment and distinction of particular 'identities', in a way which seems to work directly against the emancipatory, solidaristic potential of the *social* notion of identity. It is not so much that capitalism created new 'identities' as is sometimes claimed, but that it brought issues of difference to the fore, while at the same time turning these issues of difference to its own advantage in encouraging consumption on the basis of the idea of identity, and ultimately of different 'identities'.

Overall, then, we see that 'identity' fits well with the social logic of capitalism by facilitating the mass marketing of the same set of products globally, while at the same time appealing to (and creating) different groups' sense of distinction. In particular it plays an important role in marketing, both by helping firms to sharpen their brand and corporate images, and by helping marketers identify and appeal to target groups. Perhaps most fundamentally though, the idea of identity conforms to the social logic of capitalism in this field by significantly reinforcing the idea that self-definition can only be achieved through consumption. Ultimately, contemporary consumer culture emphasises identity as simply another way in which to extend capitalist production and create new markets, selling homogenisation under the guise of diversity. As Slater explains: 'modern capitalism involves the extension not of real diversity but rather of a single dominating form, the commodity form, which renders all diversity *equivalent*, that is to say all equal as discrete exchangeable or calculable objects' (1997: 115). This was the case in the organised capitalism and mass culture of the 1950s and 1960s, and remains the case in the neoliberal, post-Fordist capitalism that prevails today.

Notes

1. Bourdieu is a special case, since though the term identity was available when he was writing, he did not use it much in his work. I discuss this further later in the chapter.
2. While a search of the magazine archives of *Ebony* threw up 20 entries for 'identity', *Essence* registered 194.
3. The websites for these companies are available at http://www.keenbranding.com/ and http://www.kontrapunkt.dk/.

7

Identity and Capitalism in the Twenty-first Century

INTRODUCTION

The cultural materialist analysis of this book has emphasised that the emergence and consolidation of the idea of identity in western capitalist societies from the 1950s cannot be explained purely via a history of ideas, but must be understood in terms of the social and material contexts of its use. What this analysis shows is that the use of the term identity to express essentialist understandings of individuals and groups only came at a point in history when those very essentialist understandings were significantly challenged or emphasised via their *politicisation* and *commercialisation*. This reveals that there was never any original, essentialist 'identity' that was subsequently made subject to a range of challenges, as many historians of identity claim. Instead, the very idea of identity, and the politics around it, emerged with great force when the previously unremarkable assumption it captures – that there is an essential set of features which define a particular person or group – became important and contentious issues in capitalist societies. In the field of politics, the notion of identity in its social sense emerged when these essentialist understandings about selves and groups were disrupted as groups began to use them to mobilise against a range of social inequalities. In the field of popular culture and everyday life, the notion of identity in its personal sense emerged when the practices of individual distinction and emulation through consumption, once the preserve of the wealthy classes of industrial capitalism, became possible – and encouraged – on a mass scale.

What remains now is to *evaluate* the contemporary salience of identity in capitalist societies. Since the 1990s in particular, the political and academic left has been divided on this question, with the lines of battle clearly drawn by Fraser in her landmark 1995 paper. On the one hand, there is the 'social left', who regard the emphasis on identity as a distraction from the proper politics of class and capitalism, and who believe that identity politics conceal the material bases of oppression and fracture class-based movements (Gitlin, 1994; Fox Piven, 1995; Grossberg, 1996; Žižek, 1997; Scatamburlo-D'Annibale and McLaren, 2003, 2004; Gimenez, 2006). On the other hand, there is the 'cultural left', who view the class analyses of Marxist theory and the labour movement as limited, and in particular, as blind to difference, and who defend the potential of identity politics to bring about increased social and political equality for excluded and disenfranchised groups, as they mobilise around gender, sexuality, 'race' or ethnicity (Butler, 1997; Bramen, 2002; Alcoff, 2006).

Yet it is clear, even to many of these authors who may be associated with one side or other of the debate, that the capitalist economy has not evolved independently of relations of 'race', gender and sexuality, but has worked through and utilised these social divisions. There are a number of important studies which persuasively demonstrate this. For example, D'Emilio (1983) and Evans (1993) have demonstrated how the structuring of 'normal' sexuality has been bound up with the division of labour and the emergence of the heterosexual family unit required and developed by capitalism. Many socialist feminists have explored the co-evolution of capitalism and patriarchy (Delphy, 1980; Przybylowicz, 1989; Walby, 1990; Mies, 1999; Ebert, 2005), demonstrating their necessary co-imbrication in the distinction between productive and reproductive labour on which capitalism trades. Meanwhile Gilroy (2000) and Feitz (2012) have shown how the construction of 'race' and contemporary formations of racism are, and always have been, intimately connected to the commercialising and profit-seeking ambitions of global and corporate capitalism. It is clear that the development and consolidation of capitalism has always been bound up with sexual regulation, family creation and control, female oppression and race-based exploitation. Indeed, this is the theoretical perspective of this volume, as developed in Chapter 3.

The power of capitalism to do this has, moreover, relied on the presentation of the economy as a separate sphere, dissociated from these 'cultural' spaces of gendered domesticity, sexuality and 'race' relations. A distinct problem with the social vs cultural left divide, therefore, is its tendency to direct our attention away from the cross-cutting and co-evolutionary nature of these forms of oppression, by prioritising culture *or* economy, identity *or* class. Indeed, this is the key claim made by Duggan in *The Twilight of Equality* (2003), when she points out that today, as much as in any previous stage of capitalism, '[n]eoliberalism ... organizes material and political life in terms of race, gender and sexuality as well as economic class and nationality' (2003: 3). She therefore insists that '[t]he economy cannot be transparently abstracted from the state or the family, from practices of racial apartheid, gender segmentation, or sexual regulation', because it is in part constituted *through* these relations (2003: xiv). The neoliberal presentation of economics as a 'matter of neutral, technical expertise' is only the most recent way in which capitalism has maintained this fiction that the 'economy' is separate from 'culture'. By failing to recognise this, Duggan argues, and by reproducing these distinctions in the social/cultural left divide, the left has facilitated rather than challenged the workings of capitalism as it generates economic and social inequalities through the formations of 'race', gender and sexuality.

The 'identity politics' of the 1960s and 1970s, Duggan (2003) argues, were focused on questions of *both* economic *and* cultural inequality, though for a range of reasons discussed further in this chapter, they eventually lost their way, becoming balkanised movements with little to offer in the face of a globalising capitalism. However, rather than side with the 'social left' and argue for a rejection of 'identity politics', she claims that we must return to the radical vision sustaining the identity politics of the 1960s and 1970s, which did not separate culture from economy, but recognised the battles against racism, patriarchy and heteronormativity to be structurally intertwined with the battle against capitalism.

This final chapter contributes to this project and vision by evaluating the use of identity in capitalist societies, and its role in either challenging or reproducing the social logic of capitalism, from a broadly egalitarian perspective: that is, one opposed both to the forms of misrecognition, disrespect and cultural imperialism that groups marked as 'other' on account of their 'race', gender, sexuality, impairment, ethnicity or religion have had to endure, *and* to the exploitative relations inherent in capitalism and the forms of serious social, political and economic inequality that this gives rise to. The historical, cultural materialist analysis of this volume has important implications for this evaluative project, for rather than accept the existence of identity or different identi*ties* at face value, it allows us to focus on how this particular and historically recent way of construing personhood and grouphood has been actively used in a range of contexts in capitalist societies. Instead of pitting identity against class, or culture against economy, it allows us to ask: what role can the notion of identity have in either challenging or reproducing the inequalities associated with global neoliberal capitalism, which continue to reflect and manifest ethnic, racial and gender differences? And does the idea of identity hold any political utility for egalitarians who are interested in both recognition and redistribution? While this analysis focuses exclusively on the category of identity, I hope that what I have to say here will serve to illuminate, and in part resolve, some of the concerns at stake in the more general 'rift' between culture and economy, recognition and redistribution, that has characterised the social 'versus' cultural left split.

Before I begin, it is worth pointing out that as I write this in 2014, the world is still in the throes of a major capitalist economic crisis, with most states worldwide experiencing recession, 'austerity' programmes and growing economic inequality. Indeed, economic inequality under capitalism is now, after a long hiatus, firmly back on the political and popular agenda worldwide. The visibility and popular impact of the global 'Occupy' movement in 2011, which drew critical attention to the unequal wealth share held by 'the 1%' (Chomsky, 2012), and the unprecedented success of Piketty's bestseller *Capital in the Twenty-First Century* (2014), which statistically proves deeply unequal wealth concentration to be an endemic feature of capitalism, are both testament to this. In this context, a focus on identity over class is even more easily construed as misguided, and the 'identity struggles' of previous decades more readily viewed as political luxuries – not just by the social left, but by the mainstream and the right too. Yet even before this economic downturn and attendant reordering of political priorities, the more activist or visible forms of identity politics had already diminished, and some theorists were starting to claim that we lived in a 'post-identity' era (Lloyd, 2005; Millner, 2005). However, despite some waning of political and academic attention, issues and questions of identity nonetheless continue to explicitly animate the politics and discourses of multiculturalism, rights claims, legal instruments and a wide variety of group-based politics. In addition, it must be noted that it is in the *aftermath* of the supposed postmodern 'shattering' of the notion of identity (Chapters 5 and 6) that widespread use of and reference to the word identity has really taken off in popular culture and the arts, in the psychological and self-help industries, and across the corporate world of niche marketing, mass advertising and brand loyalty. The great majority of these non-academic uses of identity do *not* correspond to the 'postmodern' iterations of the concept, but instead to those 'essentialist' understandings they are imagined to have super-seded: specifically, to cultural and ethnic 'identities', to notions of individual and personal identity, and even to biological accounts of identity as 'human nature'. Given the continued widespread popular, commercial and political usage of the category of identity, including its continued use to refer to the social categories of gender, sexuality, race and ethnicity that persist as serious sources of inequality in contemporary capitalist societies, it remains an impor-tant project to assess the political value of the category of identity in neoliberal societies. Indeed, to suggest otherwise would be to contribute to that social vs cultural left rift that it is the aim of this chapter to overcome.

I begin by evaluating the use of the idea of identity, firstly, in contexts of consumption, and then secondly, in more overtly political contexts, in both cases assessing the potential for identity to be used against the social logic of capitalism, either challenging the motivations and pressures of the capi-talist system, or remedying its unequal outcomes. While the personal sense of identity is more closely associated with contexts of consumption, and the social sense more closely associated with political contexts, these two senses interact in complex ways, with the result that there is often slippage between the two senses, complicated by the fact that people tend simply to refer to 'identity', without always specifying the particular sense in which they intend it. This, of course, is precisely what makes identity a contemporary keyword, and the source of both its complexity and productive power. This analysis moves us from an examination of concrete uses of 'identity' in historical contexts that has been the subject of this book thus far, to more general claims about the value of identity in challenging or reproducing capitalist inequalities. Following this, I attempt an overall historicisation of the political uses and values of the idea of identity in the evolution of capitalism, and specifically in terms of the transition from organised to neoliberal capitalism. I conclude with some suggestions for how 'identity' might be incorporated into a broad struggle for equality today.

IDENTITY AND ANTI-CAPITALIST RESISTANCE IN THE CONSUMER SOCIETY

Can the idea of identity be put to use in anti-capitalist ways in contexts of consumption, or must it conform to the social and abstract logic of capitalism? Chapter 6 demonstrated how the very use of the personal sense of 'identity' as a way of conceptualising, ordering and regulating consumption is in part generated by, and compatible with, the social logic of capitalism. Following this line of argument to its logical conclusion would seem to entail that the idea of identity is not just *compatible* with capitalism, but more, *functional* to it, thereby leading to a deeply pessimistic assessment of its potential use in consumerist contexts in any way that would generate resistance to capitalism. Viewing this relationship from a cultural materialist perspective, however, allows us to attribute at least some agency to those individuals who deploy the idea of identity in contexts of consumption. And while it is true, as the Frankfurt School have argued, that the creation and realisation of various 'needs' and desires through consumption is both ideologically and economically conducive to the maintenance and perpetuation of capitalism, we do not need to view all needs and desires realised through consumption as wholly and *only* functional to capitalism. Here it is worth distinguishing between the needs and aspirations created by capitalist entrepreneurs, and those other needs and aspirations that arise quite independently of the capitalist system. Arguably processes of self- and other-identification are part of the human condition, and operate within a nexus of need and aspiration that pre-exists and is in many ways independent of capitalism. This is why the 'social logic of capitalism' is a useful analytical tool here, as it does not require us to claim that all social needs are functional to and created by the capitalist system, but allows us to see instead how older or independent needs and aspirations can be effectively *capitalised*, as people are encouraged to behave in ways that promote the logic of capital accumulation. On this understanding, I suggest that what we have seen in the linking of age-old processes of self- and group-identification and distinction to practices of consumption via the social logic of capitalism is precisely the alignment of a general human need to a specifically capitalist one, and its articulation in the notion of identity.

This more nuanced position suggests then that there may be some possibility for the idea of identity to be deployed *against* the social logic of capitalism in contexts of consumption. In the first place, there is evidence that the notion of identity is explicitly relevant to some anti-consumerist activists, as can be seen from several online fora and sites which discuss attempts to build an 'authentic anti-consumerist identity' as part of their projects of challenging destructive, alienating and environmentally damaging forms of capitalism (Kozinets, 2002; cf. Chatterton, 2010; Identity Campaigning, 2010). Indeed, as Callinicos suggests, 'the strongest motivation to anti-capitalist resistance today is probably the relentless spread of commodification, both because of its deadening spiritual consequences … and because of its destructive effects on the physical and social worlds alike' (2006: 72). However, the value of identity in these projects appears minimal. The 'identity campaigning' project of the World Wildlife Federation (WWF) has been criticised for attempting to change the 'basic psychology' of its audience, 're-programming people's values away from consumption, status and selfish desires and towards collective awareness and a closer relationship with our place in the natural world', in a way which implies 'there's something wrong with their personality'.[1] Indeed, this 'identity campaigning' strategy of the WWF has since been closed, which may be evidence of the weakness of an approach which relies on the personal sense of identity in order to achieve anti-capitalist change. More effective projects of anti-consumption are primarily bound up with the political projects of anarchism, eco-feminism and 'sustainable living', which reject capitalist consumption as part of a larger repudiation of the capitalist system as a whole. But these groups do not, it seems, require the idea of identity (whether personal *or* social) in order to do so, as there is little evidence of attention to 'identity' per se in these projects.

There is a second form of identity-based 'anti-capitalist' practices that is probably more widespread. This involves the construction of an 'identity' through consumption in a manner which is perceived to use the commodities of the capitalist system against it (Hall and Jefferson, 1976; Hebdige, 1979; De Certeau, 1984). Examples may include 'punks', who fashion a personal identity that presents an affront to the conservative mores of an authoritarian capitalist state, in the process creating a valuable sense of solidarity and shared purpose amongst excluded white youths in British society (Hebdige, 1979), and anarchist or anti-capitalist groups who create an active online presence or 'identity' on Facebook, using it to build group solidarity and ultimately organise various anti-capitalist campaigns. In both cases, successful politicisation arguably depends on a shift from a personal to a more social sense of identity. Furthermore, while both sets of identity-based activities may present a challenge to a capitalist way of life, or offer counter-hegemonic perspectives which challenge capitalist values, these practices can do little to subvert the systemic logic of consumption-led production. After all, there is a sense in which capitalist producers do not care what you do with products you buy, so long as you buy them. Thus you may use your computer to read online anti-capitalist or anarchist manifestos, or wear safety pins to signify a 'Punk' attitude to the capitalist state, without making much of a dent in the logic of a system which depends upon the sale of computers and safety pins. The asymmetry of power between deliberate counter-hegemonic identity construction through consumption and the prevailing logic of economic activity remains vast. This is one of the main challenges facing most anti-capitalist groups today – the degree to which the social logic of capitalism has permeated their everyday lives, including some of the resources they mobilise to engage in resistance.

But there is another problem here too, which relates directly to the very use of the category of identity as a means of constructing an anti-capitalist stance. This concerns the manner in which that anti-capitalist or anti-consumerist 'identity' itself becomes commodified, and then sold back to the original target groups, as well as to other vaguely disaffected consumers. Hebdige (1979), of course, noted this in his original analysis of the punk identity. Indeed, punk is now, more than anything else, a 'rebel' fashion statement, to the extent that *The Urban Dictionary* has an entry for 'fashion punks' ('also known as fucktards, fashion punks are individuals that exploit the subculture known as the punk movement in the name of fashion, thereby desecrating all that the punks stand for'). This tendency is also apparent in a new proliferation of 'fair trade' or 'ethical' consumption, which, as Binkley (2008) observes, is regularly promoted via the construction of an explicitly named 'anti-consumerist identity'. As he further observes, 'consumers today are increasingly asked to look beyond consumer capitalism's drab seriality and moral vacuity, to seek deeper meanings to wider life problems in a range of niche-marketed products bearing the stamp of rebellion, authenticity, simplicity, economic justice and ecological responsibility' (2008: 599). This creation of an 'anti-consumer identity' of course creates markets for the products consumed, as the savvy, ethical consumer defines herself through her (almost unavoidably conspicuous) consumption of fair trade, organic, 'green', cruelty-free or otherwise 'ethical' produce, thereby further commodifying not alone her sense of self and belonging, but this (pseudo) political stance too. I am struck here particularly by the recent proliferation of woven or 'flax' shopping bags, emblazoned with the script, 'I ♥ fair trade'. This, generally, is the thesis of McGuigan's *Cool Capitalism*, which refers to 'the incorporation of disaffection into capitalism itself' via the logic of 'cool' (2009: 1).

'Cool capitalism' assuages disaffection with, and even resistance to, the capitalist system by repackaging it as something to emulate, admire and, ultimately, ironically consume, thereby ensuring further ideological integration into a capitalist way of life. The 'solutions', as much as the problems, are to be found in practices of capitalist consumption.

Much anti-capitalist resistance today, however, does not take the form of constructing an 'anti-consumerist identity', but rather of rejecting global brands and their iconic 'brand identities' (see Chapter 6). Consumers have increasingly grasped -- thanks in no small part to the huge popularity and accessibility of Naomi Klein's *No Logo* (2002) -- the exploitative link between the consumer and the producer that is mystified in the form of the commodity itself -- what Marx referred to as 'commodity fetishism'. Opposition has taken the form of boycotts, and putting pressure on corporations over sweat-shop production that pays workers a tiny fraction of the profits accrued through the sale of the final, branded product. This form of resistance is made difficult by the tendency of these global corporations to outsource production, to the extent that their final product is the brand itself, leaving them (ostensibly) without responsibility for the manner in which the commodities they 'buy' from other producers and then subsequently 'brand' are manufactured, or for the conditions of the workers who make them. The outsourcing of the manufacture of the Apple iPhone to the Foxconn plant in China, where a number of serious labour law violations are alleged to have taken place, is the most recent, high-profile example of these practices. Whether the international media and campaigning attention to this case will make any dent in the very high volume of iPhone sales remains to be seen. Nonetheless, resistance to brand identities, where it does occur, may place serious pressures on corporations, and indeed, on the machinations of global neoliberal capitalism itself. This form of anti-capitalist resistance is thus potentially the most effective of all strands considered here -- crucially, however, it takes the form of resistance to the very *use* of identity in a consumerist context, rather than its embrace.

IDENTITY AND ANTI-CAPITALIST RESISTANCE IN POLITICS

Can the idea of identity be put to work in more directly anti-capitalist ways in the field of politics, where it is more likely to be deployed in its social rather than personal sense? A key claim of the so-called social left is that 'identity politics' cannot be said in any sense to be anti-capitalist, as they challenge neither the forms of economic inequality capitalism generates, nor the exploitative social relations at the heart of the system. There is a spectrum of views here. According to theorists associated with the cultural left, the social left typically view identity politics as a form of 'cultural politics' (Bernstein, 2005: 49), and the issues they address as 'merely cultural' (Butler, 1997). Gitlin exemplifies this position well when he witheringly remarks that 'fights over appropriate language, over symbolic representation …, over affirmative action and musical styles and shares of the public space are, to them, the core of "politics". *Just as these cohorts have their clothes and their music, they have "their politics" – the principal, even the only form of "politics" they know'* (1994: 154). Perceptions like these are argued to have led many on the social left to view identity politics as 'not real politics but a silly fad, concerned with surfaces rather than depths, with gestures rather than principles' (Bramen, 2002: 2).

Others on the social left concede that while identity politics have secured certain group-based rights, these largely civil and political rights are compatible with a wide range of social and economic inequalities and with the successful functioning of capitalism. Thus identity politics are accused 'of providing vehicles for the amelioration of grievances within the existing system' (Aronowitz, 1995: 117), and as representing, at best, 'little more than a demand … for inclusion into the metropolitan salons of bourgeois representation' (Scatamburlo-D'Annibale and McLaren, 2003: 154). More seriously still, identity politics are argued to preserve capitalism from critique (Brown, 1995). Scatamburlo-D'Annibale and McLaren hence claim that much of the social theory and politics organised around questions of identity and difference are 'either unwilling or ill equipped to grapple with the disturbing social conditions engendered by the globalization of capital' (2003: 150), while Žižek (1997) directly links the cultural emphasis on difference and identity to the failure to act politically against capitalism:

> It is effectively as if, since the horizon of social imagination no longer allows us to entertain the idea of an eventual demise of capitalism – since, as we might put it, everybody silently accepts that capitalism is here to stay – critical energy has found a substitute outlet in fighting for cultural differences which leave the basic homogeneity of the capitalist world-system intact. So we are fighting our PC battles for the rights of ethnic minorities, of gays and lesbians, of different life-styles, and so on, while capitalism pursues its triumphant march – and today's critical theory, in the guise of 'cultural studies' is doing the ultimate service to the unrestrained development of capitalism by actively participating in the ideological effort to render its massive presence invisible. (1997: 46)

Meanwhile, Žižek continues, the relentlessly growing numbers of the homeless, the ghettoised and the permanently unemployed – 'the growing and permanent reminder of how the immanent logic of late capitalism works' – are excluded from the new 'rainbow coalition' of purportedly progressive political struggles. In a similar vein, Scatamburlo-D'Annibale and McLaren argue that identity

politics have ultimately functioned to 'displac[e] a politics grounded in the
mobilization of forces against the material sources of political and economic
marginalization' (2003: 153).

Is this pessimism justified? I want to focus here on those movements which
explicitly organise their activism around the concept of identity, and not on
'race', gender or sexual politics more generally, though given the recent tendency for these social categories to be referred to as 'identities' themselves,
these two are often conflated. I contend that such forms of identity politics, so
defined, *must* be of an anti-capitalist character insofar as some of the inequalities they challenge are inequalities generated by capitalism. That is, to the extent
that capitalism plays a role in creating the inequalities structured by gender,
'race' and so on, then the 'identity politics' which challenge these are *ipso facto*
anti-capitalist. 'Identity politics' in this respect do not imply that the oppression experienced by the group in question is not *connected* to capitalism, only
that how it emerged and how it is experienced, patterned and at least partially
structured is in terms of particular 'identities'.

The capacity for identity politics, so defined, to directly challenge the injus-
tices of the capitalist system is in many respects self-evident when we look at
the successes of these movements. For example, in her work on identity and difference politics, Young (1990, 1997, 2002) provides empirical evidence to show
that these politics can and do effectively challenge economic inequalities. Young
criticises Fraser's opposition of the cultural to the social left for 'exaggerat[ing]
the degree to which a politics of recognition retreats from economic struggles',
asserting that she sees 'little evidence … that feminist or anti-racist activists, as
a rule, ignore issues of economic disadvantage and control' (1997: 148). Young
argues that the theoretical dichotomisation of culture and economy is at the
root of this analytical distortion, claiming that this leads Fraser 'to misrepresent
feminist, anti-racist and gay liberation movements as calling for recognition as
an end in itself, when they are better understood as conceiving cultural recognition as a means to economic and political justice' (Young, 1997: 148). A
similar point is made by Walby (2001: 117), who argues that recent claims that
identity or recognition politics have pushed demands for equality, economic
justice and redistribution off the agenda are in fact 'empirically incorrect'.
Walby agrees that there has been a visible shift in the surface configurations
of contemporary politics, specifically concerning the way in which claims for
equality are made, and who is imagined to be the proper subject of such claims,
but denies that identity or recognition politics have either 'replaced' class politics, or undermined their aims. She also provides evidence to show that the
new forms of politics associated with the recognition of different identities have
actually provided *alternative* means of addressing economic inequalities. Thus
Walby concludes that the politics of recognition associated with identity politics should properly be seen as the 'handmaiden' of a politics of redistribution.
Young finishes with a similar point, arguing that 'for most social movements,

what Fraser calls "recognition" is a means to the economic and social equal-ity and freedom that she brings under the category of redistribution' (Young, 1997: 152). Duggan (2003) also highlights the real successes of the identity politics of the 1960s and 1970s in particular, pointing to the effective downward redistribution of resources they achieved – in fact, she claims, the vigour of the backlash against these politics should be properly interpreted as evidence of the very real threat they were seen to pose to the economic order.

However, while identity politics can demonstrably challenge the unequal distribution of resources and power along group-based lines that are produced and maintained within capitalist societies, to what extent can they be said to challenge the exploitative relations at the heart of the system? Or to put it in the terms of this volume, can *these* identity-based movements challenge the logic of the capitalist system, in either its abstract or social form?

As we saw in Chapter 5, it has been argued that many of these identity struggles – and specifically what I have referred to as the 'defensive' identity politics around cultural identities – are in fact *directly* anti-capitalist, as they are generated specifically as forms of resistance to capitalist globalisation, and the impact of this on people's valued and customary ways of life. Castells's central hypothesis is that 'in the network society, project identity, if it develops at all, grows from communal resistance. This is the actual meaning of the new primacy of identity politics in the network society' (2004: 11–12). Thus, for Castells, 'identity politics' are the *only* politically valid response to the inequali-ties thrown up by global capitalism.

However, for this claim to be valid, we need to be sure that the category of identity plays an active role in these movements, rather than simply function-ing as a category of analysis in his account. On these grounds, we can rule out several of his case studies very quickly. In particular, there is no evidence of the Zapatistas themselves discussing the 'new Indian identity' Castells attributes to them (for example, none of the six 'Declarations of the Lancandon Jungle'[2] issued by the Zapatista Army of National Liberation between 1995 and 2002 uses the term even once), and there is scant evidence that idea of identity is deployed by Green movement activists in the way that Castells suggests it is. In short, the *idea* of identity seems to do little or no political work in these two movements. Thus while the Zapatistas and the Green movement were sym-bolically significant in the anti-capitalist movement of the 1990s, contrary to what Castells claims, this cannot be taken as evidence of the 'power of identity'. However, some of the other movements Castells documents – including the women's movement and race-based movements – have been already shown to use the idea of identity to challenge the economic inequality of capitalist socie-ties, with at least some successes. But can they be in any way said to use the idea of identity to challenge the social or abstract logic of capitalism?

What I want to suggest is that while identity politics can and do promote economic redistribution, and thus *indirectly* challenge capitalism by targeting its unequal outcomes, they are less likely to challenge either the abstract or social logic of capitalism itself. In making this claim, it is useful to distinguish between class politics and redistributive politics more generally. The important point of difference is that class politics explicitly and by definition counter and oppose the social logic of capitalism, as they arise out of, and in opposition to, the social divisions created directly by capitalism. A key strength of a Marxist class analysis is thus the recognition that people are placed *relationally* to one another on economic and political grounds in a capitalist system. 'Class', then, is pre-cisely this relation between groups of people, so that some classes profit at the expense of others. And it is these relations, which are intrinsic to the operation of capitalism, that are challenged in class politics. In distinction to this, identity politics – by which I mean politics organised specifically around the notion of identity as opposed to feminist or anti-racist struggles more generally – tend to use a categorical understanding of oppression, defining it in terms of the powerlessness and exclusions experienced by particular groups. While many contemporary theorists of identity have attempted to conceptualise identity relationally (McCall, 2005), the notion of identity itself, as I have explained it, pulls against this relational understanding towards a more categorical under-standing, as we see clearly in the continued common hypostatisation of social groups *as* 'identities'. Thus while an explicit 'identity politics' may improve the economic position of a particular group defined in terms of its identity, or may resist the incorporation of that group into a capitalist way of life, it seems unlikely to directly challenge the horizontal cleavages created by the exploita-tive class relations of capitalism.

What does this imply for the recent tendency to conceptualise class as itself an identity? Could this offer a more direct way for the category of identity to be used to challenge the exploitative relations at the heart of the capitalist system? Indeed, there has been, in recent decades, an increasing social scien-tific tendency to consider different social class positions as different 'identities', and to view class relations through an identitarian lens (Bottero, 2004). The conceptualisation of social class as an identity certainly has some advantages: it generates important insights into the lived reality and personally damaging effects of social class on individuals; it emphasises the subjective aspects of social class formation; and it offers a means of naming a class position in a potentially empowering way for the individuals and groups concerned. However, it is also problematic for how it encourages a shift from a relational to a categori-cal understanding of class. The central Marxist insights concerning the social relations of capitalism are lost, as capitalism as a system is understood apart from those very social relations that constitute it, and social classes become simply dif-ferent groups within capitalism. As a result, challenging 'class inequality' comes to be about challenging 'classism' – that is, the notion that it is wrong to *discrimi-nate* on the basis of social class – rather than objecting to the very existence of classes. As Gimenez (2006: 431) puts it, 'Class … is not just another identity, another "subject position"; it is a social relation among people mediated by their relationship to the means of production.' And as Eagleton reminds us, it is not that 'some individuals manifest certain characteristics known as "class" which then results in their oppression; on the contrary, to be a member of a social class just *is* to be oppressed' (1998: 289). Once 'prejudice' towards different classes rather than class relations themselves is perceived to be the central problem, this can do precious little to challenge either the social logic of capitalism, as it accommodates people to a capitalist way of life, or the abstract logic of the system itself, which is based on the very existence of social classes.

   None of this is to suggest that class itself does not operate in racialised and gendered ways, and on these grounds, many have argued that we must rethink traditional categories of class themselves (cf. Gilroy, 1987; Aronowitz, 1992; Skeggs, 1997; Reay, 1998; Arnold, 2008). However, any rethinking of the category of class must retain its relational character, and thus rethinking class *as* an identity is not a useful way to proceed. On the whole, then, while the social left are wrong to claim that identity politics cannot promote greater economic equality, they are right to be concerned by the displacement of class politics by identity politics, or their reconstitution in identitarian form. The fact that identity politics can achieve economic redistribution does not mean that they can be regarded as doing the same job as class politics, particularly in terms of challenging the social or abstract logic of capitalism directly. For those who are concerned to challenge the capitalist system itself, much of value is lost with the removal of class from the analytic and political arsenal, or its reconceptualisation through an identitarian frame.

IDENTITY IN THE EVOLUTION OF CAPITALISM: THE CONSOLIDATION OF NEOLIBERALISM

To fully understand and evaluate the relation of identity to capitalism, we must recontextualise the intertwined use of the personal and social senses of identity in the history of their deployment in capitalist societies, from their early uses in the period of 'organised capitalism', up to and including their current uses in the neoliberal capitalist societies of today. Against accounts which trace the transition to neoliberalism in economic and class-based terms only, Duggan (2003: xii) argues that we may distinguish five successive phases in the 'construction of neoliberal hegemony' from the 1950s, each of which 'relied on identity and cultural politics'. She specifies that although neoliberalism developed primarily in the US, these patterns were nonetheless reproduced to different degrees in the 'secondary' development of neoliberalism across Western Europe. According to Duggan, this construction of a neoliberal hegemony, which accompanied and facilitated the structural economic shifts, depended crucially on both overt

attacks on progressive identity politics (and not only class politics, as is more
generally claimed), and on a concerted and increasingly successful effort to
present the economy as <u>detached from</u> relations of gender, race and sexuality.
While Duggan does not explicitly focus on the idea of identity as I do, her
framework nonetheless provides a useful basis for exploring how the idea of
identity, and not just the politics activated in its name, was deployed by both
progressive and regressive actors in the transition to and consolidation of neoliberal capitalism, and for evaluating the overall egalitarian potential of the idea
of identity in capitalist societies.

According to Duggan, the first phase in the construction of a neoliberal
hegemony occurred in the 1950s and 1960s, and was characterised by 'attacks
on the New Deal coalition, on progressive unionism, and on popular front
political culture and progressive redistributive internationalism' (2003: xii). This
was still the period of Fordist–Keynesian capitalism, but Duggan nonetheless
identifies some early attempts to dismantle the accord between labour and
capitalism that had characterised this period. It is interesting that while many
view this period in terms of a peaceful and socially beneficial deal between
capital and labour, Marxist commentators, as we saw, view this less positively as
a clear deradicalisation of unions, and the incorporation of the labour movement into the management of capitalism. From this perspective, the 'accord' did
not so much restrain and regulate capitalism as lay the way for the neoliberal
hegemony that was to come. Indeed, Chapter 5 identified a clear shift in political discourse at this time, and an increased motivation to name grievances in
non-class terms. Furthermore, and relatedly, in this period the social logic of
capitalism began to work in a way that made people less likely to view capitalism as a problem, and more likely to view it as capable of delivering on its
promises of opportunity, success and wealth for all. This period then provided
the initial context for the emergence of the idea of identity, as it came to underpin both progressive politics and practices of consumption from the 1960s in
particular. Indeed, from this point on, the use of identity in politics exploded,
and a large number of radical movements emerged which used the idea of
identity to challenge the oppression experienced by women, African Americans
and gay and lesbian people. While the roughly coterminous suppression of class
politics and emergence of identity politics were both consequences of the same
set of social forces that animated this first phase of the construction of a neoliberal hegemony, it would be a mistake nonetheless to accept the Marxist view
that these identity politics were, by definition, part of a hegemonic capitalist
project. As this book has shown, 'identity politics' had definite progressive and
redistributive successes in this period.

The second phase identified by Duggan in the construction of a neoliberal
hegemony was constituted by 'attacks on downwardly redistributive social movements, especially the Civil Rights and Black Power movements, but including
feminism, lesbian and gay liberation, and countercultural mobilizations during

the 1960s and 1970s' (2003: xii). It was precisely the power of these movements to challenge the capitalist social and economic order that prompted this virulent response – and construction of an alternative – from the political and business elites of the time. The struggles against which these elites reacted cannot be characterised as prioritising culture over economy, as they have since been construed by the social left. As this book has shown, and as Duggan also points out, '[g]ay liberation newspapers included anti-imperialist manifestoes and analyses of the racist legal and prison system. Black feminists set out to track the interrelations of capitalism, patriarchy, and racism' (2003: xvii). Indeed, she continues, 'the overall emphasis that connected the progressive-left social movements was the pressure to level hierarchies and redistribute down – redistribute money, political power, cultural capital, pleasure and freedom' (2003: xvii). In fact, it was precisely their capacity to link culture and economy in such a radical way that invited the sustained and damaging attack they came to endure in this period.

However, it was not just the external attacks on these radical movements that led to their undoing, but also, arguably, something internal to these politics themselves. Duggan notes that although these different movements did not all share the same aim or goal, they shared some similar practices, policies, concepts and languages. In particular, as I have shown, they all shared and were animated by the concept of identity. As demonstrated, the use of the idea of identity by these movements was not happenstance or a 'mistake', but in place for all the political and social reasons that rendered sensible the use of the term in the first place (see Chapter 4). But the crystallising of these movements around the concept of identity would eventually undermine them. This was in part due to the predominance of the personal sense of identity as it became increasingly implicated in the growth of mass consumption, and thus compatible with capitalism. The fact that people spoke mainly of 'identity' as a single concept, not explicitly differentiating between the personal and more radical social senses of the term, made it more likely that such a slippage would occur.

But this is not simply a question of conceptual slippage. Rather, the contexts in which identity evolved and came to be used (that is, contexts of consumption and group-based politics) already had an elective affinity. As Chasin (2000) has observed, different groups have been targeted as consumers at precisely the point in time that they have started to successfully win political campaigns for group rights. Thus, she notes, women were targeted as consumers in an unprecedented way at the same time as they were granted the constitutional right to vote in the US; African Americans were targeted as consumers in the immediate aftermath of the successful 1960s civil rights campaigns; and, most recently, gay and lesbian people have been targeted as consumers just as they have engaged in a series of successful anti-discrimination and equal rights initiatives. 'Why would there be such a pattern?' she asks. 'Why would social groups that had worked so long for enfranchisement become ripe for niche marketing in their moments of apparent success?' (2000: xvi).

Focusing on the intersection between the movement constituencies and target markets for the gay and lesbian community, Chasin tells us that the 'short answer' to her question is that 'the capitalist market makes possible, but also constrains, social movements whose central objective is the expansion of individual political rights' (2000: xvii). This is because market mechanisms allow for the consolidation of a group identity, 'which can then form the basis of a political movement for equal rights equal to other citizens' (2000: 24). However, Chasin contends, this very acquisition of rights furthermore promotes the constitution of that group as a niche market, which in turn acts to deflect and defuse the group's politics. 'The corollary effect is that consumption becomes a form of political participation, perhaps supplanting other, more direct, models of participation' (2000: 24).

What the argument of this book suggests is that the conceptualisation of individuals and groups in terms of the idiom of identity can only reinforce and amplify the pattern Chasin identifies. That is, from the 1950s and 1960s onwards, the idea of identity came to both express *and* consolidate the already existing affinity between rights-based social movements and group-based consumer markets, as it facilitated both the realisation of group rights and the promotion of individual and group-based forms of consumption. Crucially, however, in a context where the social logic of capitalism is dominant, and where the social and personal senses of identity are not fully separable, the individualist, consumerist meanings associated with the personal sense are likely to take precedence over, and indeed shape, the collectivist, progressive meanings associated with the social sense. The very use of the idea of identity in group politics and patterns of group-based consumption thus further strengthens the tendency, noted by Chasin, for market forces to win out over the progressive potential of particularist group politics. Together, these complex tensions between the marketisation and politicisation of group formations in capitalist societies, intensified by the use of 'identity' to express both, and the sustained attack on identity politics from various establishment and right-wing political forces, would ultimately lead to the demise of identity politics in their most progressive formulations.

The third phase identified by Duggan is characterised by 'pro-business activism during the 1970s, as U.S.-based corporations faced global competition and falling profit rates, previously conflicting big and small business interests increasingly converged, and business groups organized to redistribute resources upward' (2003: xii). The further consolidation of this pro-business alliance under Reagan and Thatcher in the 1980s gave rise to the set of 'resolutions' and capitalist restructurings that we now know as 'neoliberalism'. But this was not just an economic project. Rather, as Duggan emphasises, it 'was built on, and further developed, a wide-ranging political and cultural project – the reconstruction of the everyday life of capitalism, in ways supportive of upward redistribution of a range of resources, and tolerant of widening inequalities of many kinds'

(2003: xi). In this context of widening inequality, the radical social movements began to disintegrate under growing economic pressures and increased imperatives for fundraising, and where they remained, to concentrate their efforts on the lobbying and litigations strategies that were most likely to succeed in such a restrictive climate. In effect, writes Duggan, 'large portions of the organized efforts of social movements succumbed to liberalism's paltry promise – engage the language and institutional games of established liberal contests and achieve equality' (Duggan, 2003: xviii). Many involved in these movements recognised the limits of the kind of equality on offer – that is, 'equality disarticulated from material life and class politics, to be won by definable "minority" groups, one at a time' (2003: xviii) – yet were pushed into such a position as they had few other feasible options. Relatedly, the very concept of identity employed by these movements began to shift under these pressures, as it came to be increasingly used in the context of legislative and court-room battles. The social sense of identity became increasingly subjugated to the personal sense, as the latter remained more compatible with the political and cultural structural shifts in capitalist societies. ④

This brings us to Duggan's fourth phase, the 'domestically focused "culture wars" attacks on public institutions and spaces for democratic public life, in alliances with religious moralists and racial nationalists, during the 1980s and 1990s' (2003: xii). One of the notable successes of the identity politics of the 1960s and 1970s had been to legitimise the study of 'race', gender and sexuality through their institutionalisation in the various 'women's studies', 'queer studies' and 'African American' and other 'ethnic minority' studies programmes that sprang up across university campuses in the West. By the 1980s, as a result of the increased privatisation that had shrunk the spaces available for democratic debate and political or cultural expression, these campuses became one of the few spaces in which radical political debate and theorisation was possible. As such, they also became the focus of a sustained attack from both the 'mainstream', and elements of the left itself. Combining discourses of moral and fiscal responsibility, the mainstream attacked the 'politically correct' battles of these academic programmes for presenting an affront to the moral sensibilities of the heterosexual two-parent family unit, and being a waste of 'tax-payers' money'. Meanwhile, elements of the left began to dissociate themselves from, and more, attack these programmes, and the identity politics they were perceived to have developed from, for ironically, 'fragmenting the left' (Gitlin, 1994). Although it was arguably the construction of a neoliberal hegemony via overt attacks on identity politics and the political spaces in which they had operated that had forced the retrenchment of the more radical forms of identity politics into university departments, elements of the left now began to blame these proponents of identity politics for the position in which they found themselves, and further, for splintering the left into 'distinct, mutually exclusive groups without a common ground so that potential alliances are thwarted in the name of

special interests' (Bramen, 2002: 1). It was only at this point in time that the
'"economics/culture" split ... appear[ed] as a major and sustained divide in
U.S. progressive-left politics' (Duggan, 2003: xvii), and indeed, that the 'social vs
cultural left' split began to manifest.

From the perspective of this book, however, it is not the supposed 'turn' to
questions of identity and culture that was the problem, as the newly consolidat-
ing social left began to suppose, but rather the Left's acceptance of this whole
way of looking at things. As argued, the distinction between economic and
cultural issues has worked to the advantage of the right, as the entire neoliberal project relies on normalising and entrenching distinctions of gender, 'race'
and sexuality in order to achieve and cement its goals of privatisation, profit-
creation and the upward channelling of wealth. Although the social left largely
recognise that capitalism exploits those very forms of difference challenged by
identity politics, they failed at this point and since then to fully recognise the
counterpart: that identity politics – in their more radical forms – draw attention
precisely to the inseparability of culture and economy that a class politics alone
risks ignoring.

We have now arrived at the final phase of Duggan's historicisation of the
construction of a neoliberal hegemony, a period of '"multicultural", neoliberal "equality" politics – a stripped-down, nonredistributive form of "equality"
designed for global consumption during the twenty-first century, and compatible with continued upward redistribution of resources' (2003: xii). While a
range of economic and political forces have led to this situation, we cannot fully
understand its development without a proper appreciation of the progressive
and regressive uses of the idea of identity in getting here. As we have seen, these
include: the series of attacks on those identity politics that promoted recognition
as well as redistribution, as they recognised the intertwined nature of cultural and
economic oppression; the problems inherent in deployment of the very category
of identity in these politics, as the more radical 'social' sense became gradually
undermined by the more individualist 'personal' sense in a context of capitalist
consumerism; and the reaction – and indeed, *self*-creation – of the 'social left',
which reinforced rather than challenged the culture/economy and identity/
class divide.

As a consequence of these factors, we see now that certain contemporary
forms of identity politics positively reinforce elements of neoliberal ideology,
especially where they converge in their promotion of cultural relativism, freedom of expression and the celebration of difference and diversity (Kauffman,
1991; Ray and Sayer, 1999; Scatamburlo-D'Annibale and McLaren, 2003). As
a result, there is no contradiction in supporting a multicultural identity politics
and economic conservatism at the same time. As Shivani writes, 'No matter
how retrograde your views on class and economics, no matter how cravenly
you abandon the working class, you can always fall back on your multiculturalist
credentials to legitimate your discourse as liberal' (Shivani, 2002: unpaginated).

We find evidence of this in the fact that neoliberals are quite happy to support anti-discrimination measures and to promote policies that would increase the racial and gender balance 'at the top', so long as the economic gap between those 'at the top' and everyone else is left untouched. This is why, argues Walter Benn Michaels,

> the real (albeit very partial) victories over racism and sexism represented by the Clinton and Obama campaigns are not victories *over* neoliberalism but victories *for* neoliberalism: victories for a commitment to justice that has no argument with inequality as long as its beneficiaries are as racially and sexually diverse as its victims. (2008: 34)

A parallel development is the emergence of what might be called a 'libertarian' identity politics, which is completely divorced from the notion of social identity on which the progressive identity politics of the 1960s and 1970s were founded. This form of 'identity politics' fixates on individual rights and rejects an 'interventionist state' it accuses of interfering with the personal freedoms of sovereign individuals. Chasin also notes the small but growing number of 'gay libertarians' who reject collective activism, 'quotas' and group-based associations in favour of individual rights to self-expression and freedom. This libertarian politic, she argues, 'places a high premium on individual choice – the right and ability to self-define, the right and ability to act freely in the market, and the right and ability to self-define through action in the market' (2000: 222–3). The notion of personal identity has here been totally dissociated from the social sense, and instead works to promote an extreme form of possessive individualism by reinforcing a 'conception of the individual as essentially the proprietor of his own person or capacities, owing nothing to society for them' (Macpherson, 1964: 2). As Eisenstein wrote, 'a woman who self-identifies as a feminist must be able to see herself as an individual defined by a group status; without that connection, there is no feminist consciousness. There is just a woman seeing an individual female. Gay activists recognize a similar connection: their identity as gay cannot be recognized without the group status naming the identity' (1996: 72–3). In those libertarian identity politics that exist today, the social sense of identity to which Eisenstein alludes has been completely eroded: in these contexts, 'there is just a woman seeing an individual female', and indeed, just a gay man seeing an individual citizen.

The convergence of contemporary identity politics and neoliberalism is also evident in the continued marketisation of identity groups as sites of consumption, a trend Chasin also documents in her tellingly named book, *Selling Out: The Gay and Lesbian Movement Goes to Market*. She concentrates on exposing the myth that visibility in the marketplace indicates equality for gay and lesbian people, arguing that private identity-based consumption is inimical to progressive social change as it promotes rather than challenges (anti-egalitarian)

capitalist structures and values. The connections between the 'processes of commodification and the formation of lesbian and gay identities' are also explored
by Rosemary Hennessy (2000), who does not view the new visibility of gay
and lesbian identities in the mass media not as a significant challenge to heteronormativity, nor as a sign of a new acceptance of gay and lesbian communities,
but rather as an indication of the potential for the marketisation and commodification of these identities. She insists that such visibility must be 'considered
critically in relation to capital's insidious and relentless expansion. Not only is
much recent gay visibility aimed at producing new and potentially lucrative
markets, but as in most marketing strategies, money, not liberation, is the bot-
tom line' (Hennessy, 1995: 32).

While these two commentators focus exclusively on the commodification
of gay and lesbian 'identities', what this book has shown is that it is not the
'content' of an identity that makes it ripe for commodification, but rather the
construal of a particular group *as* an identity in the first place. Although there
may be a number of reasons why gay and lesbian people are particularly visible
and/or targeted in the marketplace today – including marketing assumptions
around the 'pink pound'– it remains the case, as Chapter 6 documented, that
other 'identities' too are highly commodified in contemporary neoliberal societies. In each case we see how the idea of identity has recently worked to pull
these groups into circuits of capitalist consumption, primarily integrating them
into a capitalist way of life rather than enabling them to develop modes of
resistance to it.

In general, then, this final and current phase of the construction of a
hegemonic neoliberal project has seen an evisceration of the *social* sense of
identity, with the result that the concept of identity that is now prominent
is seriously impoverished. This is the context in which '*[i]dentity politics*, in the
contemporary sense of the rights-claiming focus of balkanized groups organized
to pressure the legal and electoral systems for inclusion and redress, appeared
out of the field of disintegrating social movements' (Duggan, 2003: xviii).
The part has replaced the whole. Attention to the concept of identity itself –
particularly as a category of practice rather than a category of analysis – helps us
see how this happened: primed for adaptation to an individualised, rights-based
orientation, in a context where its social senses have been actively attacked, the
idea of identity had nowhere else to go. Political victories have therefore come
to be increasingly construed in terms of 'representation', in a manner which
is quite compatible with the aims of neoliberalism. And the notion of identity
continues to encourage intensive group-based and individual forms of consumption, an aggressive targeting of consumers by 'identity' market groups
and the proliferation of global 'identity brands'. We have reached a time when
identity operates primarily to facilitate consumption on a global scale, while
at the same time informing a version of politics that remains compatible with
the architecture of neoliberalism.

STRATEGIES FOR RESISTANCE: IDENTITY AS PART OF A GLOBAL CLASS-BASED, ANTI-CAPITALIST MOVEMENT?

Duggan (2003: xx) argues that 'as long as the progressive-left represents and reproduces itself as divided into economic vs. cultural, universal vs. identity-based, distribution vs. recognition-oriented, local or national vs. global branches, it will defeat itself'. Instead, she argues that '[e]ffective resistance to the culture war strategy of neoliberal economic, political, and cultural restructuring requires a vision of the significant links among various cultures of downward redistribution in a context of multiple, overlapping inequalities' (Duggan, 2003: 41). She identifies the anti-globalisation movement as a possible site for the rejoining of these different struggles, noting that 'this remains a possibility, and not an achievement' (2003: xix–xx). Since she was writing, we have also seen the emergence of a new set of social movements under the 'Occupy' and related labels, as well as in the so-called 'Arab Spring' across the Middle East and Northern Africa. While these movements have been criticised for failing to produce a coherent strategy or alternative economic model, they have nonetheless begun once more to link questions of economic with cultural equality, and to provide a democratic public space – typically overtly so, in public squares and parks – for articulating these concerns. In particular, the struggles of the Arab Spring have linked questions of religion, autonomy, female emancipation and gay and lesbian rights to questions of democratic control and economic equality. There is little evidence, however, that the idea of identity has played much of a role in these movements. Has it lost any progressive potential altogether?

Those who maintain a faith in the idea of identity have argued that it should be integrated into a broader movement working for economic equality. Thus, for example, Chasin argues that we should 'rethink' identity as the basis for political organising, calling 'for political alliance, for a multi-issue, multiconstituency collation focused on economic justice' (2000: 27). This, she argues, would address the needs of specific identity groups by winning back the right to organise, and then by addressing identity-based needs without being 'identity-specific' (2000: 241).

But to focus on how 'identity politics' could be *integrated* into a broader project of economic justice runs the risk of reiterating that unhelpful dissociation and hierarchisation of economy and culture. It does not explain how the concept of identity – in its social or personal sense, and whether theorised as singular, multiple or intersectional – could contribute to such a project. Against this implicit devaluation of the concept of identity in Chasin's proposal, Nicholson suggests that there is value in the concept of identity itself, arguing that the 'identity politics' of the 1960s and 1970s are important, at the very least, for the manner in which they helped us to think differently:

Identity politics stretched our notion of what constituted a legitimate political issue. It forced us to recognize that since identity affects life possibilities,
it needs to be addressed on a political level. While identity politics often
expressed a view of identity that was crude and simplistic, it also inaugurated
a discussion about identity that we continue to need today. Therefore, identity
politics represents neither a lost nirvana nor a simple wrong turn. Rather it
is best viewed as a useful beginning of a discussion in which we still need to
be engaged. (2008: 186)

Alcoff articulates more specifically still why the very concept of identity is
worth retaining, and how it might itself contribute to a broad based social
and global justice movement. She argues that 'the recognition of the political
relevance of identities is *required* for, rather than opposed to, unity and effective
class struggle' (2006: 46). Identities should not be seen as specific interest groups
where shared experiences determine a singular outlook and set of concerns and
aims – which is how the concept has evolved politically today – but as embodied
interpretative frameworks which render one's subjective and objective social
location intelligible by linking, through narrative, contemporary collective and
individual experiences with group history and memory. 'In reality', she argues,

> identities are not lived as a discrete and stable set of interests, but as a site
> from which one must engage in the process of meaning-making and thus from
> which one is open to the world ... On this account, identity does not deter-
> mine one's interpretation of the facts or constitute a fully formed perspective;
> rather ... identities operate as horizons from which certain aspects or layers
> of reality can be made visible. (2006: 43)

Although Alcoff takes the existence of 'identities' at face value, she nonetheless
may be read as offering a cultural materialist account of how the idea of
identity *may* be operationalised by people struggling to make sense of their
individual histories and opportunities, as these are at least in part collectively
shared and forged with similar others with the same experiences and
expectations. An 'identity' thus understood provides a particular vantage point
from which to view the social world. This fits well with Alcoff's endorsement
of participatory democracy as the cornerstone of any transformative class
politics, as she claims that a truly participatory democracy is not based on
separation of interests and aims from one's vantage point, but on a wholly
inclusive dialogue informed and justified by what one's vantage point allows
one to see. Thus true rationality and the possibilities for clear and democratic
argument come, not with objective and purportedly interest-free deliberation,
but with *awareness* of the origin of ostensibly neutral beliefs, and the inclusion
of these in democratic discussion.

What does the concept of identity contribute to all this? After all, *all* social
actors enter the public or political domain with a perspective that is already

dependent on background experience and values, though these may be so normalised as to appear non-existent or invisible. The sets of interests presumed to be attached to particular 'identities', then, whether a broad category like 'women' or an intersectional category like black, working class women, are no more and no less exclusivist or separatist than the sets of interests attached to any other vantage point on the world. The value of claiming a particular 'identity' – and thus the value of the very *idea* of identity in enabling this – is to give real credibility and authority to previously disregarded viewpoints; to make visible and authorise previously dismissed perspectives and experiences. The inclusion of these marginalised viewpoints and perspectives is essential for achieving participatory democracy and the transformations it would foster.

As this book has shown, the prioritisation and popularisation of the idea of identity has made it possible for certain people to speak with confidence and pride about the importance of their own experience. This experience need not be a classed one, nor be specifically related to the social logic of capitalism, but it need not exclude these issues either. And when it does work to address them, it demonstrates how the category of identity can contribute to a broader challenge to the social logic of capitalism, as it gives space for people to speak about the effects of capitalism in terms of the experiences they share with others who are similarly positioned. This represents an advance over the social left accounts which, by assuming a universal voice and ignoring or depreciating 'identity', may end up failing to recognise the diversity of experiences shaped by capitalism, the multiplicity of ways in which it works and, therefore, crucially, the full range of potential points of resistance to the system.

The choice between identity politics and class politics is thus a false opposition – *even* when considering forms of resistance to contemporary capitalism. Challenging capitalism means challenging both its structural features, which requires engaging with it as a global system, and its invidious daily effects as these are perpetuated via the social logic of capitalism, which often means engaging at more local levels with immediate problems of poverty, disempowerment and group-based oppression. Identity and identity politics have at least some roles to play in these engagements, and thus within the only type of anti-capitalist movement that seems to offer hope in today's world.

FINAL COMMENTS

In *Sovereign Individuals of Capitalism*, Abercrombie et al. describe what they call 'The Discovery of the Individual', by which they mean a long historical process in Western societies that gradually developed a particular concept of the individual by emphasising both 'the difference between individuals and the importance of individuals' (1986: 189). While they posit that this 'discovery' 'refers to very general properties of individuals....[and] does not pick out specific characteristics of persons for emphasis', they also note that there are at the same time 'more specific discourses of the individual, which do place an emphasis on particular qualities as important' (1986: 189). Of the four discourses they identify, 'individualism', 'individuality', 'anarchism' and 'socialism', they focus individualism as the most important of these, and indeed, this is the main subject of their book, as they explore the co-evolution of the discourse of individualism with the development of capitalism. Contrary to what they claim is the widespread assumption that capitalism and individualism co-evolved in a functional manner, they argue that the relationship between individualism and capitalism is contingent only, and that for most of their history, 'individualism and capitalism develop independently and separately' (1986: 190). But at a particular point in their co-histories, the paradigm of individualism and the structures of capitalism came to operate in a manner where each helped shape the other:

> Individualism shapes capitalism in a particular mould, in that it provides a particular type of economic subject, namely, the individual and individual property ownership. Capitalism influences individualism by confirming its discursive dominance and emphasizing the possessive aspects of individualistic theory. Individualism and capitalism are contingently related. We do not argue that capitalism causes individualism or vice versa. Furthermore, the capitalist mode of production does not have any necessary ideological conditions of existence. (1986: 190)

This book has shown that 'identity' operates as another such 'specific discourse of the individual', as it is concerned with 'the difference between individuals and the importance of individuals', while also placing 'emphasis on particular qualities as important'. As such, this book has charted a closely related set of connections, between capitalism and the idea of 'identity'. As I have shown, 'identity' is not a perennial feature of human life, but we have come to use the idea of identity to construct a particular conception of the individual and its relation to others – one that is fundamentally concerned with qualities of sameness and difference. While the idea of identity has a long pre-history, at the point of its emergence it operated in a very particular way in relation to capitalism. Similarly to what Abercrombie et al. say about individualism, this relationship is contingent, co-evolutionary and neither necessary nor predictable. The picture is complicated by the fact that two senses of the word evolved at the same time, senses that pull against, and work with, each other in different ways. Politically, the idea of identity can be deployed in ways which challenge both the effects of capitalism and, to a lesser extent, the social logic of capitalism. Meanwhile, within the field of popular culture and everyday life, the idea of identity is far more likely to be deployed in a way which is amenable to the social logic of capitalism, though there is some small scope for it to enable counter-hegemonic perspectives and ways of life.

Though remarkably recent in origin, the idea of identity shows no sign of disappearing. Nor, as I have shown, should it be thought of as merely cultural, and confined to claims of recognition. Rather than rejecting identity, then, egalitarians should develop those of its understandings and meanings which help to advance equality. By coming to understand the idea of identity and the different ways in which it works, we can actively use it in ways that promote socially progressive values, and challenge those uses which facilitate capitalism.

The relationship between the idea of identity and capitalism, then, is far from predetermined. In the current historical period, there are some progressive uses of the idea of identity, but the 'personal' sense is dominant, and dovetails with the social logic of capitalism. Whether or not this continues to be the case depends on the uses to which the category of identity is put, and the willingness of the left to work strategically with those uses. I have shown that attempting to separate questions of identity from questions of class and capitalism is analytically mistaken and politically counter-productive. What we need to do instead is to think critically about the use of identity as a category of analysis and as a category of practice, as it is deployed in a capitalist context, and to promote those understandings and actions which work best to achieve the outcome of a more equal and socially just world. Finally, it should now be clear that this book is not a 'critique' of identity, nor a 'defence': rather, it offers an exploration of the meanings and uses of the idea of identity in capitalist societies, in the understanding that as political actors we can influence the uses to which a particular idea is put, and thereby shape our collective history.

Notes

1. A summary of the online debate around this issues is available at http://peopleand-place.net/on_the_wire/2010/1/5/consumerism_and_identity_campaigning.
2. See EZLN Communiques, at http://www.struggle.ws/mexico/ezlnco.html.

References

Abercrombie, Nicholas and Turner, Bryan S. (1978) 'The Dominant Ideology Thesis', *British Journal of Sociology*, 29(2): 149–70.

Abercrombie, Nicholas, Hill, Stephen, et al. (1986) *Sovereign Individuals of Capitalism*. London: Allen and Unwin.

Adorno, Theodor (2005 [1938]) 'On the Fetish Character in Music and the Regression of Listening', in Andrew Arato and Eike Gebhardt (eds), *The Essential Frankfurt School Reader*. Oxford: Blackwell.

Adorno, Theodor and Horkheimer, Max (1972 [1948]) 'The Culture Industry: Enlightenment as Mass Deception', in James Curran, Michael Gurevitch and Janet Woollacott (eds), *Mass Communication and Society*. London: Edward Arnold.

Agger, Ben (1992) *Cultural Studies as Critical Theory*. London: The Falmer Press.

Aglietta, Michel (1979) *A Theory of Capitalist Regulation: The US Experience*. London: NLB.

Akerlof, George and Kranton, Rachel (2000) 'Economics and Identity', *Quarterly Journal of Economics*, 115(3): 715–53.

Albert, Michael (2011) 'Social Media and Revolution: Znet/Zsocial and The Alternative to Corporate Facebook/Twitter', lecture given at UCD Dublin, 12 October.

Alcoff, Linda Martin (2006) *Visible Identities: Race, Gender and the Self*. Oxford: Oxford University Press.

Ali, Tariq and Watkins, Susan (1998) *1968: Marching in the Streets*. London: Bloomsbury.

Allen, Robert L. (1992 [1969]) *Black Awakening in Capitalist America: An Analytic History*. Trenton, NJ: Africa World Press.

Amin, Ash (ed.) (1994) *Post-Fordism: A Reader*. Oxford: Blackwell.

Andrade, Nathanael J. (2013) *Syrian Identity in the Greco-Roman World*. Cambridge: Cambridge University Press.

Arnold, Kathleen R. (2008) *America's New Working Class: Race, Gender, and Ethnicity in a Biopolitical Age*. University Park: Pennsylvania State University Press.

Aronowitz, Stanley (1992) *The Politics of Identity: Class, Culture, Social Movements*. New York: Routledge.

Aronowitz, Stanley (1995) 'Reflections on Identity', in John Rajchman (ed.), *The Identity in Question*. London: Routledge.

Atkins, Ben (2013) 'The Cambridge Graduates Grateful to Earn £7 an Hour as Amazon Drones', *The Daily Mail*, 19 December.

Atkinson, Will (2007) 'Beck, Individualization and the Death of Class', *The British Journal of Sociology*, 58(3): 349–66.

Baker, Richard T. (1964) 'The Impact of Mass Communications', in Roger Shinn (ed.), *The Search for Identity: Essays on the American Character*. New York: Harper & Row.

Balibar, Etienne and Wallerstein, Immanuel (1991) *Race, Nation, Class: Ambiguous Identities*. London: Verso.

Baudrillard, Jean (1988 [1976]) 'Symbolic Exchange and Death', in Mark Poster (ed.), *Jean Baudrillard: Selected Writings*. Oxford: Polity Press.

Bauman, Zygmunt (1996) 'From Pilgrim to Tourist – or a Short History of Identity', in Stuart Hall and Paul du Gay (eds), *Questions of Cultural Identity*. London: Sage.

Bauman, Zygmunt (2004) *Identity: Conversations with Benedetto Vecchi*. Cambridge: Polity.

Bauman, Zygmunt (2005) *Work, Consumerism and the New Poor*. Maidenhead: Open University Press.

Bauman, Zygmunt (2007) *Consuming Life*. Cambridge: Polity.

Beck, Ulrich (1992) *Risk Society: Towards a New Modernity*. London: Sage.

Beck, Ulrich and Beck-Gernsheim, Elizabeth (2002) *Individualization: Institutionalized Individualism and its Social and Political Consequences*. London: Sage.

Beck, Ulrich, Giddens, Anthony and Lash, Scott (1994) *Reflexive Modernization: Politics, Tradition and Aesthetics in the Modern Social Order*. Cambridge: Polity.

Bell, Daniel (1973) *The Coming of Post-industrial Society: A Venture in Social Forecasting*. New York: Basic Books.

Bell, David and Hollows, Joanne (eds) (2006) *Historicizing Lifestyle: Mediating Taste, Consumption and Identity, 1900s to 1970s*. Aldershot: Ashgate.

Bello, Walden (2008) 'Wall Street Meltdown Primer', *Foreign Policy in Focus* (http://www.fpif.org/fpiftxt/5560).

Bendle, Mervyn F. (2002) 'The Crisis of "Identity" in High Modernity', *British Journal of Sociology*, 53(1): 1–18.

Benedict, Ruth (1934) *Patterns of Culture*. New York: Houghton Mifflin.

Benjamin, Marina (1993) *A Question of Identity: Women, Science, and Literature*. New Brunswick, NJ: Rutgers University Press.

Benn Michaels, Walter (2008) 'Against Diversity', *New Left Review*, 52: 33–6.

Bennett, Tony, Grossberg, Lawrence, et al. (eds) (2005) *New Keywords: A Revised Vocabulary of Culture and Society*. Oxford: Blackwell.

Berman, Marshall (1983) *All That is Solid Melts into Air: The Experience of Modernity*. London: Verso.

Bernstein, Mary (2005) 'Identity Politics', *Annual Review of Sociology*, 31: 47–74.

Best, Steven and Kellner, Douglas (1997) *The Postmodern Turn*. New York: Guilford Press.

Binkley, Sam (2008) 'Liquid Consumption', *Cultural Studies*, 22(5): 599–623.

Blunden, Andy (2005) 'The Subject' (http://home.mira.net/~andy/works/the-subject.htm).

Boltanski, Luc and Chiapello, Eve (2005a) *The New Spirit of Capitalism*. London: Verso.

Boltanski, Luc and Chiapello, Eve (2005b) 'The New Spirit of Capitalism', *International Journal of Politics, Culture and Society*, 18(3–4): 161–88.

Bottero, Wendy (2004) 'Class Identities and the Identity of Class', *Sociology*, 38(5): 985–99.

Bourdieu, Pierre (1984) *Distinction: A Social Critique of the Judgement of Taste*. London: Routledge and Kegan Paul.

Bourdieu, Pierre (1986) 'The Forms of Capital', in J.G. Richardson (ed.), *Handbook of Theory and Research for the Sociology of Education*. Westport, CT: Greenwood.

Bourne Taylor, Jenny (2007) 'Psychology at the Fin de Siècle', in Gail Marshall (ed.), *The Cambridge Companion to the Fin de Siècle*. Cambridge: Cambridge University Press.

Bramen, Carrie Tirado (2002) 'Turning Point: Why the Academic Left Hates Identity Politics', *Textual Practice*, 16(1): 1–11.

Braudel, Ferdinand (1973) *Capitalism and Material Life, 1400–1800*. London: Weidenfeld and Nicolson.

Brown, Wendy (1995) *States of Injury: Power and Freedom in Late Modernity*. Princeton, NJ: Princeton University Press.

Brubaker, Roger and Cooper, Frederick (2000) 'Beyond "Identity"', *Theory and Society*, 29(1): 1–47.

Buechler, Steven M. (1995) 'New Social Movement Theories', *The Sociological Quarterly*, 36(3): 441–64.

Butler, Judith (1990) *Gender Trouble: Feminism and the Subversion of Identity*. London: Routledge.

Butler, Judith (1997) 'Merely Cultural', *Social Text*, 52/53 (Autumn–Winter): 265–77.

Butler, Marilyn and Todd, Janet (eds) (1989) *The Works of Mary Wollstonecraft*. London: Pickering and Chatto Publishers.

Calhoun, Craig (1993) '"New Social Movements" of the Early Nineteenth Century', *Social Science History*, 17(3): 385–427.

Calhoun, Craig (1994) 'Social Theory and the Politics of Identity', in Craig Calhoun (ed.), *Social Theory and the Politics of Identity*. Oxford: Blackwell.

Callinicos, Alex (2006) *The Resources of Critique*. Cambridge: Polity Press.

Campbell, Colin (1995) 'The Sociology of Consumption', in Daniel Miller (ed.), *Acknowledging Consumption: A Review of New Studies*. London: Routledge.

Canny, Nicholas and Pagden, Anthony (eds) (1987) *Colonial Identity in the Atlantic World, 1500–1800*. Princeton, NJ: Princeton University Press.

Carol, Estelle (1968) 'Chapter Report, Chicago', *Voice of the Women's Liberation Movement*, 1 March.

Carter, Kate (2008) '"What's Next for Me? World Domination!" Gok Wan Speaks to Kate Carter', The *Guardian*, 16 June.

Castells, Manuel (1996) *The Information Age: Economy, Culture and Society, Vol I: The Rise of the Network Society*. Oxford: Blackwell.

Castells, Manuel (2004) *The Information Age: Economy, Culture and Society, Vol II: The Power of Identity*. Oxford: Blackwell.

Chambers, Jason (2008) *Madison Avenue and the Color Line: African Americans in the Advertising Industry*. Philadelphia: University of Pennsylvania Press.

Chaney, David (1996) *Lifestyles*. London: Routledge.

Chasin, Alexandra (2000) *Selling Out: The Gay and Lesbian Movement Goes to the Market*. Basingstoke: Palgrave.

Chatterton, Paul (2010) 'Autonomous Spaces and Social Centres: So What Does it Mean to be Anti-capitalist?' (http://socialcentrestories.wordpress.com/2008/04/29/autonomous-spaces-and-social-centres-so-what-does-it-mean-to-be-anti-capitalist/).

Chomsky, Noam (2012) *Occupy*. London: Penguin.

Collini, Stefan (1985) 'The Idea of "Character" in Victorian Political Thought', *Transactions of the Royal Historical Society*, 35: 29–50.

Collins, Patricia Hill (2000) *Black Feminist Thought: Knowledge, Consciousness, and the Politics of Empowerment*. London: Routledge.

Combahee River Collective (1979 [1977]) 'A Black Feminist Statement', in Zillah R. Eisenstein (ed.), *Capitalist Patriarchy and the Case for Socialist Feminism*. New York: Monthly Review Press.

Cooley, Charles H. (1902) *Human Nature and the Social Order*. New York: Scribner's.

Corbett, J. (1994) 'A Proud Label: Exploring the Relationship between Disability Politics and Gay Pride', *Disability and Society*, 9(3): 343–57.

Cornes, Judy (2008) *Madness and the Loss of Identity in Nineteenth Century Fiction*. Jefferson, NC: McFarland and Company Inc.

Covey, Stephen R. (1989) *The Seven Habits of Highly Successful People*. New York: Simon and Schuster.

Crenshaw, Kimberle (1989) 'Demarginalizing the Intersection of Race and Sex: A black feminist critique of antidiscrimination doctrine, feminist theory, and antiracist politics', *University of Chicago Legal Forum*, 14: 538–54.

De Certeau, Michel (1984) *The Practice of Everyday Life*. Berkeley: University of California Press.

Delphy, Christine (1980) 'The Main Enemy', *Gender Issues*, 1(1): 23–40.

Demetriou, Denise (2012) *Negotiating Identity in the Ancient Mediterranean: The Archaic and Classical Greek Multiethnic Emporia*. Cambridge: Cambridge University Press.

D'Emilio, John (1983) 'Capitalism and Gay Identity', in Ann Snitow, Christine Stansell and Sharon Thompsen (eds), *Powers of Desire – The Politics of Sexuality*. New York: Monthly Review Press.

D'Emilio, John (1998) *Sexual Politics, Sexual Communities*. Chicago: University of Chicago Press.

Du Cille, Ann (2004) 'Dyes and Dolls: Multicultural Barbie and the Merchandising of Difference', in Jacqueline Bob, Cynthia Hudley and Claudine Michel (eds), *The Black Studies Reader*. New York: Routledge.

Duggan, Lisa (2003) *The Twilight of Equality? Neoliberalism, Cultural Politics and the Attack on Democracy*. Boston: Beacon Press.

Durant, Alan (2006) 'Raymond Williams's Keywords: Investigating Meanings "Offered, Felt for, Tested, Confirmed, Asserted, Qualified, Changed"', *Critical Quarterly*, 48(4): 1–26.

Eagleton, Terry (1976) 'Criticism and Politics: The Work of Raymond Williams', *New Left Review*, 95: 3–23.

Eagleton, Terry (1998) 'Defending the Free World', in Stephen Regan (ed.), *The Eagleton Reader*. Malden, MA: Blackwell.

Ebert, Teresa L. (2005) 'Rematerializing Feminism', *Science and Society*, 69(1): 33–55.

Eder, Klaus (1993) *The New Politics of Class: Social Movements and Cultural Dynamics in Advanced Societies*. London: Sage.

Eisenstein, Zillah (1996) *Hatreds: Racialized and Sexualized Conflicts in the 21st Century*. New York: Routledge.

Erikson, Erik (1950) *Childhood and Society*. New York: W.W. Norton.

Erikson, Erik (1959) *Identity and the Life Cycle*. London: W.W. Norton.

Ernst, Waltraud and Harris, Bernard (eds) (1999) *Race, Science and Medicine: 1700–1960*. London: Routledge.

Evans, David T. (1993) *Sexual Citizenship: The Material Construction of Sexualities*. London: Routledge.

Facebook (2013) 'Facebook Reports First Quarter 2013 Results' (http://investor. fb.com/releasedetail.cfm?ReleaseID=761090).

Fearon, James (1999) 'What is Identity (As We Now Use the Word)?' (http://www. stanford.edu/~jfearon/papers/iden1v2.pdf).

Featherstone, Mike (1990) 'Theories of Consumer Culture', *Sociology*, 24(1): 5–22.

Featherstone, Mike (1991) *The Body in Consumer Culture*. London: Sage.

Feitz, Lindsey (2012) 'Creating a Multicultural Soul: Avon, Race, and Corporate Responsibility in the 1970s', in Laura Warren Hill and Julia Rabig (eds), *The Business of Black Power: Community Development, Capitalism and Corporate Responsibility in Postwar America*. Rochester: University of Rochester Press.

Fine, Ben (2006) 'Addressing the Consumer', in Frank Trentmann (ed.), *The Making of the Consumer: Knowledge, Power and Identity in the Modern World*. Oxford: Berg.

Foote, Nelson N. and Cottrell, Leonard S., Jr (1955) *Identity and Interpersonal Competence: A New Direction in Family Research*. Chicago: University of Chicago Press.

Foucault, Michel (1977) *Discipline and Punish*. New York: Pantheon.

Foucault, Michel (1998) *The History of Sexuality Vol. 1: The Will to Knowledge*. London: Penguin.

Fox Piven, Francis (1995) 'Globalizing Capitalism and the Rise of Identity Politics', *The Socialist Register*, 31: 102–16.

Fraad Baxandall, Rosalyn (2007) 'Catching the fire', in Rachel Blau Duplessis and Ann Snitow (eds), *The Feminist Memoir Project: Voices from the Women's Liberation Movement*. New Brunswick, NJ: Rutgers University Press.

Frank, Thomas (1997) *The Conquest of Cool: Business Culture, Counterculture, and the Rise of Hip Consumerism*. Chicago: University of Chicago Press.

Fraser, Nancy (1995) 'From Redistribution to Recognition? Dilemmas of Justice in a Post-socialist Age', *New Left Review*, 212: 68–93.

Fraser, Nancy (1997a) 'Heterosexism, Misrecognition, and Capitalism: A Response to Judith Butler', *Social Text*, 52/53: 279–89.

Fraser, Nancy (1997b) *Justice Interruptus: Critical Reflections on the 'Post-socialist' Condition*. London: Routledge.

Fraser, Nancy (1997c) 'A Rejoinder to Iris Young', *New Left Review*, 223: 126–9.

Frazier, Nishani (2012). 'A McDonald's That Reflects the Soul of a People: Hough Area Development Corporation and Community Development in Cleveland', in Laura Warren Hill and Julia Rabig (eds), *The Business of Black Power: Community Development, Capitalism and Corporate Responsibility in Postwar America*. Rochester: University of Rochester Press.

Freud, Sigmund (1920) *Dream Psychology: Psychoanalysis for Beginners*. New York: The James A. McCann Company (http://www.gutenberg.org/files/15489/15489-h/15489-h.htm).

Friedan, Betty (1963) *The Feminine Mystique*. New York: W. W. Norton.

Gallagher, Catherine (1992) 'Raymond Williams and Cultural Studies', *Social Text*, 30: 79–89.

Garnham, Nicholas (1998) 'Political Economy or Cultural Studies: Reconciliation or Divorce?', in John Storey (ed.), *Cultural Theory and Popular Culture: A Reader*. London: Prentice Hall.

Gibson, Marion, Trower, Shelley, et al. (eds) (2013) *Mysticism, Myth and Celtic Identity*. London: Routledge.

Giddens, Anthony (1990) *The Consequences of Modernity*. Cambridge: Polity.

Giddens, Anthony (1991) *Modernity and Self-identity: Self and Society in the Late Modern Age*. Cambridge: Polity.

Gilligan, Chris (2007) 'The Irish Question and the Concept "Identity" in the 1980s', *Nations and Nationalism*, 14(4): 599–617.

Gilroy, Paul (1987) *'There Ain't no Black in the Union Jack': The Cultural Politics of Race and Nation*. Chicago: University of Chicago Press.

Gilroy, Paul (1997) 'Diaspora and the Detours of Identity', in Kathryn Woodward (ed.), *Identity and Difference*. London: Sage/Open University.

Gilroy, Paul (2000) *Against Race: Imagining Political Culture Beyond the Color Line*. Cambridge, MA: Harvard University Press.

Gimenez, Martha E. (2006) 'With a Little Class: A Critique of Identity Politics', *Ethnicities*, 6(3): 423–39.

Giroux, Henry (1994) 'Consuming Social Change: The "United Colors of Benetton"', *Cultural Critique*, 26 (Winter 1993–1994): 5–32.

Gitlin, Todd (1994) 'From Universality to Difference: Notes on the Fragmentation of the Idea of the Left', in Craig Calhoun (ed.), *Social Theory and the Politics of Identity*. Oxford: Blackwell.

Gitlin, Todd (1995) *The Twilight of Common Dreams: Why America is Wracked by Culture Wars*. New York: Metropolitan Books/Henry Holt and Company.

Glasser, William (1972) *The Identity Society*. New York: Harper & Row

Gleason, Philip (1983) 'Identifying Identity: A Semantic History', *Journal of American History*, 69(4): 910–31.

Glyn, Andrew (2006) *Capitalism Unleashed: Finance, Globalization and Welfare*. Oxford: Oxford University Press.

Goffman, Erving (1963) *Stigma: Notes on the Management of Spoiled Identity*. Englewood Cliffs, NJ: Prentice Hall.

Goldie, Peter (2004) *On Personality*. London: Routledge.

Gooding-Williams, Robert (1994) 'W.E.B. du Bois: Of Cultural and Racial Identity', *The Massachusetts Review*, 35(2): 168.

Graham, Stedman (2012) *Identity: Your Passport to Success*. Upper Saddle River, NJ: Pearson Education Inc.

Gramsci, Antonio (1971) *Selections from the Prison Notebooks*. London: Lawrence and Wishart.

Grossberg, Lawrence (1996) 'Identity and Cultural Studies: Is That All There Is?', in Stuart Hall and Paul du Gay (eds), *Questions of Cultural Identity*. London: Sage.

Gruen, Erich S. (ed.) (2011) *Cultural Identity in the Ancient Mediterranean*. Los Angeles: Getty Research Institute.

Gumbs, Alexis Pauline (2012) 'Black (Buying) Power: The Story of *Essence* Magazine', in Laura Warren Hill and Julia Rabig (eds), *The Business of Black Power: Community Development, Capitalism and Corporate Responsibility in Postwar America*. Rochester: University of Rochester Press.

Gunther-Canada, Wendy (2001) *Rebel Writer: Mary Wollstonecraft and Enlightenment Politics*. DeKalb: Northern Illinois University Press.

Hall, Stuart (1992) 'The Question of Cultural Identity', in Stuart Hall, David Held and Tony McGrew (eds), *Modernity and its Futures*. Cambridge: Polity Press in association with the Open University.

Hall, Stuart (1996) 'The Problem of Ideology: Marxism without Guarantees', in David Morley and Kuan-Hsing Chen (eds), *Stuart Hall: Critical Dialogues in Cultural Studies*. London, Routledge. (Originally published in B. Matthews (ed.), (1983) *Marx: 100 Years On*. London: Lawrence and Wishart.)

Hall, Stuart and Jefferson, Tony (eds) (1976) *Resistance Through Rituals: Youth Subcultures in Post-war Britain*. London: Hutchinson in association with the Centre for Contemporary Cultural Studies, University of Birmingham.

Hancock, Ange-Marie (2007) 'When Multiplication doesn't Equal Quick Addition', *Perspectives on Politics*, 5(1): 63–79.

Hartmann, Heidi (1979) 'The Unhappy Marriage of Marxism and Feminism: Towards a More Progressive Union', *Capital and Class*, 3(2): 1–33.

Harvey, David (1989) *The Condition of Postmodernity: An Enquiry into the Origins of Cultural Change*. Oxford: Basil Blackwell.

Harvey, David (2005) *A Brief History of Neoliberalism*. Oxford: Oxford University Press.

Harvey, David (2010) *The Enigma of Capital and the Crises of Capitalism*. London: Profile Books.

Hayden, Casey and King, Mary (1965) *Sex and Caste: A Kind of Memo from Casey Hayden and Mary King to a number of other women in the peace and freedom movements*. (http://www.uic.edu/orgs/cwluherstory/CWLUArchive/memo.html.)

Hearn, Alison (2008) 'Insecure: Narratives and Economies of the Branded Self in Transformation Television', *Continuum: Journal of Media and Cultural Studies*, 22(4): 495–504.

Hebdige, Dick (1979) *Subculture: The Meaning of Style*. London: Methuen.

Heilbroner, Robert L. (1985) *The Nature and Logic of Capitalism*. London: W.W. Norton & Company Ltd.

Hennessy, Rosemary (1995) 'Queer Visibility in Commodity Culture.' *Cultural Critique*, 29 (Winter 1994–1995): 31-76.

Hennessy, Rosemary (2000) *Profit and Pleasure: Sexual Identities in Late Capitalism*. New York: Routledge.

Hetherington, Kevin (1998). *Expressions of Identity: Space, Performance, Politics*. London: Sage.

hooks, bell (1984) *From Margin to Centre*. Boston, MA: South End Press.

hooks, bell (2001) 'Postmodern Blackness', in Simon Malpas (ed.), *Postmodern Debates*. Basingstoke: Palgrave.

Hume, David (2000 [1739]) *A Treatise of Human Nature*. Oxford: Oxford University Press.

Identity Campaigning (2010) 'What is Identity Campaigning?' (http://www.identitycampaigning.org/what-is-identity-campaigning/).

Ingham, Geoffrey (2003) 'Schumpeter and Weber on the Institutions of Capitalism', *Journal of Classical Sociology*, 3(3): 297–309.

Ingham, Geoffrey (2004) *The Nature of Money*. Cambridge: Polity.

Ingham, Geoffrey (2008) *Capitalism*. Cambridge: Polity.

Inglehart, Ronald (1990) *Culture Shift in Advanced Industrial Society*. Princeton, NJ: Princeton University Press.

Iversen, Roberta Rehner and Armstrong, Annie Laurie (2006) *Job's Aren't Enough: Towards a New Economic Mobility for Low Income Families*. Philadelphia: Temple University Press.

James, William (1890) *The Principles of Psychology* (2 vols). New York: Henry Holt.

Jameson, Frederic (1991) *Postmodernism: Or, the Cultural Logic of Late Capitalism*. London: Verso.

Jenkins, Richard (2008) *Social Identity*. London: Routledge.

Jessop, B (2002) *The Future of the Capitalist State*. Cambridge: Polity Press.

Johnston, Hank, Larana, Enrique, et al. (1994) 'Identities, Grievances and New Social Movements', in Enrique Larana, Hank Johnston and Joseph R. Gusfield (eds), *New Social Movements: From Ideology to Identity*. Philadelphia: Temple University Press.

Jones, Lisa (1991) 'A Doll is Born', *Village Voice*, 26 March.

Kail, Robert V. and Cavanaugh, John C. (2010) *Human Development: A Life-span View*. Wadsworth, CA: Cengage Learning.

Katten, Michael (2005) *Colonial Lists/Indian Power: Identity Formation in Nineteenth Century Telugu Speaking India*. New York: Columbia University Press.

Kauffman, L.A. (1991) 'New Age Meets New Right: Tofu Politics in Berkeley', *The Nation*, 253(8): 294–6.

Kaufman, Cynthia (2003) *Ideas for Action: Relevant Theory for Radical Change*. Cambridge, MA: South End Press.

Kellner, Douglas (1995) *Media Culture: Cultural Studies, Identity and Politics. Between the Modern and Postmodern*. New York: Routledge.

Kelly, Gordon (2014) 'The Majority of iPhone Users Admit to "Blind Loyalty" – Why This is a Problem for Apple', *Forbes*, 21 March (http://www.forbes.com/

sites/gordonkelly/2014/03/21/the-majority-of-iphone-users-admit-to-blind-loyalty-why-this-a-problem-for-apple/2/).

Klein, Naomi (2002) *No Logo: No Space, No Choice, No Jobs*. London: Flamingo.

Kozinets, Robert V. (2002) 'Can Consumers Escape the Market? Emancipatory Illuminations from Burning Man', *Journal of Consumer Research*, 29(1): 20–38.

Kumar, Krishan (1995) *From Post-industrial to Post-modern Society: New Theories of the Contemporary World*. Oxford: Blackwell.

Langman, L. (1994) 'From Capitalist Tragedy to Postmodern Farce: The Eighteenth Broomstick of H. Ross Perot', *Rethinking Marxism*, 7(4): 115–37.

Lapavistas, Costas (2014) 'Finance's Hold on our Everyday Life must be Broken', The *Guardian*, 1 January.

Lasch, Christopher (1985) *The Minimal Self: Psychic Survival in Troubled Times*. London: Pan Books.

Lash, Scott and Urry, John (1987) *The End of Organized Capitalism*. Cambridge: Polity.

Lee (Pseudonym), Reba and Hastings Bradley, Mary (1956) *I Passed for White*. London: Peter Davies.

Lewis, Tania (2008) 'Revealing the Makeover Show', *Continuum: Journal of Media and Cultural Studies*, 22(4): 441–6.

Lipietz, Alain (1992) *Towards a New Economic Order: Postfordism, Ecology and Democracy*. Cambridge: Polity.

Lloyd, Moya (2005) *Beyond Identity Politics*. London: Sage.

Loyal, Stephen (2003) *The Sociology of Anthony Giddens*. London: Pluto Press.

Lynd, Helen Merrell (1958) *On Shame and the Search for Identity*. New York: Harcourt, Brace.

Mackenzie, William J.M. (1978) *Political Identity*. Harmondsworth: Penguin.

Macpherson, Crawford Brough (1964) *The Political Theory of Possessive Individualism: Hobbes to Locke*. Oxford: Oxford University Press.

Malcolm X (1963) 'God's Judgement of White America (The Chickens Come Home to Roost)', 4 December (http://www.malcolm-x.org/speeches/spc_120463.htm).

Malcolm X (1965) 'After the Bombing / Speech at Ford Auditorium', 14 February (http://www.malcolm-x.org/speeches/spc_021465.htm).

Marcuse, Herbert (1991 [1964]) *One-dimensional Man: Studies in the Ideology of Advanced Industrial Capitalism*. London: Routledge.

Marx, Karl (1973 [1939]) *Grundisse*. New York: Vintage.

Marx, Karl (1976 [1867]) *Capital, Vol 1: A Critique of Political Economy*. London: Penguin.

Marx, Karl (1994 [1859]) 'Preface to "A Contribution to the Critique of Political Economy"', in Lawrence H. Simon (ed.), *Karl Marx: Selected Writings*. Cambridge: Hackett Publishing Company, Inc.

Matthewman, Steve, Lane West-Newman, Catherine, et al. (eds) (2007) *Being Sociological*. Basingstoke: Palgrave Macmillan.

Matthews, Sean (2001) 'Change and Theory in Raymond Williams's Structure of Feeling', *Pretexts: Literary and Cultural Studies*, 10(2): 179–94.

Max-Neef, Manfred A. (1991) 'Development and Human Needs', in Manfred A. Max-Neef, Antonio Elizalde and Martin Hopenhayn (eds), *Human Scale Development: Conception, Application and Further Reflections*. New York: Apex.

McAdam, Doug (1986) 'Recruitment to High-risk Activism: The Case of Freedom Summer', *American Journal of Sociology*, 92(1): 64–90.

McCall, Leslie (2005) 'The Complexity of Intersectionality', *Signs: Journal of Women in Culture and Society* 30(3): 1771–1800.

McGuigan, Jim (2009) *Cool Capitalism*. London: Pluto Press.

McGuigan, Jim and Moran, Marie (2014) 'Raymond Williams and Sociology', *The Sociological Review*, 62(1): 167–88.

McIntyre, Lisa (2006) *The Practical Skeptic: Core Concepts in Sociology*. London: McGraw Hill Higher Education.

Mead, George Herbert (1934) *Mind, Self and Society from the Standpoint of a Social Behaviorist*. Chicago: University of Chicago.

Meiksins Wood, Ellen (1995) *Democracy against Capitalism: Renewing Historical Materialism*. Cambridge: Cambridge University Press.

Meiksins Wood, Ellen (1997) 'Modernity, Postmodernity or Capitalism?', *Review of International Political Economy*, 4(3): 539–60.

Mellor, Mary (2010) *The Future of Money: From Financial Crisis to Public Resource*. London: Pluto Press.

Melucci, Alberto (1988) 'Getting Involved: Identity and Mobilization in Social Movements', in Bert Klandermans, Hanspeter Kriesi and Sidney Tarrow (eds), *International Social Movement Research, Vol. 1, From Structure to Action*. Greenwich, CT: JA1 Press Inc.

Mercer, Kobena (1990) 'Welcome to the Jungle', in Jonathan Rutherford (ed.), *Identity*. London: Lawrence and Wishart.

Meyerson, Emile (1930) *Identity and Reality*. London: Allen and Unwin.

Mies, Maria (1999) *Patriarchy and Accumulation on a World Scale: Women in the International Division of Labour*. London: Zed Books.

Miles, Robert (2009) 'Apropos the Idea of "Race" … Again', in Les Back and John Solomos (eds), *Theories of Race and Racism: A Reader*. London: Routledge.

Miller, Daniel (ed.) (1995) *Acknowledging Consumption: A Review of New Studies*. London: Routledge.

Millner, Michael (2005) 'Post Post-identity', *American Quarterly*, 57(2): 541–54.

Milner, Andrew (1993) *Cultural Materialism*. Melbourne: Melbourne University Press.

Mirowski, Philip (2009) 'Postface: Defining Neoliberalism', in Philip Mirowski and Dieter Plehwe (eds), *The Road from Mont Pelerin: The Making of the Neoliberal Thought Collective*. Cambridge, MA: Harvard University Press.

Morley, David and Chen, Kuan-Hsing (eds) (1996) *Stuart Hall: Critical Dialogues in Cultural Studies*. London: Routledge.

Morley, David and Robins, Kevin (1995) *Spaces of Identity*. London: Routledge.

Mostern, Kenneth (1999) *Autobiography and Black Identity Politics: Racialization in Twentieth-century America*. Cambridge: Cambridge University Press.

Nicholson, Linda (2008) *Identity Before Identity Politics*. Cambridge: Cambridge University Press.

Nicholson, Linda and Seidman, Steven (eds) (1995) *Social Postmodernism: Beyond Identity Politics*. Cambridge: Cambridge University Press.

Noonan, Harold (2009) 'Identity', in Edward N. Zalta (ed.), *The Stanford Encyclopedia of Philosophy*, Winter 2009 edn (http://plato.stanford.edu/archives/win2009/entries/identity/).

NOW (National Organization for Women) (1966) 'The National Organization for Women's 1966 Statement of Purpose', adopted at NOW's first National Conference in Washington, DC, 29 October.

Oakley, Ann (2005) *The Ann Oakley Reader: Gender, Women and Social Science*. Bristol: Policy Press.

O'Neill, John (1998) *The Market: Ethics, Knowledge and Politics*. London: Routledge.

Osborne, Peter (1992) 'Modernity is a Qualitative, not a Chronological, Category: Notes on the Dialectics of Differential Historical Time', in Francis Barker, Peter Hulme and Margaret Iversen (eds), *Postmodernism and the Re-reading of Modernity*. Manchester: Manchester University Press.

Oxford University Press (2008) 'Key Theorists' (http://www.oup.com.au/titles/higher_ed/social_science/sociology/9780195550979/key_theorists).

Pakulski, Jan and Waters, Malcolm (1996) *The Death of Class*. London: Sage.

Park, Robert (2009 [1950]) 'The Nature of Race Relations', in Les Back and John Solomos (eds), *Theories of Race and Racism: A Reader*. London: Routledge.

Paterson, Mark (2006) *Consumption and Everyday Life*. London: Routledge.

Perina, Kaja (2009) 'iPhone, Therefore I Am', *Psychology Today*, 42(5): 5.

Phillips, Anne (1997) 'From Equality to Difference: A Severe Case of Displacement?', *New Left Review*, 224: 143–53.

Piketty, Thomas (2014) *Capital in the Twenty-First Century*. Cambridge, MA: The Belknap Press of Harvard University Press.

Przybylowicz, Donna (1989) 'Toward a Feminist Cultural Criticism: Hegemony and Modes of Social Division', *Cultural Critique*, 14 (Winter): 259–301.

Pye, Lucian Wilmot (1962) *Politics, Personality and Nation Building: Burma's Search for Identity*. New Haven, CT: Yale University Press.

Quine, W.V. (1980) *From a Logical Point of View*. Cambridge, MA: Harvard University Press.

Radicalesbians (1970) 'The Woman Identified Woman' (http://scriptorium.lib.duke.edu/wlm/womid/).

Rajchman, John (ed.) (1995) *The Identity in Question*. New York: Routledge.

Ray, Larry and Sayer, Andrew (1999) 'Introduction', in Larry Ray and Andrew Sayer (eds), *Culture and Economy after the Cultural Turn*. London: Sage.

Reay, Diane (1998) 'Rethinking Social Class: Qualitative Perspectives on Class and Gender', *Sociology*, 32(2): 259–75.

Richmond, Mary (1938) *Concealed Identity*. London.

Riesman, David (1961 [1950]) *The Lonely Crowd: A Study of the Changing American Character*. New Haven, CT: Yale University Press.

Robins, Kevin (1991) 'Tradition and Translation: National Culture in its Global Context', in John Corner and Sylvia Harvey (eds) *Enterprise and Heritage: Crosscurrents of National Culture*. London: Routledge.

Rowden, Mark (2000) *The Art of Identity: Creating and Managing a Successful Corporate Identity*. Burlington, VT: Gower.

Ruvio, Ayalla A. and Belk, Russell W. (eds) (2013) *The Routledge Companion to Identity and Consumption*. London: Routledge.

Sassatelli, Roberta (2007) *Consumer Culture: History, Theory and Politics*. London: Sage.

Savage, Mike (2000) *Class Analysis and Social Transformation*. Buckingham: Open University Press.

Sayer, Andrew (2002) 'What are You Worth? Why Class is an Embarrassing Subject', *Sociological Research Online*, 7(3) http://www.socresonline.org.uk/7/3/sayer.html.

Sayer, Andrew (2005) *The Moral Significance of Class*. Cambridge: Cambridge University Press.

Scatamburlo-D'Annibale, Valerie and McLaren, Peter (2003) 'The Strategic Centrality of Class in the Politics of "Race" and "Difference"', *Cultural Studies, Critical Methodologies*, 3(2): 148–75.

Scatamburlo-D'Annibale, Valerie and McLaren, Peter (2004) 'Class Dismissed? Historical Materialism and the Politics of "Difference"', *Educational Philosophy and Theory*, 36(2): 183–99.

Schultz, Majken, Hatch, Mary Jo, et al. (eds) (2000) *The Expressive Organization: Linking Identity, Reputation, and the Corporate Brand*. Oxford: Oxford University Press.

Scurlock, James D. (2007) *Maxed Out: Hard Times, Easy Credit*. London: Harper Collins.

Sen, Amartya (1999) *Reason Before Identity: The Romanes Lecture for 1998*. Oxford: Oxford University Press.

Sen, Amartya (2000) 'Other People', *New Republic*, 18 December.

Shinn, Roger (ed.) (1964) *The Search for Identity: Essays on the American Character*. New York: Harper & Row.

Shivani, Anis (2002) 'From Redistribution to Recognition: A Left Critique of Multiculturalism', *CounterPunch*, weekend edition 19–21 October (http://www.counterpunch.org/2002/10/19/a-left-critique-of-multiculturalism/).

Shoemaker, Sydney (2006) 'Identity and Identities', *Daedalus*, 135(4): 40–8.

Simmel, Georg (1957 [1904]) 'Fashion', *American Journal of Sociology*, 62(6): 541–58.

Simmel, Georg (1990 [1907]) *The Philosophy of Money*. London: Routledge.

Skeggs, Beverley (1997) *Formations of Class and Gender: Becoming Respectable*. London: Sage.

Skeggs, Beverley (2004) *Class, Self, Culture*. London: Routledge.

Slater, Don (1997) *Consumer Culture and Modernity*. Cambridge: Polity.

Somers, Margaret R. (1994) 'The Narrative Constitution of Identity: A Relational and Network Approach', *Theory and Society*, 23(5): 605–49.

Storey, John (1998) 'Rockin' Hegemony: West Coast Rock and America's War in Vietnam', in John Storey (ed.), *Cultural Theory and Popular Culture: A Reader*. Harlow: Prentice Hall.

Strong, Amy L. (2008) *Race and Identity in Hemingway's Fiction*. Basingstoke: Palgrave Macmillan.

Sullivan, Martin and Lane West-Newman, Catherine (2007) 'Being: Identity', in Steve Matthewman, Catherine Lane West-Newman and Bruce Curtis (eds), *Being Sociological*. Basingstoke: Palgrave Macmillan.

Thomson, Mathew (2006) *Psychological Subjects: Identity, Culture, and Health in Twentieth-century Britain*. Oxford: Oxford University Press.

Tirosh, Yofi (2007) 'Adjudicating Appearance: From Identity to Personhood', *Yale Journal of Law and Feminism*, 19(1): 49–123.

Torfing, Jacob (1999) *New Theories of Discourse: Laclau, Mouffe and Žižek*. Oxford: Blackwell.

Tormey, Simon (2004) *Anti-capitalism: A Beginner's Guide*. Oxford: Oneworld.

Touraine, Alain (1981) *The Voice and the Eye: An Analysis of Social Movements*. Cambridge: Cambridge University Press.

Van Riel, Cees B.M. and Balmer, John M.T. (1997) 'Corporate Identity: The Concept, its Measurement and Management', *European Journal of Marketing*, 31(5/6): 340–55.

Veblen, Thorstein (1925 [1899]) *The Theory of the Leisure Class: An Economic Study of Institutions*. London: George Allen and Unwin Ltd.

Von Grunebaum, Gustave Edmund (1962) *Modern Islam: The Search for Cultural Identity*. Berkeley: University of California Press.

Wagner, Peter (2001) *A History and Theory of the Social Sciences: Not All That is Solid Melts into Air*. London: Sage.

Walby, Sylvia (1990) *Theorizing Patriarchy*. Oxford: Blackwell.

Walby, Sylvia (2001) 'From Community to Coalition: The Politics of Recognition as the Handmaiden of the Politics of Equality in an Era of Globalization', *Theory, Culture and Society*, 18(2–3): 113–35.

Walby, Sylvia (2006) *Rethinking the Concept of System: Multiple Social Inequalities and Complexity Theory*. Paper presented to the Complexity Seminar, Lancaster University, 1 March.

Walder, Dennis (ed.) (2001) *The Nineteenth-century Novel: Identities*. London: Routledge.

Wallerstein, Immanuel (1983) *Historical Capitalism*. London: Verso.

Weber, Brenda R. (2009) *Makeover TV: Selfhood, Citizenship and Celebrity*. Durham: Duke University Press.

Weber, Max (1976 [1930]) *The Protestant Ethic and the Spirit of Capitalism*. London: Allen and Unwin.

Webster, Frank (2006) *Theories of the Information Society*, 3rd edn. London: Routledge.

Weigert, Andrew J., Teitge, J. Smith, et al. (1986) *Society and Identity: Towards a Sociological Psychology*. Cambridge: Cambridge University Press.

Whyte, William H. (1956) *The Organization Man*. Garden City, NY: Doubleday.

Williams, Raymond (1958) *Culture and Society, 1780–1950*. New York: Columbia University Press.

Williams, Raymond (1961) *The Long Revolution*. London: Chatto and Windus.

Williams, Raymond (1973) 'Base and Superstructure in Marxist Cultural Theory', *New Left Review*, 82: 3–16.

Williams, Raymond (1974) *Television: Technology and Cultural Form*. Glasgow: Collins.

Williams, Raymond (1976) *Communications*. Harmondsworth: Penguin.

Williams, Raymond (1977) *Marxism and Literature*. Oxford: Oxford University Press.

Williams, Raymond (1979) *Politics and Letters: Interviews with 'New Left Review'*. London: Verso.

Williams, Raymond (1981a) *Culture*. London: Fontana.

Williams, Raymond (1981b) 'Marxism, Structuralism and Literary Analysis', *New Left Review*, 129: 51–66.

Williams, Raymond (1983) *Keywords: A Vocabulary of Culture and Society*, 2nd edn. London: Fontana.

Williams, Raymond (1989 [1958]) 'Culture is Ordinary', in Raymond Williams (ed.), *Resources of Hope*. London: Verso.

Williams, Robin (2000) *Making Identity Matter: Identity, Society and Social Interaction*. Mill Valley, CA: Sociology Press.

Wilson, Sloan (1955) *The Man in the Gray Flannel Suit*. New York: Simon and Schuster.

Wirth, Louis (1928) *The Ghetto*. Chicago: University of Chicago Press.

Wolfreys, Julian (2004) *Critical Keywords in Literary and Cultural Theory*. Basingstoke: Palgrave Macmillan.

Wollstonecraft, Mary (2002 [1796]) *A Vindication of the Rights of Woman, with Strictures on Political and Moral Subjects* (http://www.gutenberg.org/cache/epub/3420/pg3420.html).

Woodward, Kathryn (ed.) (1997) *Identity and Difference*. London: Sage.

Worldwatch Institute (2013) *The State of Consumption Today* (http://www.worldwatch.org/node/810).

Wrong, Dennis (1992) 'Disaggregating the Idea of Capitalism', *Theory, Culture and Society*, 9(1): 147–58.

Young, Iris Marion (1990) *Justice and the Politics of Difference*. Princeton, NJ: Princeton University Press.

Young, Iris Marion (1995) 'Gender as Seriality: Thinking about Women as a Social Collective', in Linda Nicholson and Steven Seidman (eds), *Social Postmodernism: Beyond Identity Politics*. Cambridge: Cambridge University Press.

Young, Iris Marion (1997) 'Unruly Categories: A Critique of Nancy Fraser's Dual Systems Theory', *New Left Review*, 222: 147–60.

Young, Iris Marion (2002) *Inclusion and Democracy*. Oxford: Oxford University Press.

Zaretsky, Eli (1994) 'Identity Theory, Identity Politics: Psychoanalysis, Marxism and Post-structuralism', in Craig Calhoun (ed.), *Social Theory and the Politics of Identity*. Oxford: Blackwell.

Zaretsky, Eli (1995) 'The Birth of Identity Politics in the 1960s: Psychoanalysis and the Public/Private Division', in Mike Featherstone, Scott Lash and Roland Robertson (eds), *Global Modernities*. London: Sage.

Žižek, Slavoj (1997) 'Multiculturalism, or, the Cultural Logic of Multinational Capitalism', *New Left Review*, 225: 28–51.

Index

Paterson, M. 129, 131
'personal' identity 35, 36, 38, 42–5
    problem of 86–7
    see also under consumerism
'personality' and 'individuality' 38, 43–4
Piketty, T. 158
popular discourse 19–22, 43
popular psychology 137–8
possessive individualism 70, 103, 173
post-Fordism 141–53
postmodern identity 124–5, 142–3, 146
postmodernist perspective 123–5, 141–53
postwar era 102–3
privatization 75–6, 171–2
property 38, 45, 50
psychoanalytical tradition 123
    see also Freud, S.
psychological self 94–6
psychology 15–16, 43, 45
    popular 137–8
'punks' 160–1

Quine, W.V. 42

'race' 16, 47–9
    and culture 98
    gender and sexuality 156–7
    hierarchies and distinctions 87–8
    see also African Americans
'Radicalesbians' 112
rebel consumer 138
recognition politics 46–7
reflexive self 148–9
Regulation School 55–6, 66, 134–5
resistance *see* anti-capitalist resistance
Riesman, D. 20, 137
Robins, K. 144, 145

sameness 35, 36–8, 46–7
    and difference 131–2, 135–6
Sassatelli, R. 116, 129, 131
Sayer, A. 78, 150, 152
Scatamburlo-D'Annibale, V. and McLaren, P.
    163–4
science *see* biology/nature
'self-branding' 151
'self-creation' 149–50
sex
    and gender 111–12
    hierarchies and distinctions 87–8
sexuality, gender and 'race' 156–7
Shakespeare, W. 17
Shinn, R. 137–8
Shivani, A. 172

Shoemaker, S. 37, 42
signification 62, 63
Simmel, G. 131–2
Slater, D. 129, 130, 134–5, 143, 150, 154
social constructionism vs essentialism debate 6,
    50–2, 142–3
'social' identity 35, 36, 45–7
    in consumer society 139–41
    and social characteristics 49–50
social language 63–5
social logic of capitalism 65–9, 77–8, 93, 177
    and consumption 133, 152, 153–4, 159–60
    in neoliberal societies 72–6
    in practice 69–72
social movements 13, 23
    and neoliberalism 168–71
    'new' 105, 109, 116–17, 119
    see also identity politics
social sciences 18–19, 47–8, 93–4, 137
    see also academia
social status and consumption 130–2
sociological self 92–9
Somers, M.R. 120
Spencer, H. 36
spirit of capitalism 66–7, 77
'structure of feeling' 95–6
subjectivisation 4–5
synchronistic and diachronistic meanings 31–2

'taste' and 'distinction' 150, 152
Tormey, S. 70–1
trade unions 102–3, 107

Veblen, T. 129–31, 135, 150
Vietnam War 106–7
Voice of the Women's Liberation Movement 112

Walby, S. 71–2, 121, 164
Weber, M. 66–7
Webster, F. 66
Williams, R. 4, 8, 14, 27, 30, 31–2, 33, 34, 35, 37,
    52–3, 59–65, 95, 97, 98
Wollstonecraft, M. 16
Women's Liberation movement 110–11, 112, 113
'Women's Radical Action Project' 112
Woolf, V. 16
World Wildlife Federation (WWF) 160
Worldwatch Institute 128
Wrong, D. 71

Young, I.M. 8, 164–5

Zaretsky, E. 6, 95, 134, 135
Žižek, S. 118, 163